Contents

To the memory
of
Corena Crowley

Acknowledgements

This book came to me as a surprise. I had felt for some time that a new vision was beginning to unfold in the contemporary British novel, but found myself at a loss as to how to talk about it in critical terms. This changed fundamentally as I discovered the philosophy of Jean-Luc Nancy, which I encountered for the first time in Timothy C. Baker's doctoral thesis, imminently forthcoming from Edinburgh University Press as *George Mackay Brown and the Philosophy of Community*. Timothy's application of Nancean ideas was majorly instrumental in setting me on my way.

A trip to Chennai in March 2008, initiated and impeccably organised by Renuka Rajaratnam, brought to life Nancy's theorising. I remain incredulous at the sheer marvel of Chennai, whose miraculous urban beauty took my breath away, and whose daily bustle came to epitomise to me Nancy's inoperative community far beyond all preconceived images of chaos or exotic splendour. The people of Chennai are Nancean 'being singular plural'. No two people I saw in the streets of the city were ever even remotely alike, and yet they all seemed to belong together. There was none of that blind, hectic indifference and uniformity that work to automatise and dishearten life in many western cities (most notably London). Every passer-by I met in the streets of Chennai appeared to seek out my gaze, searching for clues as to who I might be, who I had assumed I was before coming to their city and, most urgently, why I had come. I cannot express enough my gratitude to Renuka for thus opening my eyes to India and the dynamic of its ceaseless cosmopolitan world-creation. Great thanks are due also to Susan Oommen of Stella Maris College, C. T. Indra in the English Department at Madras University, and Shantha Gabriel of the British Council in Chennai, all of whom generously extended their hospitality to me.

The Cosmopolitan Novel could never have reached completion without the support of the English Research Institute at Manchester

Metropolitan University. I simply could not wish for a better or more generous team of colleagues. Special thanks are due to Sue Zlosnik, Janet Beer and Peter Gilroy for paving the way to my long-awaited research leave in 2008, and to Andrew Moor and Anna Powell for shouldering many a burden that would normally have been mine. Nicole Weickgenannt Thiara and Christopher Perriam volunteered to read the final draft of the book, and I am greatly indebted to them for their friendship, enthusiasm and critical perspicacity. Needless to say I am solely responsible for any errors that remain.

Thank you also to Helen Rogers, Fiona McCulloch and Gill Plain, who commented on work in progress and provided moral support throughout. Similarly, Stephen Smith and Richard Sandover never tired of listening to yet another account of my academic plights and pleasures. Thanks as well to Jackie Jones at Edinburgh University Press for her prodigious energy and unwavering faith in the project. I am also indebted to Nancy Armstrong, unrivalled among critics of the novel, whose shrewd wisdom proved inestimable, as always. Finally, thanks are due to my students on the MA programme in Contemporary Literature and Film, who listened to many wild flights of fancy and cheerfully thrashed them out with me. And how could I not also thank Sheila, Queen of the Daleks, who sphinx-like sat through it all, never in any doubt that sooner or later this flurry of human agitation, too, would pass.

Many years ago in the summer of 1985, on the third-floor balcony of the Ulrich-Zasius-Haus in Freiburg im Breisgau, Corena Crowley introduced me to the art of cosmopolitan conversation. This book is dedicated to her memory. Many thanks to Karen Krauss for getting in touch and reminding me.

At times, [its] endless flexibility borders on chaos. But thanks to it, the novel becomes the first truly planetary form: a phoenix always ready to take flight in a new direction, and to find the right language for the next generation of readers.

Franco Moretti

In the present circumstances, I'd say the only thing worth globalizing is dissent.

Arundhati Roy

Introduction

Ever since Roland Robertson defined globalisation as 'the compression of the world and the intensification of a consciousness of the world as a whole' (1992: 8), sociological research on the increasing tightening of a global web of communal interaction and interdependency has proliferated massively, prompting an equally dramatic growth in cosmopolitan theory. Arguably affecting different spheres of life (economic vs. social/cultural), globalisation and cosmopolitanisation have come to be perceived as twin phenomena working to fix, as Zygmunt Bauman puts it, 'the intractable fate of the world' (1998: 1). Only recently have there been any notable efforts to theorise cosmopolitical models of agency and resistance, such as Ulrich Beck's promotion of a 'methodological cosmopolitanism'. In *The Cosmopolitan Vision* Beck calls on communities to unlearn their nationalist modes of self-identification and start contributing to global culture instead, always equipped with, as Beck specifies, '[their] own language and cultural symbols' (2006: 21). Conceiving of responsible world citizenship as based on the paradox that 'there are no others . . . [there are] *many* cultural others' (Tomlinson 1999: 194), contemporary cosmopolitanism promotes a departure from traditional internationalist perspectives while stressing the significance of local cultures for the development of any meaningful and viable world-communal future.

According to Bauman, 'we are all being "globalized"' (1998: 1). Reduced to a state of powerlessness and passivity by a plethora of anonymous forces, initiative – both individual and collective – becomes mere wishful fantasy as the world is quite literally taken out of our hands and transported 'beyond the reach of the design-and-action capacity of anybody in particular' (60). Although some of us benefit considerably more than others from the current world-systemic dynamic of globalisation, which, as Jürgen Habermas asserts, works to split world society into 'winner, beneficiary and loser countries' (2006: 12), no one person or group of persons is ultimately in charge in the sense of plotting or controlling the general course of events. History *per se* appears to be slowing down, heading for dystopian homeostasis, as our capacity for political agency is dilapidating into crisis management. How can humanity still hope to make a difference and shape such a world by turning the quasi-inevitable to its advantage? In *Liquid Love* Bauman suggests the answer lies in imagining 'the *global* community', and although he admits to being puzzled as to how such imaginative work could ever become strategically effective without the support of an institutional framework like that of a world state to prescribe and promote it, he concludes simply by reassuring us 'that "history is still with us and can be made"' (2003: 148, 150). This is where, as 'a counter to globalization', cosmopolitanism as an attitude and disposition gains momentum. In Walter Mignolo's definition, globalisation is assumed to incorporate 'a set of designs to manage the world while cosmopolitanism is a set of projects toward planetary conviviality' (2002: 157). Yet not only ought one to be wary of Mignolo's understanding of globalisation as 'manageable', but his neat dichotomy conceals an imbalance between individual cosmopolitan agency on the one hand and, on the other, a globalised pattern of systemic co-optation structurally and ideologically buttressed by governmental and corporate sanction. It is problematic to conceive of cosmopolitanism as a ready-made panacea for globalisation without addressing also the question of how individuals and communities might actually learn to go about living with everyone else in the world, rather than merely coexisting, especially since what cosmopolitanism is, or might be, remains as yet to be clearly defined.

Traditionally cosmopolitanism has been regarded as the 'privileged and irresponsible detachment' of a self-professed elite of select individuals 'held to be incapable of participating in the making of history, doomed to the mere aesthetic spectatorship that [they are] also held secretly to prefer' (Cheah and Robbins 1998: 4). This view of cosmopolitanism seems substantiated by 'Cosmopolitans and Locals in World Culture' (1990), an early essay by Ulf Hannerz, one of the pioneers in the field of cosmopolitan theory. Enthused by the gift of world citizenship, made all the more attractive by the new communication technologies as well as cheap global travel, Hannerz's cosmopolitan manifesto reveals a strikingly naive lack of political purpose, commitment and ethical responsibility. Although barely twenty years old, Hannerz's essay now reads like wishful blue-skies philosophising as, without very much critical reflection or engagement, it trumpets the merits of a new world order to be enjoyed to the full by everybody except, possibly, a few inveterate 'locals'. Hannerz's critical unselfconsciousness, fuelled by the close of the Cold War, finds expression in his curiously aestheticising statement that 'to become acquainted with more cultures is to turn into an *aficionado*, to view them as art works', as well as his crypto-imperialist inference that 'competence with regard to alien cultures itself entails a sense of mastery [. . .] One's understandings have expanded, a little more of the world is somehow under control' (Hannerz 1990: 239–40). As Hannerz's statements also reveal, traditional cosmopolitanism was at permanent risk of invalidation by its own intrinsic class-blindness. Who has ever really enjoyed the kind of untrammelled access to the world eulogised by Hannerz? And whose lives, by contrast, continue to be blighted by this access being in actual fact available only to a privileged few? As Shaobo Xie points out:

> Although technological revolution, transnational corporations and global restructuring of capitalism have made the world increasingly interdependent and interconnected, radically altering our concepts of time, space, politics, and relations, this has in no way changed the fundamental fact that the West still poses or imposes itself as the centre of the world. The mythology of a world already decentred politically, culturally, economically, and ideologically papers over the lived global power-relations between the developed West and the underdeveloped Rest. (2006: 55)

Despite the fact that mobility now ranks with 'the uppermost among the coveted values' (Bauman 1998: 2), its desirability as a commodity is by no means unproblematic; it remains a fraught and divisive manifestation of the unequal distribution of both socio-economic and cultural capital. Crucial distinctions need to be upheld between the mobility of tourists, economic migrants and refugees. The mobility of the latter two is enacted under duress, propelled by inhospitable local circumstance rather than catalysed by the allure of a worldwide opening up of limitless opportunity. Rather than 'freedom', then, mobility in this sense often denotes deracination as a direct consequence of economic expulsion.

A similarly enthusiastic utopianism to Hannerz's, if of an intellectually more engaging and sophisticated order, can be found in two recent British contributions to cosmopolitan theory. In *After Empire* Paul Gilroy blames identity politics for obfuscating the actual cosmopolitan conviviality that informs everyday metropolitan existence. By conviviality Gilroy means 'the process of cohabitation and interaction that have made multiculture an ordinary feature of social life in Britain's urban areas and in postcolonial cities elsewhere'. It is this open intercommunality, he argues, that 'makes a nonsense of closed, fixed, and reified identity' (2004: xi). But how successful really is Gilroy's largely intuitive talk on convivial openness and fluidity in dismantling the rigidity of traditional cultures which all of us live among on a daily basis and, in particular also, the frequently phobic and paranoid self-encapsulation of minoritarian monocultures within British society? More often than not, what opens up between communities is a perilous rift or gap, an *ou*-topia or 'non-place', rather than a comfortably inhabitable 'Third Space' enabling mutual encounter. Everyday living practices remain at the mercy of ideological control, and any openness there is, more often than not strictly confined to the relative inconsequentialities of everyday intercourse, can effectively be proscribed at a moment's notice. What renders Gilroy's views inspirational is therefore not so much his impressive optimism as his exchange of the very terminology of globalisation for a new vocabulary of planetary self-realisation. To him, envisionings of our human existence as 'planetary' specify 'a smaller scale than the global, which transmits all the triumphalism and complacency of ever-expanding imperial universals' (xi–xii). Like snapshots of Earth from outer space they evoke an emotionally engaging sense of the planet's exposure and vulnerability. In other words, they identify the globe primarily as a precariously fragile residential locus rather than an endlessly resourceful and repackageable unit of economic management and commercial pursuit.

Informed by a similar rejection of identity theory and politics, and indeed conventional intellectual enquiry as such, Mica Nava's partly autobiographical *Visceral Cosmopolitanism* follows Gilroy's study in prioritising everyday living over ideological pigeonholing by attempting to retrieve a sense of how people in Britain have actually lived, and continue to live, their lives. Nava aims to uncover a multicultural history of British anti-racism by focusing on 'the unconscious, non-intellectual, emotional, inclusive features of cosmopolitanism, on feelings of attraction for and identification with otherness' (2007: 8). Citing London as the perfect example, Nava – like Gilroy – is taken in by the city's 'increasingly undifferentiated, hybrid, post-multicultural, lived transformations which are the outcome of diasporic cultural mixing and indeterminacy' (13). There is no mention that to a new arrival the colossal unwieldiness of London might appear far from hospitable, relentlessly processing its bustle of stressed-out commuters while cultivating a marked lack of solicitous eye contact with the stranger. Another problem with Nava's enquiry is of course that emotionality as such is no safeguard against communal exclusion; indeed, the opposite is the case, as xenophobia and racism tend to be virulently visceral, kneejerk expressions of deep-seated fears impervious to cosmopolitan reasoning. Significantly, recent sociological research reveals

Nava's perspective as paradigmatic of middle-class London's largely disingenuous pretensions at cosmopolitan living. Studying gentrification processes in Islington, Tim Butler undermines Nava's self-professed cosmopolitanism when he writes that 'in a city which is massively multiethnic, its middle classes, despite long rhetorical flushes in favour of multiculturalism and diversity, huddle together into essentially White settlements in the inner city' (2003: 2469). Butler outlines 'the formation of a metropolitan habitus in which values such as diversity, social inclusion and social integration form an important element of the narrative [. . .] which, in its practice, is one of social exclusivity' (2471). He shows cosmopolitan self-portraits like Nava's to be deeply marred by self-delusive wishful 'feeling', fuelled by class bias. According to Butler, middle-class London 'values the presence of others [. . .] but chooses not to interact with them' (2484), a fact that transpires most eloquently in respect to where, and with whom, parents decide to send their kids to school. Multiculturalism and ethnic diversity serve as mere exotic wallpaper to the self-fashioning of middle-class identities, whose quality of life and sense of self are appealingly enhanced by being able to 'feel cosmopolitan' due to the apparent, yet far from actively neighbourly, proximity of 'others'.

In both theory and practice cosmopolitanism continues to harbour manifold shortcomings, and its exact relationship to globalisation remains difficult to determine. As a strategy of resistance, can it ever dare dream of extricating itself from the densely wrought web of power relations it seeks to expose, analyse and undo? Cosmopolitans must stay alert to their own positionality as well as the complex enmeshment of other people's historical legacy, economic capital, and ensuing degree of cosmopolitan competence and ambition. Any unilateral declaration or pursuit of cosmopolitanism, however well-intentioned, is no cosmopolitanism at all. Hannerz's euphoric opening, 'there is now a world culture' (1990: 237), remains problematic because it paints 'an idealized view of society as a place of "togetherness" where "otherness" has been banished to less civilized times' (Haylett 2006: 187). We live in no homogenised or consensual world of perfect equality, in which the core–periphery axiomatic of past imperialisms has dissolved. Rather than assuming a state of accomplished globality, therefore, it appears more productive to conceive of the world as merely global*ised*, that is, as caught up in an ongoing – some might say 'unremitting' – process of globalisation.

According to Malcolm Waters, 'in a fully globalized context, no given relationship or set of relationships can remain isolated or bounded. Each is linked to all the others and is systematically affected by them' (2001: 15). Yet, at the same time, no relationship could be claimed as already (or ever) definitively set or sorted. Whereas everybody's 'style of cultural experience and identification is bound to be affected by the complex and multiform interrelations, penetrations and cultural mutations that characterize the globalization of our current stage of modernity' (Tomlinson 1999: 105), the global order remains far from consistent or rounded, suggesting there continues to be plenty of room for fruitful communal manoeuvre and intervention. 'As the sort of cultural disposition people living in a globalized world need to cultivate' (194), therefore, John Tomlinson recommends a non-globalist kind of cosmopolitanism. By this he means a locally resourced political agency rooted in the realisation that in the twenty-first century the world constitutes an all-encompassing network in which whatever as individuals we do, or fail to do, is bound to have repercussions and consequences for us all.

While it is possible to record a long history for both globalisation (as a process involving the whole of humanity) and cosmopolitanism (as a corresponding body of political ideas), I am primarily interested in their creative, literary-cultural phenomenology as particular manifestations of the contemporary. For the purposes of my study the origins of 'the contemporary' are tracked down to two 9/11 events: the fall of the Berlin Wall on 9 November 1989 and the World Trade Center attacks on 11 September 2001. (Depending on which calendric format is used – global or US American – '9/11' can refer to both 9 November and 11 September.) Because I have a special interest in contemporary Britishness and the potentialities of a distinct British cosmopolitanism, it seems uncanny that devolution, which has begun to define domestic politics within the United Kingdom, is equally marked by a 9/11 inscription: Scotland's second, successful referendum on national self-rule was held on 11 September 1997. Hence a total of three 9/11s can be cited as determining Britain's contemporaneity, and in my view it is important that, in cultural-historical terms, one 9/11 is not allowed to eclipse one's view of the other two, even – or especially – if the events in question are so easily ranked not only according to their perceived traumatic severity but also within a local/global hierarchy. The latter might suggest, for instance, that Scotland's devolution is more 'local' than the fall of the Berlin Wall, which, in turn, might be regarded as less 'global' in its impact than the terror attacks on the World Trade Center. What is clear is that contemporary Britain finds itself in a unique cultural and political position as a post-imperial and increasingly devolved nation sandwiched between neo-imperial US America and supranational 'Old'

Europe. It is this in-between position and internal diversification that define contemporary Britain's specific globality: as part of its imperial heritage, it is linked to over three quarters of the world, and many of its twenty-first-century citizens retain close familial ties with what used to be the Empire's colonies. Britain is also composed of at least four nations under one state roof: England, Scotland, Wales and Northern Ireland. Moreover, it is linked to Europe, and it entertains a special relationship with US America, supported by a common language and shared historical heritage. As a result, it appears at times hard to think of a place more thoroughly globalised than twenty-first-century Britain.

My suggestion that contemporary cosmopolitanism takes its beginnings in 1989 is not entirely original. Robert Fine identifies 'a form of radicalism that has flourished since the fall of the Berlin Wall in 1989 and goes by the name of the new or actually existing cosmopolitanism', adding that 'it was only after 1989, at the close of the Cold War, that a new configuration of cosmopolitan practices seemed to change the very character of the epoch' (2003: 452, 456). Yet if the new cosmopolitanism was indeed inspired by the events of 1989, it is certainly equally true that it was forced to undergo significant recasting in the aftermath of 2001. As Norman Denzin and Yvonna Lincoln assert, 'the world changed on 11 September 2001' (2003: xiii). Somewhat more elaborately, Thomas Friedman differentiates between 'two competing forms of imagination at work in the world today: the creative imagination of 11/9 and the destructive imagination of 9/11':

> One brought down a wall and opened the windows of the world [. . .] It unlocked half the planet and made the citizens there our collaborators and competitors. Another brought down the World Trade Center, closing its Windows on the World restaurant forever and putting up new invisible and concrete walls among people at a time when we thought 11/9 had erased them for good. (2005: 543)

Estranged from the optimism of Hannerz's generation, who were free to indulge in cosmopolitanism as an attractive lifestyle option, these days all of us are aware that in order to serve any relevant purpose at all cosmopolitanism must always mean 'realistic cosmopolitanism' (Beck 2006: 57). In other words, it must be definitive of ethical responsibility and firm political commitment. As the Berlin Wall came down, signalling the close of the Cold War, the world could conceive of itself momentarily as an entirety. Yet hope for a fairer and less oppositional future, devoid of hatred and paranoia, was traumatically nipped in the bud in 2001. Not only was the world 'once more turned into a list of supporters and detractors [. . .] of what became the names of an ominous global enemy: terror, terrorism, terrorists', there was also very little time or room for cosmopolitan deliberation as the then US government under George W. Bush asserted quite unequivocally that 'abstentions were not permitted' (Appadurai 2006: 20). The new cosmopolitanism had come of age; it had lost its carefree innocence in response to a paroxysm of atrocious violence followed on its heel by a period of oppressive worldwide duress.

All the more astonishing, then, that contemporary British literary history should have remained largely untouched by these massive contextual upheavals, indicative of a major, quite literally epoch-making world-political mood swing from celebratory euphoria at the close of the Cold War to traumatic shock, gross political disillusionment and cultural despondency in the aftermath of 2001. In *The Contemporary British Novel* James Acheson and Sarah Ross gesture only vaguely in the direction of 'an increasingly complex contemporary world' (2005: 1), while Dominic Head's *Introduction to Modern British Fiction* (2002) is hampered by his given calendric remit of 1950–2000, which obfuscates the dates and events that truly defined British history and culture in the second half of the twentieth century, namely the Suez Crisis of 1956 and, of course, the events of 1989 and 2001. James English equally overlooks the actual determinants of British contemporaneity by tracing 'the contours of the British fiction scene in all its national particularity' back to the Thatcher revolution of the 1980s. English does hint at 'a global framework within which those contours have assumed their contemporary shape', but by this, as it turns out, he means ultimately only those parts of the world that used to belong to the British Empire (2006: 3–6). Less nostalgic is Philip Tew and Rod Mengham's *British Fiction Today* (2006), which professes to pay attention to 'certain larger perspectival qualities that characterize the historical differences between the pre-millennial and post-millennial phases of British creativity' (xiv), and even more promising is Tew's *Contemporary British Novel*, which sets out to capture 'the current contemporary British scene [as] a globalized locality' (2007: x). Tew's objective echoes Brian Finney's realisation that an ever larger component of contemporary British literature is written in immediate response to 'a world which is so thoroughly interconnected that it is no longer possible to treat any part of it as unaffected by everything else in it' (2007: 2).

The only work of literary criticism, however, that explicitly attributes significance to 1989 and 2001 as 'two events, standing at either end of the 1990s, [which] had a crucial political and symbolic resonance for British culture' (2005: 2) is Nick Bentley's *British Fiction of the 1990s*. But Bentley chooses to characterise the 1990s as 'the only decade in the twentieth century [when] the possibility of global war has not had a significant effect on the cultural imagination', which must seem rather odd, especially since he himself notes 'the abundance of regional wars during the 1990s in the Balkans, Africa and the Middle East' (3). Bentley appears to believe that in our rapidly globalising world it continues to be possible to distinguish meaningfully between global and regional wars, quite as though the conflicts ravaging Yugoslavia, Somalia, Rwanda and Palestine had remained safely contained within their countries of origin rather than unleashing repercussions well beyond the boundaries of the nation state. As I see it – with regard to political accountability and worldwide socio-economic expedience, as well as humanitarian questions of conscience and ethical responsibility – in the era of globalisation a world at war regionally is inevitably a world at war *in toto*.

Arjun Appadurai's reassessment of the 1990s as 'a decade of superviolence' seems more astute than Bentley's global compartmentalisation. Equally perceptive is Appadurai's prognosis that in the long term globalisation 'could expose severe pathologies in the sacred ideologies of nationhood' (2006: 1). As Laura García-Moreno and Peter Pfeiffer suggest, nations are inclined to assert themselves most vehemently whenever their boundaries are drawn into doubt by being revealed as porous, arbitrary or transient. A fierce vying for predominance is set in motion between the local and the global which, in the end, only serves to consolidate the fact of their tight mutual imbrication and interdependency:

> The end of the Cold War seemed to make the idea of a world not solely mapped as nation states more possible than ever before. Reaffirmations of nationhood and new forms of regionalism, however, soon asserted themselves as the principal foundations of political, social, and cultural organization. At the same time, the force of globalization in both the economy and information technology disavows the primacy of the local or regional that has become so prominent in political and cultural discourses. (1996: vii)

Chantal Mouffe not only concurs with García-Moreno and Pfeiffer by stipulating that the post-1989 world had indeed witnessed 'the emergence of new global antagonisms'. She also re-accentuates the global-local valency of these antagonisms by designating them as 'a sort of global civil war'. Mouffe's hope is for what she terms 'a cosmopolitan democracy', the establishment of which she finds impeded by a facile, politically ineffective cosmopolitanism 'that has imagined the possibility of eliminating antagonisms' (2004: 70). Critics like Mouffe deserve to be reassured that the new post-1989 cosmopolitanism has shed its former starry-eyedness and grown realist. Far from ironing out all agitation, anxiety and conflict, which after all determine the human condition as inalienably as humanity's capability for peace and harmony, the new cosmopolitanism is centred on the development of a strong sense of global community in order to pre-empt war and terrorism, be they motivated by nationalism, religious fundamentalism, or any other arch-ideological conviction or belief. Acknowledging and cherishing human life for what it is – that is, embracing its diversity and inveterate imperfections – the new cosmopolitanism is rooted in the realities of the present rather than mobilising for the future fulfilment of any one or other set of utopian ideals.

Notably, both globalisation and cosmopolitanisation have been apprehended as glib euphemisms for Americanisation. As Timothy Brennan alerts us, the sudden increase in the expression of well-intentioned cosmopolitan sentiments everywhere deserves careful intellectual scrutiny. In Brennan's view the practitioners of what he calls 'cosmo-theory' cultivate far too optimistic a stance towards the allegedly 'new' post-Cold War world order, blinding themselves to their own corporate instrumentality in providing convenient rhetorical cover for economic as well as cultural oppression and exploitation. Cosmopolitanism, as Brennan sees it, is invariably the carrier of 'a veiled Americanism' (2001: 682). Deeply vexed by his peers' 'explicit failure to see cosmopolitanism as less an expansive ethos than an expansionist policy: a move not toward complexity and variety but toward centralization and suffocating stagnation' (1997: 55), he con-demns cosmopolitan theory as the ideological vehicle of a wholly dele-terious process of globalisation induced, orchestrated and covered up by 'the West'. 'Globalization bears on cosmopolitanism as structure to idea', he asserts. 'It is that purportedly new material reality to which the new ethos – cosmopolitanism – responds' (2001: 662).

In opposition to Brennan, who feels compelled to disparage all western cosmopolitanism as collusive with the neo-imperialist project of American world domination, I would like as far as possible to disen-tangle my investigation from US politics, literature and theory, and what I see as their traditional burden of utopianist emplotment, mis-sionary zeal and hyperbolic universalism. Instead, following in the footsteps of Umberto Eco and Jürgen Habermas, I will aim to fore-ground Europe's cosmopolitan heritage as foundational to a more complex and complicated sense of the present, which is multi-causal and multi-perspectival rather than issuing from a single moment of aggression, suffering, fear and retaliation as the be-all and end-all of 'civilised' life in the contemporary world (see Eco 2005: 16; Habermas 2006: 96). To elucidate my position, I would like to draw attention to

Katie Trumpener's response to the '2004 American Comparative Literature Association Report on the State of the Discipline'. Trumpener pointedly charges her academic compatriots with world-blindness and a debilitating proclivity for cultural indifference in all but the most basic statistical terms, thus seriously calling in question whatever cosmopolitical aspirations they believe themselves to be entertaining:

> So how has the radically changed situation of the last decade reshaped our cognitive patterns and maps? At least so far, fifteen years from the 1989 breakdown of a bifurcated Europe, the ensuing political, economic, and demographic transformations of Europes East and West, and their concurrent partial reconsolidation under the sign of the European Union, have had remarkably little effect on the North American study of European literatures and cultures. (So too the long-anticipated or long-feared devolutionary 'breakup of Britain' now in progress has had virtually no impact on the American study and teaching of 'English' literature.) Only the demographics of our graduate programs changed markedly in the 1990s, as record numbers of Eastern European students have begun studying at our universities. In contrast – and this is a mark of our inherent institutional and disciplinary conservatism – only a tiny number of Eastern European humanists were recruited to move to North American universities. There may be ongoing excitement about a few Eastern European thinkers, dead (Mikhail Bakhtin) and alive (Slavoj Zizek), but there is no large-scale infusion of Central and Eastern European faculty, methods, and literary sensibilities into the North American academy – at least nothing comparable to the period from the 1930s to the 1950s, when our universities were intellectually reinvigorated by the arrival of émigrés fleeing fascism or communism. (2006: 191–2)

Trumpener's excoriating assessment of the state of her discipline, which by definition specialises in multicultural discourse and transnational enquiry, paints a very bleak picture of US American academia's knowledge of, and interest in, contemporary cosmopolitan Europe, allegedly its ideologically closest ally. Meanwhile, US American academia's cosmopolitan engagement with the cultures and living conditions of the whole of 'the rest of the world' is virtually non-existent.

The present study rebuts critical views like Brennan's that refer to 'the West' monolithically and elide distinctions between US America on the one hand and Britain and Europe on the other. Wrongly, in my view, Brennan refers to 'the great conformist family of European and North American man' (1997: 309). What I will suggest is that we may currently be witnessing the emergence of a new British cosmopolitanism, whose emergence is accompanied by the rise of a new kind of novel – 'the cosmopolitan novel'. It is the themes and formal particularities of this new kind of narrative that I intend to define in the following with reference to current debates in globalisation studies and cosmopolitan theory. But how, in turn, might cosmopolitan theory and politics benefit from literary criticism and the study of the contemporary novel in particular? How might novelistic portrayals of the world relate – and, more importantly, what might they be shown to contribute – to contemporary conceptualisations of globality? Whereas traditionally the rise of the novel has been studied in intimate association with the rise of the nation state, might increasing globalisation currently be prompting the development of a less homebound and territorialist sub-genre of the novel, more adept than its national and postcolonial counterparts at imagining global community?

In *Imagined Communities* (1983) Benedict Anderson defines the nation as an act of the communal imagination. 'The members of even the smallest nation will never know most of their fellow-members, meet them, or even hear of them', he writes, 'yet in the minds of each lives the image of their communion' (2006: 6). Anderson singles out the novel and the newspaper as the two most widely circulating and hence readily available 'means for "re-presenting" the *kind* of imagined community that is the nation' (25) and for 'creating that remarkable confidence of community in anonymity' (36). In his analysis of a handful of novels from different parts of the world Anderson insists that the genre remains confined to imagining a panoramic *tour d'horizon*, tracing and reinscribing the content, shape and boundaries of the nation rather than proliferating beyond it into the limitless vistas of an all-encompassing and essentially open-ended *tour du monde* (30). In 'The National Longing for Form', Brennan's influential essay on nation and narration, one finds Anderson's perspective reiterated in essentially unaltered form. Brennan asserts that 'it was the *novel* that historically accompanied the rise of nations [. . .] by mimicking the structure of the nation [. . .] its manner of presentation allowed people to imagine the special community that was the nation' (1990: 49–50). My own chief question in the following will be whether, in our increasingly globalised world, the novel may already have begun to adapt and renew itself by imagining the world instead of the nation. If so, how might novels currently be going about 'mimicking the structure of the [world]'? What exactly characterises 'the special community that is the [world]', and what might be the impact of these characteristics on the novel's 'manner of presentation'? My enquiry is more radically paradigm-shifting than Patrick Parrinder's, which concludes 'that twenty-first-century novelists will continue to participate in the making and remaking of English identity' (2006: 414), or Bruce King's, which suggests that what we are currently witnessing is the writing of 'a new national literature' (2004: 324). It is the contemporary British novel as *tour du monde*, as a practice of communal world-narration of which Anderson declares it quite categorically incapable, that stands at the centre of my investigation. Nothing less, in fact, than the world as a whole will do as the imaginative reference point, catchment area and addressee of the cosmopolitan novel.

There is nothing that ought to prevent us imagining the world as one community or capturing it inside the vision of a single narrative. As Anderson concedes, in the eighteenth century, when the novel first began to take shape, the nation itself must have appeared equally unmanageable in its scope and anonymous diversity, and besides, today we enjoy much-improved communication technologies and information resources that considerably facilitate our access to the world at large. According to Matthew Rofe, it is Anderson's theorising that enables us to make that creative leap from the national to the cosmopolitan in the first place. 'Acknowledging community as a form of "collective imagining" enhances the ability to conceptualise the existence of communities beyond the constraints of territory' (Rofe 2003: 2518). At the same time as this formation of transterritorial communities exceeds all spatialities in equal measure, be they global or local, it also strengthens and renews our sense of rootedness and belonging by requiring us to define who we are, or strive to be, within an ever-broadening spectrum of contexts. Already Robertson linked the development of a global consciousness to an increase in the perception and representation of 'the world as an "imagined community"' (1992: 183). More recently, Anthony Appiah has argued that 'a world in which communities are neatly hived off from one another seems no longer a serious option, if it ever was' (2006: xx). In this light, then, any novel that continues to be tied to a narrowly nationalist agenda must appear as an inept, possibly even fraudulent anachronism. But precisely what implications might imagining the world instead of the nation have for the form of the novel *per se*? Is the shift in perspective and scope likely to remould the very morphology of the genre? And what exactly *is* the structure of the world to be mimicked in the cosmopolitan novel?

In *Globalization and Culture* Tomlinson approaches the subject by problematising the world's new 'complex connectivity' and 'increasing global-spatial proximity', which are prone to confound our experiential sense of the 'undeniable, stubbornly enduring physical distance between places and people in the world' (Tomlinson 1999: 1–4). The globe appears to be shrinking, yet to the majority of people this is little more than a baffling *trompe l'œil* of somebody else's projection. As Tomlinson explains, 'the paradigmatic experience of global modernity for most people [. . .] is that of staying in one place but experiencing the "displacement" that global modernity *brings to them*' (9). Consequently, cosmopolitan representation's possibly greatest challenge lies in bridging the rift between the world of globalised business, marketing and political decision-making, on the one hand, and its countless sub-worlds of powerless, disenfranchised daily living, on the other. Globalisation has levelled the planet in more than one sense through homogenisation, deracination and compartmentalisation. Our lives are lived quite literally at different levels: an elevated sphere travelled by the privileged is upheld by innumerable lower levels whose apparent solidity depends on their inhabitants' social immobility and hopeless economic entrapment. Whereas the privileged have a clear view of the whole world but can easily avert their gaze, the disenfranchised are doomed to watch as 'distant events and powers penetrate [their] local experience' (Tomlinson 1999: 9), frequently at random and without much prior warning. Cosmopolitan representation must convey this synchronicity of the incongruous, multifarious and seemingly disconnected at the same time as it does its best to capture the streaming flow of a newly emergent contemporaneity. Its manner of presentation will most certainly include juxtaposition, as in Anderson's example of newspaper reporting, and it is indeed very likely to cast up similar ruminations:

> Why are these events so juxtaposed? What connects them to each other? Not sheer caprice. Yet obviously most of them happen independently, without the actors being aware of each other or of what the others are up to. The arbitrariness of their inclusion and juxtaposition [. . .] shows that the linkage between them is imagined. (Anderson 2006: 33)

Yielding to fruitful interpermeation only intermittently, and precariously held together by the author's vision and reader's imagination, at its best this kind of juxtaposition results in the cosmopolitan novel's compositeness, which is not at all the same as fragmentation.

Episodic yet cohesive, compositeness forges narrative assemblage out of a seemingly desultory dispersion of plot and characterisation. Cosmopolitan representation resorts to the montage techniques of contemporary cinema, effecting rapid shifts in focus and perspective with the aim of cramming as many story lines and clashing imageries as possible into one and the same mise en scène. A good example of such cosmopolitan film-making is *Babel* (2006) by the Mexican director Alejandro González Iñárritu, in which stories from California, Japan, Mexico and Morocco coalesce to create one traumatised world. However, none of the individual locations and sets of characters in *Babel* ever relinquishes its edgy, boxed-in solipsism, and the gaping wound of their encounter remains unstaunched as ultimately the picture refuses to heal remedially into one. Juxtaposing modern five-star tourism with economic migration and the plight of eking out a quasi-medieval existence in the African desert, the one-world imagery of *Babel* is blighted by global inequality and crushed into an accident-prone mosaic of misfitting segments that push and press one on the other, yet remain worlds apart. To fulfil the representational challenges of the contemporary world, representation as we know it must change and adopt what Beck calls a 'cosmopolitan outlook' while steering clear of becoming either starry-eyed utopia or defeatist jeremiad. In this respect *Babel*'s most commendable feature is its unflinching realism. The film employs the image of a gun – originally used by a tourist on safari, then passed on as a gift, and finally fired off by children at play, seriously wounding another tourist – as a poignant image of what currently binds our planet into one. What is so remarkable about *Babel* is how well it captures the self-encapsulated isolation of each individual life-world, how communal enclaves reach deeply into each other yet, protectively gloved, fail to sense the heartbeat of each other's hopes, dreams and anxieties, how the world lies shattered into stories bound into differently paced and oriented trajectories while all the time, undisavowably, the common truth of humanity's vulnerability and mutual interdependence obtains.

Following the representational example of *Babel*, as well as Beck's catalogue of cosmopolitical caveats and imperatives, the contemporary cosmopolitan novel must aim 'to break out of the self-centred narcissism of the national outlook and the dull incomprehension with which it infects thought and action, and thereby enlighten human beings concerning the real, internal cosmopolitanization of their lifeworlds and institutions' (Beck 2006: 2). It must do its best to demonstrate that 'in a world of global crises and dangers produced by civilization, the old differentiations between internal and external, national and international, us and them, lose their validity and a new cosmopolitan realism becomes essential to survival' (14). Such a radical refocusing of the literary imagination from the national to the global will bring about truly paradigm-shifting change, heralding the beginning of a new era in both critical and creative thought. As Don Kalb and Marco van der Land explain, 'in the birthact of the social sciences, as well as in historiography and literature, a view was inscribed of a global mosaic of human cultures', resulting in scholars more or less exclusively 'describing and explaining what went on, and what had to be going on, within any single part of the mosaic, that is within the boundaries' (2000: 273–4). In the twenty-first century the task is to venture beyond our nationally demarcated horizons into the world at large and understand the domestic and the global as weaving one mutually pervasive pattern of contemporary human circumstance and experience, containing both dark and light.

Unlike other national literatures, some might argue, very little should stand in the way of contemporary British writing evolving into this kind of 'world literature' of cosmopolitan human experience, if it has not in fact already made the transition. This is chiefly to do with its anglophone disposition combined with 'the ability of "English literature" to stand for literature in English as well as literature by the English', which means it has never fully complied in the first place with the normative standards of what a national literature ought ideally to be (Connell 2004: 81). English is the world's new lingua franca and, as the medium of choice for literary self-expression by an ever-increasing number of non-native and/or bilingual writers, it tends to absorb quite literally a whole world of national differences while finding its own original distinctiveness profoundly hybridised by continual re-appropriation. At the same time, more inexorably than any other literature, literature in English is subject to the vicissitudes of global market forces. And yet, as Simon Gikandi demonstrates, although English literature constitutes 'one of the most universal cultural phenomena, a pantheon that can be traced all the way from the Outer Hebrides of Scotland to Suva in Fiji, [it remains] constantly associated with very provincial geographies and concerns' (2001: 650). Despite its apparent diversity and worldliness English literature still fundamentally serves a 'mosaic' of nations. The simple fact that so many different national perspectives cluster and converge within its imaginative realm renders English literature international, but not necessarily also cosmopolitan. Global circulation and popularity do not guarantee a cosmopolitan outlook; neither does an author's choice of the world as their central topic, or their targeting of a world readership, even though this is certainly important. What matters in the end is a particular stance towards the world, which must come to be shared by author and reader, but whose manifestation and effect obviously rely first and foremost on the author. As Jon Binnie and his co-editors suggest in *Cosmopolitan Urbanism*, ideally cosmopolitanism should meld 'a philosophy of world citizenship which simultaneously transcends the boundaries of the nation-state and descends to the scale of individual rights and responsibilities [with] a particular set of skills and attitude towards diversity and difference' (2006: 13). Applied to the work of the cosmopolitan novelist, it is crucial that these cosmopolitan skills are not confused with calculated manipulative control. Rather, they must be understood as integral to the author's capability to open up and yield to the structuring of the world as she or he finds it, however bewildering, turbulent or self-contradictory.

A first intuitive inkling of a new genre stirring within the tradition of the English novel crystallises in Steven Connor's *The English Novel in History* (1996), even though his enquiry continues largely to be faithful to the worn-out novel/nation paradigm. Commenting on works by Salman Rushdie and Kazuo Ishiguro, Connor detects 'a skeptical dissatisfaction with the inherited forms in which the condition of England has been represented [. . .] combined with a continuing faith in the capacities of narrative to effect kinds of collective symbolic transformation and solidary connections'. By interrogating 'the essential integrity of the nation' Rushdie and Ishiguro are seen to 'add to that picture of harmonious interdependence some awkwardly unassimilable facts and experiences', while pioneering 'the possibility of forms of mutual belonging which do not depend upon such a smooth annulment of conflict and difference' (89). It is Connor's reflection on the renegotiation and reconstitution of national community in the works of literary 'outsiders' such as Rushdie and Ishiguro – that is, how in their works solidarity and dissent, identification and difference, tend to converge rather than prove incommensurable – that potentially points to the rise of the cosmopolitan novel. Practising an imagining of community that is dedicated, even loyal, to the idea of the nation, yet at the same time refutes the nationalist myths of essence, homogeneity and perfect integrity, in Rushdie's and Ishiguro's writing the nation is surrendered to the unruly heterogeneity of individual experience and modes of belonging that resist uniform incorporation.

Connor's reading of the nation as represented by Rushdie and Ishiguro displays an interesting affinity with the French philosopher Jean-Luc Nancy's reflections on 'community' and 'world-formation' in works such as *The Inoperative Community* (1986), *Being Singular Plural* (1996) and the recently translated *The Creation of the World or Globalization* (2002). As I will demonstrate, the very tentativeness of Nancy's outline of community as 'inoperative being-in-common' – that is, as a collective human necessity without fixed teleological function – proves instructively illuminating for literature imagining global community beyond 'the people' or (united) nations, and outside the utopian/dystopian framework of ideological modelling or transcendent meaning-making. Intent on saving the world from definitive subsumption within any worked-out global formation, Nancy introduces 'community' – be it global, national, familial or otherwise – always simply as the unwieldy structure of our shared existence, which at any moment remains prone to affiliation and capable of dispersion.

Central to the cosmopolitan novel is its representation of worldwide human living and global community. This one would expect to be driven by sound ethical commitment and political conscientiousness, while abstaining from the projection of any particular destiny for humankind as a whole lest it result in the formation of a new grand narrative inclined to reframe the globe rather than releasing its inherent world-creative potential. Unsurprisingly the issue of community pervades current critical debates on globalisation. Thus, Bauman blames global commerce for 'the invasion and colonization of *communitas*' resulting in a 'persistent crumbling away of the skills of sociality'. In his view 'human solidarity is the first casualty of the triumphs of the consumer market' (2003: 74–6). By contrast, while agreeing that the ever-tighter commodification of our daily lives is taking its toll on traditional ties and bonds, Tomlinson deems the complexity and depth of human relations ultimately far more resilient than Bauman allows for. In his view the manifold lived microstructures of 'identity' – such as personal relationships, local affiliations, traditional customs, as well as other everyday practices and experiences of belonging – are not so easily reined in, let alone smoothly homogenised. According to Tomlinson, it is in fact the quotidian microstructural '"thickening" of cultures that [. . .] chafes against the smooth advance of a uniform capitalist culture' (1999: 88).

Whereas Bauman comes to the conclusion that only a global community institutionally organised into a world state stands a chance of saving humanity from the grim dystopia of socio-economic totalitarianism, Tomlinson remains doubtful of the feasibility, necessity and ultimate desirability of such large-scale centralisation. In Tomlinson's view, it is imperative that all of us learn to live as 'neighbours', both locally and globally, which in an increasingly populous world means first and foremost that we stop feeling cornered and threatened by each other, and that everyday life in the immediate present is prioritised over the pursuit of any grand utopian designs of unanimity and perfection. Indeed, perfect harmony and consensus ought never to be the ultimate goal of community and are probably best discarded altogether. As Tomlinson reminds us, 'it is a characteristic of neighbours that we don't choose them, but have to live alongside them' (182). Instead of requesting the delivery of a new form of global governance that would corral us all into the entirety of one global people, Tomlinson proposes we choose 'to become cosmopolitans without the prospect of a cosmopolis' (199). This would help us make the most of our newly acquired proximity by developing a locally rooted sense of global community, marked by a common agenda of sharing, mutual support and responsibility, yet also by diversity, cultural difference and ample opportunity for political dissent.

Imagining global community without lapsing into either utopia or dystopia is well-nigh impossible. As Tomlinson details, globalisation as 'the emergence of one single culture embracing everyone on earth and replacing the diversity of cultural systems that have flourished up to now' (71) is widely abhorred and resisted. By contrast, if globality might somehow be able to abolish centuries-old enmities and inequalities without also dissolving our individual and collective particularities, it would probably be welcomed by many as the best of all possible worlds. But embarking on an imagined future is always problematic. Invariably it involves a process that risks losing sight of the very practicalities of departure, the difficulty of choosing the right vehicle and road map and, most importantly, the crucial task of ensuring nobody is left behind or falls by the wayside. This is essentially what globalisation as a universal dynamic shares with the initiative of anti-globalisation movements, all of which appear not only to rely on a division between leaders and followers, but also proceed in reaction to an actual or perceived rift between 'us' and 'them' and thus from the start fail to think in genuinely holistic world-communal terms. In this respect, then, Appadurai's (2001: 3) well-intentioned championing of 'grassroots globalization' or 'globalization from below' as 'a series of social forms [that] has emerged to contest, interrogate, and reverse' globalisation proves deeply fallacious. From the work of Michel Foucault we are aware that power must never be regarded *simply* as diametrically opposed to powerlessness, that is, as discretely isolated from its counterpart by a neat hierarchical chasm; rather, power and powerlessness are always of necessity implicated in one another. Therefore, to speak of agencies that 'create forms of knowledge transfer and social mobilization that *proceed independently* of the actions of corporate capital and the nation-state system' (Appadurai 2001: 3; my italics) can only be erroneous, perpetuating a Marxian notion of 'struggle' not – in Nancean terms – as world-communal 'agitation' and 'effervescence' (Nancy 2007: 55), but as two or more partisan factions forever categorically pitted against each other. As Ronaldo Munck explains, the real challenge is to devise 'a new paradigm or framework that will allow us to understand how globalization and contestation (or anti-globalization, to put it crudely) are inextricably bound up with one another' (2007: ix).

Far more successful than Appadurai with regard to their conceptualisation of global resistance are Michael Hardt and Antonio Negri in *Empire* (2000), even though they express their ideas in a language that 'attempts to articulate the utopian longings of Leftist traditions' (McCallum and Faith 2005: 16). What commends Hardt and Negri's approach is their definition of globalisation as 'a decentered and deter-ritorializing apparatus of rule that progressively incorporates the entire global realm within its open, expanding frontiers' (xii). Globalisation is understood in terms of its self-perpetuating systemic impact rather than the doing of any one specific human agency of management or control. Instead of an apparatus that segregates humanity into factions, globali-sation is seen as an all-pervasive, anonymous mechanism whose work-ings do not exclusively affect groups of people from 'below' or the margins; nor are these workings likely ever to be successfully resisted by them alone. Rather, what Hardt and Negri refer to as a 'multitude' – that is, presumably, humanity as a whole – needs to rally from within the system itself 'to reorganize [these workings] and redirect them towards new ends' (xv).

In their review of *Empire* Pamela McCallum and Wendy Faith explain that Hardt and Negri use the term 'multitude' not only 'to avoid the passivity implied in "masses"' but also 'to imagine a group within whom resistance is immanent'. Yet crucially, at the same time as 'the multitude embodies a great refusal, an existential stance of "being-against" [whose] subversive energies [. . .] cannot be controlled by national boundaries and [. . .] exert an insurgent will against any forces of containment' (16), it is also – as Hardt and Negri insist – 'the creative forces of the multitude that sustain Empire' (xv). Put differently, it might no longer be possible to discriminate unequivocally between those who resist Empire, on the one hand, and its functionaries, help-meets and accomplices, on the other. Moreover, as a system Empire can only ever be restructured, yet never dismantled. As culprits and inno-cents, the privileged and the wretched, we inhabit one world propelled by one and the same set of agglomerative forces. We are confronting the same global risks, and only as one community can we ever hope to intervene and creatively alter or channel globalisation's course. Where we are headed matters to all of us, especially since our future is likely to offer increasingly less room for detachment, compartmentalisation or self-encapsulation. Foreigners, migrants, the poor and the starving are already our neighbours, no matter if we choose to deny them entry, deport them or look the other way.

Yet 'how are people even to *think* of themselves as belonging to a global neighbourhood [and] what does it mean to have a global iden-tity, to think and act as a "citizen of the world"' (184)? Tomlinson's questions make it sound as if recognising oneself first and foremost as a human being of and in this world – as vulnerable, culturally deter-mined, exposed to historical circumstance, yet equipped also with a capacity for political agency, however limited – poses a greater challenge than keeping up the appearances of a particular nationality or any other category of belonging. To call oneself a cosmopolitan involves not so much excising one's local affiliations, or rounding off one's personal repertory of identities with a final outer finish, as opening oneself up to a radical unlearning of all definitive modes of identification. It involves stepping out of narrow, self-incarcerating traditions of belonging. The new cosmopolitanism promotes an open and flexible practice of community that can accommodate the whole world, which is quite different from assimilating or containing it. Recalling Immanuel Kant's original Enlightenment conception of the cosmopolitan idea, such a global community would never quite assume the fixity of a neat, seamless entity; rather, it would forever remain a momentary composition enduringly particular and productively conflictual with regard to all its constituents. As Timothy Garton Ash and Ralf Dahrendorf explain:

> Not only did Kant know that power exists, but he thanked nature 'for cantankerousness, for jealous vanity always seeking competition, for the insatiable desire to possess and even to rule.' Only through the 'unsociable sociability' of people, that is, through multiplicity and fission, through 'antagonism,' can people escape from the Arcadian idyll, in which 'in a condition of absolute harmony, frugality and mutual love, all talent would forever wither in the bud.' (2005: 142)

Contemporary cosmopolitanism projects a community that bears rupturing and indeed thrives on recurrent reassemblage – a community that will always tear as well as mend untidily, avoiding clear-cut contours or perfect patterns. This community has no *telos* except its own continuation, which remains resolutely finite and of this world.

This kind of indeterminate, open-ended imagining of world community could only have started to be put into practice towards the end of the twentieth century. As Jérôme Bindé explains, pointing to the fall of the Berlin Wall as a paradigmatic case in point, 'our era has seen the collapse of most ideologies founded on the definition of common salvation and the symbolic representation of a collective destiny' (2001: 91–2). But not only can the fall of the Berlin Wall be read as signposting the end of all radically utopian politics, its very demise was brought about by the spontaneous emergence of a particular kind of communal solidarity, impulsive and improvised to the point of being desultory and chaotic. In the marked absence of ideological directives or governmental management, if possibly motivated vaguely by an originary sense of cultural-historical togetherness and belonging, the forcibly estranged next-door neighbours of East and West Germany mustered a common will to topple that obscene local hallmark of global partitioning that was the Berlin Wall. Perversely, its erection in 1961 had been justified by Communist functionaries as a measure to safeguard the gestation of World Communism, that is, a now thankfully obsolete, strictly regulated project of establishing global community.

The fall of the Berlin Wall exemplifies the revolutionary potential and radical-political clout of what Jean-Luc Nancy theorises in terms of an 'inoperative community'. Not only the popular unruliness that led to the demolition of the Wall, but even more so perhaps the worldwide euphoric optimism that surged in its wake, created momentarily a Nancean 'community without essence (the community that is neither "people" nor "nation," neither "destiny" nor "generic humanity," etc.)' exercising a kind of solidary politics 'that does not stem from the will to realize an essence' (Nancy 1991: xxxix–xl). The event crystallised as an impromptu celebration of ecstatic togetherness across the Iron Curtain frontier, propelled by a pristine yearning to free and to be free. As the Wall came down, nobody had political reunification in mind; most certainly nobody was making definite plans for it. Only once the event as such had occurred did conservative politics choose to identify the agency that toppled the Wall as owned by the German people, triumphantly reunified in the assertion of their sovereignty and their desire for self-completion through accomplishing single-statehood. This retrospective invocation of an essence of Germanness – the nationalist fraudulence of which showed after Reunification in the fiercely partisan rifts between *Wessies* and *Ossies* – stripped the event of its radically *trans*national, cosmopolitan momentum. It also distorted what Fred Dallmayr identifies as the 'relational character' of Nancean community, which is 'predicated on the very rupture or ecstatic transgression of compactness' (1997: 179). Many of the young Germans (and not only Germans) partying in euphoric self-abandon among the debris of the Wall had never conceived of Germany as one and, accordingly, their jubilation was little to do with wresting national unity from a history of tyrannical partitioning. 'Inoperative', in Nancy's vocabulary, describes 'a bond that forms ties without attachments, or even less fusion [. . .] a bond that unbinds by binding' (Nancy 1991: xl). In my view, this captures extremely well the kind of communal spirit that brought down the Berlin Wall, but then wound up stifled, as the expediencies of traditional nation-building resumed their highly predictable course.

In his reading of *The Inoperative Community* Dallmayr writes that by 'reflecting a mutuality [. . .] without fusion, [Nancean] community signals the place of "the *between* as such", that is, a dash or incision: "you *and* I (between us) – a formula in which the *and* does not imply juxtaposition, but exposition"' (1997: 182; see also Nancy 1991: 29).

Applied to the 'inoperative' popular struggle that led to the fall of the Berlin Wall, this suggests that far from finding common ground in their allegedly ineradicable Germanness, East Germans and West Germans in fact shared very little beyond the blank at the core of their national designations as East and West Germans respectively, marking the trauma of either's nationalist overspecification. Yet the conspicuous lacuna splitting 'East' and 'West' from 'German' is also what vitally enabled their communal exposition and mutuality. As Dallmayr comments, 'located in the interstices of mutual exposure [. . .] community is not producible or "workable", but rather marked by a basic lack or absence: the lack of a substance or stable identity that could be fixated once and for all' (1997: 182). It was the very irretrievability of traditional Germanness that contributed to the toppling of the Wall, which – uninhibited by any plan, specific purpose or 'work' – never constituted a project as such. The German revolution had no programme or manifesto, and no leader. It was not carried out in accordance with a fixed political agenda.

What should be clear by now is that 'the absence of communitarian substance does not mean a lack of bonding, just as the accent on "in-operation" does not entail a lapse into indifference or apathetic inaction' (Dallmayr 1997: 191). In other words, inoperative community *is* properly communal, and it also does 'work' in the sense of bringing about political results. What it militates against is ideological organisation and teleology, as well as any other form of 'management', both extraneous and from within. As Ian James explains, Nancean community 'does not refer to a specific social formation or mode of organization, but rather is thought in terms of the very structure of a shared existence' (2006: 176–7). Only by cultivating such an anarchical, radically existential disposition can it effectively 'serve as a bulwark both against a totalizing globalism (dominated by hegemonic powers) and against the surrender of politics to the relentless self-interest of atomistic agents (be they states, corporations, or private individuals)' (193). Commenting on the failure of Soviet Communism, Nancy expresses one of his greatest fears, which is that in our globalised present politics 'is no longer even a question of community' (1991: 23). Globalisation proves even more catastrophic in its impact than Communism because it represents a form of totalitarian rule that has no interest in a controlled restructuring of community after some rigid ideal of perfection; rather, community is regarded as operationally redundant. Globalisation is rendering the planet 'an enclosure in the undifferentiated sphere of a unitotality' (2007: 28). Instead of evolving into an open realm of burgeoning neighbourhoods, in which humanity could thrive on its own multi-relational being-in-common, the planet has begun to agglomerate into mere heapage, a 'piling up' of people and things into disastrously calculable projects of construction. Individuals atomise, while humanity as a whole is corralled into fiercely self-contained, inimical identities. As Nancy warns, in future the globe may come to manifest only as 'its double, *glomus*', signifying 'an indefinite growth of techno-science [. . .] a correlative exponential growth of populations [. . .] a worsening of inequalities of all sorts within these populations'. Humanity will succumb to the 'unworld' of globalisation (34) or, in other words, to *glomicity*, which stands for 'the suppression of all world-forming of the world' (50). The only antidote against this lethal stranglehold is what Nancy designates as *mondialisation* or 'the creation of the world'. As a term, concept and dynamic, mondialisation is as all-encompassing as globalisation. What renders it fundamentally different, however, is that it originates and stays rooted in the specific, unassimilable singularities of the local.

Lest globality forfeit for good 'its capacity to "form a world"' (34), mondialisation promotes cosmopolitan agency as non-directive 'struggle' – by which Nancy means both agitation and effervescence, as well as agitation that is effervescence, and effervescence that is agitation – intent not so much on radically re-imagining the world or rehabilitating humanity as simply exercising 'itself and its contagious communication as propagation of an enjoyment' (55). In certain respects, this Nancean 'enjoyment' appears to take the shape of an embrace, and indeed active fostering, of what in the final chapter of *Liquid Life* Bauman deplores as 'togetherness dismantled'. In Nancy's view, unsettling deconstructive processes are absolutely integral to any productive creation of community, always provided they result in diversification and renewal rather than atomisation and annihilation. Insofar as Nancy could at all be said to envision world community in any concrete form, his vision remains strictly focused on the world as such, on how it is, uninhibited and undistorted by any model, interpretation or rule of itself. The world is at once singular and plural, radically finite and ineradicably rooted in itself; it *is* its own destiny. As he expresses it in 'Cosmos Baselius', one of the segments constituting *Being Singular Plural*:

> The unity of a world is not one: it is made of a diversity, and even disparity and opposition. [. . .] The unity of a world is nothing other than its diversity, and this, in turn, is a diversity of worlds. A world is a multiplicity of worlds; the world is a multiplicity of worlds, and its unity is the mutual sharing and exposition of all its world – within this world.
>
> The sharing of the world is the law of the world. The world has nothing other; it is not subject to any authority; it does not have a sovereign. (2000: 185)

Inclusive and all-encompassing, the world is existence rather than the organisation or management of existence; it is what is happening rather than what is planned or scheduled to happen. Globalisation as 'glomicity' threatens to alienate the world from itself by rendering it an assumed and abstract, marketable thing rather than a place for living. As a result, the world shrinks into *ou*-topia, a 'non-place'. Articulated in Nancy's own terms, 'a world is precisely that in which there is room for everyone: but a genuine place, one in which things can genuinely *take place* (in this world). Otherwise, this is not a "world": it is a "globe" or a "glome," it is a "land of exile" and a "vale of tears"' (2007: 42).

It is time now to pose a number of more immediately literary questions. What defines the new British cosmopolitan novel's position with regard to the traditional status of English literature as 'world literature' as well as its more recent postcolonial diversification? If cosmopolitan writing differs from postcolonial writing, it is presumably to do with cosmopolitanism's attempt at untying and moving beyond imperialism's core–periphery axiomatic: how might this be credibly accomplished, especially when instigated by strictly English-identified writers? How might the cosmopolitan novel be shown to represent 'mondialisation', accommodate and practise Nancean world-creation, as well as 'work' (or 'think') as a mode of resistance to the largely passively endured fate of globalisation?

Highly sensitive to historical and socio-economic shifts in polarity and perspective, literature is equipped with a unique pioneering capacity for envisioning the world. Significantly, literary realism is never interested just in an accurate portrayal of reality, but invariably also – if not indeed always much more so – in the latter's imaginative reconfiguration. As Paul Gilroy notes, it is important that as critics of globalisation we not only stay alert to how politics contrives to recast our world, but also that we implement the right to intervene in this recasting, especially when it comes to making decisions on how to handle the appearance of alleged civilisational rifts within an ever-more tightly compressed world, as well as the very phenomenon of this compression itself. 'As the postcolonial and post-Cold War model of global authority takes shape and reconfigures relationships between the overdeveloped, the developing, and the developmentally arrested worlds', Gilroy writes, 'it is important to ask what critical perspectives might nurture the ability and the desire to live with difference on an increasingly divided but also convergent planet' (2004: 3). What Gilroy's exclusive focus on politics and the selection of appropriate critical perspectives occludes is that there are creative practices, such as literature, whose reconfiguration of the world constitutes at the same time a critique of contemporary politics and, potentially at least, a nurturing of global conviviality. By making this point I intend to draw attention to a curious omission on Gilroy's part, an omission that effectively eclipses the political, critical and world-creative potentialities of art – narrative or otherwise. In *Linked Histories: Postcolonial Studies in a Globalized World* McCallum and Faith display a greater awareness of literature's ability to recast the world, that is, its ability not only to record or represent but indeed to initiate momentous paradigm shifts, both critically and politically. Despite their foregrounding of criticism, the challenges of articulation and reconceptualisation highlighted in their questioning clearly bear equal relevance for contemporary literature's practice of world-creation:

> How might it be possible to articulate and facilitate potential sites of cross-cultural exchange without situating genders, races, classes as the 'others' of Europe? How does a renewed interest in the intersections of culture and materialism challenge postcolonial criticism to rethink categories of marginality and subalternity? How might identity be reconceived by a postcolonial criticism sensitive to the nuances of complicity and compromise within global economic structures? (2005: 4–5)

Urging us to interrogate and move beyond, or at the very least to improve on, conventional postcolonialist enquiry, McCallum and Faith's catalogue of questions also touches on the generic shape and imaginative tenets of the cosmopolitan novel.

As already noted, Binnie and his co-editors define cosmopolitan practice by drawing up 'a set of skills which are applied in the encounter with difference' (Binnie et al. 2006: 8), involving in particular 'the ability to map one's own socio-cultural position vis-à-vis the diversity encountered'. Following this promising opening their outline becomes problematic, especially in its specification of the purposes and benefits of cosmopolitan practice, which appears to take us back to the crypto-imperialist early cosmopolitan theory of Hannerz's generation. Or how else are we to interpret statements seemingly resurrecting the Orientalist self/other imagery of a metropolitan observer competently organising the object of his enquiry, which is the 'other' culture? Whatever risks of exposure the observer takes on 'are overcome by [his] ability and willingness [. . .] to make sense of and move through different societies, gathering not only knowledge of the particular culture in question but also enhancing a disposition and attitude that reduces the shock of the new or the different in other circumstances'. The cosmopolitan envisaged in *Cosmopolitan Urbanism* looks like an intrepid explorer bravely contributing to our culture's accumulation of knowledge by 'navigating and negotiating difference', all the while wearing cosmopolitanism like some kind of protective shock-proof overcoat (2006: 8). In stark contrast, the skills of cosmopolitan novelists must be of an entirely different order, as their aim is, in Nancean fashion, to reveal the anachronism of these kinds of hegemonic distinctions between self and other. Faced with a contemporary global-human condition that exposes all indigenous positions in equal measure, subsuming them in the vertiginous order of an all-pervasive imperial regime that strictly inhibits the crystallisation of a clear-cut centre or margins, it is becoming increasingly difficult to discriminate categorically between victims and perpetrators, or explorers and explored, since ultimately no one controls globalisation or could be said to be exempt from the diffusive pull of its systemic subjection. As Hardt and Negri explain, globalisation 'manages hybrid identities, flexible hierarchies, and plural exchanges through modulating networks of command. The distinct national colors of the imperialist map of the world have merged and blended in the imperialist global rainbow' (2000: xxii–xxiii).

In order to resist the allure of this colourfully homogenised new globality, which not only in the same breath promotes and extinguishes individual difference but also gives rise to a dazzling worldwide diversity of the quite-similar, the cosmopolitan novelist must create the world by yielding to it as it is: exposed, finite, inoperative, powerless. Tearing up the veils of sovereignty, autonomy and independence, the cosmopolitan novelist embarks on a *tour du monde* that concentrates on who we really are, and what in order to survive we have at our disposal. Cosmopolitan narration assembles as many as possible of the countless segments of our being-in-common into a momentarily composite picture of the world – quite like a child's kaleidoscope held still for only a second before collapsing into new, equally wondrous, yet perfectly plausible constellations. Cosmopolitan narration proceeds without erasing the essential incongruousness or singularity of these individual segments, which are left intact, even though they remain subject to continual re-assortment. Most significantly, the cosmopolitan novel has abandoned the vertebrate structures of the traditional novel's *tour d'horizon* and begun instead to experiment with what are more cellular modes of representation. The specific terminology of 'vertebrate' and 'cellular' used in this context is derived from Appadurai's distinction in *Fear of Small Numbers* between different systems of political rule and agency, in which 'vertebrate' refers to the old fixed traditions of internationalist statehood whereas 'cellular' stands for the contingency of contemporary global and transnational flows (2006: 21–31). Compelled to mimic this shift in the 'texture' of global politics, the creation of the world as instigated by the vertebrate novel – that is, the novel that imagines the nation – gives way to the 'mondialising' techniques and strategies of the cosmopolitan novel – that is, the novel that imagines the world.

Both the compositeness and the cellularity of the cosmopolitan novel deserve to be taken seriously. Every cosmopolitan novel requires to be understood in its entirety, even if whatever composite integrity it displays remains at best a precarious balancing act of momentarily resisting the pull into dispersion. Sadik Al-Azm realises this very well in his appraisal of what is without doubt the single most important prototype of the contemporary cosmopolitan novel: Salman Rushdie's *The Satanic Verses* (1988), hailed by Al-Azm as 'the multicultural, multinational world-novel *par excellence*' (2000: 48). Led by the novel's arrangement as a multiplicity of differently located narratives telescoped one into the other, Al-Azm infers that in Rushdie's text:

> India, England, Islam, Europe, Iran, the West, the Arabs – as a settled past, as a live present and as an anticipated future – do not simply coexist and impact each other at the periphery [. . .] nor are they merely contemporaneous with and adjacent to each other, but mesh and interpenetrate at all conceivable levels: economic, commercial, scientific, colonial, anti-colonial, political, ideological, religious, cultural, artistic, personal, sexual, etc. [. . .] [They] become, by force of global circumstance, seriously constitutive of each other in an unprecedented manner and in unheard-of ways. (2000: 49)

By contrast, in deciding in her own reading of the novel to 'engage only the main narrative [. . .] set primarily in London, with interludes in Bombay' (2002: 44, n1), Gillian Gane fails to apprehend the cosmopolitan design and outlook of Rushdie's work. Gane believes *The Satanic Verses* falls into main- and sub-narrative strands that can be read discretely. As a result, Rushdie's project of assigning far-fetched and half-forgotten local narratives the same significance and pride of place as noisily attention-seeking metropolitan narratives eludes her, as does his conviction that ultimately there is only one narrative to narrate, and that is the world's in its entirety. The rationale behind the cosmopolitan novel's apparent predilection for constituting as a seemingly unfinished quilt of small *récits*, more often than not outside any safely contextualising frame, can be explained via Tim Gauthier's proposition that 'since we no longer possess a system whereby meaning might be immediately conferred upon an event, the creation of the "little narratives" becomes our only source for such signification' (2006: 5). Importantly, however, in the cosmopolitan novel this turn to the small is no second-best compromise, but the actually preferred mode of representation, strategically necessitated by apprehending globalisation as a powerfully meaning-enforcing system whose impact can be allayed only by mobilising the entire microcosmic 'nitty-gritty' of global multiplicity. The most crucial skill of the cosmopolitan novelist is not to map or navigate the world, or simply to go with the flow, but to take the plunge and like everybody else start mingling among the world's vast, inoperative being-in-common, that is, the world as such rather than any one of its projected models or interpretations.

Unlike many of the new media, such as television, blockbuster cinema or the internet, which supply the bulk of illustrative material for contemporary globalisation studies and cosmopolitan theory, the novel continues to thrive despite rather than because of its successful commercial commodification. This remains the case even though ubiquitous Creative Writing courses have begun to churn out an endless stream of cleverly plotted and smoothly written, yet often quite inconsequential texts conceived and commissioned more for their salability and short-term topical appeal than their artistic merit or in-depth engagement with the allegedly old-fashioned literary matters of truth, justice, community and beauty. Notably, in their introduction to a special issue of the *South Atlantic Quarterly* on 'The Globalization of Fiction', Susie O'Brien and Imre Szeman feel compelled to assert that literature is in fact 'fast becoming a vestigial cultural form' possessing little relevance 'for politically minded intellectuals interested in tracing the seismic tremors of contemporary culture back to the shifting of tectonic plates of the political and the economic', and making a suitable object of study only for 'cultural historians fascinated with long-forgotten practices whose imaginative grip it is now hard to comprehend' (2001: 612). O'Brien and Szeman's oppositioning implies not only that cultural historians may not be intellectuals, but also that what makes art worthy of critical attention is what it reveals about politics and economics rather than its own imaginative initiative and investment, and finally also that popular impact and significance are irreconcilable with 'high' art, which is assumed to be an esoteric thing of the past that no longer has any bearing at all on the contemporary.

Rather than providing a shrewd commentary on the alleged obsolescence of literature and literary study, what O'Brien and Szeman actually draw attention to is a critical malaise within cultural studies, of which their own analysis appears symptomatic. Literature's arcane representational strategies are read as a sign of its unworldliness and rapidly fading niche-market appeal rather than its intransigent, world-creative resistance to ideological vehicularisation. If literature is indeed becoming a residual art form, then this ought to give rise to great critical concern since its vanishing is bound to play into the hands of those who benefit most from our culture, namely the engineers, managers and censors of the very same 'seismic tremors of contemporary culture' that self-professed intellectuals like O'Brien and Szeman so pride themselves on detecting. My study defends the contemporary cosmopolitan novel as an art form – 'vestigial' or not – in which the realities of the political and economic are subjected to imaginative scrutiny and recasting instead of undergoing a process of simple rendition. The latter – as O'Brien and Szeman's view illustrates – not only encourages trendy, marketable consumption but moreover works to facilitate an equally trendy and marketable critique.

Steven Connor usefully opens his *English Novel in History* by characterising the novel 'not just as passively marked with the imprint of history, but also as one of the ways in which history is made, and remade'. Importantly he then adds that 'the processes we associate with the making and substantiation of fictional worlds are [also] to be seen at work within the making of the real, historical world' (1996: 1–2). In Connor's view, then, literature is equipped with powerful world-creative capabilities that either emulate, intimately correlate with, or simply share reality's. And yet, in his eyes even a text as explosively paradigm-shifting as Rushdie's *Satanic Verses* only confirms what is typical of the novel as 'the form which in its name has always promised news or novelty'; accordingly, even the most innovative or experimental novel is never really quite new because, looked at more closely, it only fulfils what is definitive of the genre. Therefore, although Connor does recognise that the contemporary novel is caught up in some 'process of refashioning' (127), this recognition has no immediate impact on his own critical outlook, which, in continuing to grasp the fate of the novel as inextricably tied to the nation's, remains inured to emergent paradigm shifts in creative perspective. Connor imagines the nation as endowed with integrity and autonomy, whose preservation is threatened by the self-interest of other nations as well as more general processes of globalisation and increasing multiculturalism. The novel he describes thus turns out to be not really world-creative at all, but creative only of the nation. Symptomatically, he speaks of Britain's post-1945 'eviction from historical self-possession' exacerbated by 'an increasingly hostile "outside" press[ing] in upon Englishness, in the ever more aggressive relations of military superpowers and the ever more rampant and uncontrollable dynamisms of a capitalism organised in multinational forms'. Not a word here of Britain's embedment within Europe or the world; instead, Britishness hardens and contracts into Englishness, eclipsing the nation's multicultural make-up and global openness, which Connor dares express only quite negatively as 'the multiplication of alternative forms of belonging and self-definition [that cause] the very idea of what Englishness meant [. . .] to come apart on the inside' (3). The nation's story, which is also the novel's, is portrayed consistently as one of disintegration and decline, leaving little room for the more productive cosmopolitan envisioning of a trajectory of deconstructive diversification and renewal.

Connor's commentary on the creative capabilities and functions of the novel both complements and fruitfully contrasts with my own, which is inspired by Nancean philosophy. In his reading of 'Myth Interrupted' and '"Literary Communism"', two constitutive segments of Nancy's *Inoperative Community* (1991: 43–70, 71–81), Ian James comes to define art within the framework of Nancy's thought as 'that movement of sense which is, or opens up, world-hood itself in all its singular plurality' (2006: 203). This definition chimes harmoniously with Connor's assertion that 'it is hard to think of another kind of evidence [apart from the novel] which so abundantly and yet so economically concentrates together representations of how the world is, or seems to be, with the shaping force of fantasy or imagination; which balances, in other words, reality and desire' (1). The crucial difference is that Nancy would baulk at Connor's virtually synonymous use of 'imagination', 'fantasy' and 'desire' as, to Nancy, imagination constitutes a far more earthbound and deeply immanent faculty than Connor appears to allow for, sourced and nourished by the experience of actual human living. Connor's association of literature with 'desire' heightens its susceptibility to the utopian fallacy, that is, the possibility that it might succumb to a yearning beyond the world as it is, and resort to projecting or replicating a particular ideological model of the world rather than engaging in inoperative world-creation.

The Nancean understanding of history is equally resolute in its refutation of *telos* and transcendence of any kind, and in its emphatic insistence upon life's finitude. It is important to recognise the vital role literature is assigned within such a radically immanent dynamic of generative disruption: 'Historical change cannot be conceived in terms of a dialectical or teleological process, but rather in terms of a constant birth or becoming of singular-plural sense that interrupts established foundational narratives and opens the way for future narratives to emerge' (James 2006: 199). Inhibited by the persistent circulation of myths and dominant ideologies that so enduringly work to rigidify the globe, humanity's literary impulse still somehow manages to tap into 'the contingent and plural mess of historical becoming', out of which might then crystallise 'other divergent or emergent narratives, or new and different forms of sense' (199). James concludes that according to Nancy, literature, far more elemental a force than what appears cast in stone about who we are supposedly, 'is the very sharing of sense which reveals to us our being-in-common [. . .] a practice of thought and of writing, of thought in and as writing, which articulates our shared being beyond any figure of identity' (200). In this light, then, the cosmopolitan novel must be seen not only to express, like any other ethically informed writing practice, 'a specific manner of being-in-the-world, and a specific way of comporting oneself toward the world and toward the existence of others' (201), but also as fruitfully disruptive of the myth-like matrix installed by preceding narrative forms of similarly inclined communal self-expression.

The introduction of sociological concepts of globalisation into literary studies will form a major feature of the following interpretative chapters. By also conducting my readings with close reference to current debates in cosmopolitan theory, I am seeking to make a contribution to current debates on global culture, communal identification, literary creativity and political agency. What distinguishes my study markedly from other recent work on the contemporary British novel is my interest in global community rather than exclusively national concerns, as well as in literature as a specialised set of ethical tools for cultural critique and creative world-formation. My study must not be mistaken for a simple overview or catalogue of exemplary case studies. Its focus on contemporary British fiction as a response to new economic and socio-cultural formations within the world as a whole sets out to challenge traditional critical and creative paradigms by tracing the development of a new narrative modus operandi.

While I agree wholeheartedly with Liam Connell's endeavour 'to depart from much of the current thinking about globalisation and the literary, which has tended to talk primarily in terms of the meta-structures of circulation and commodification of postcolonial texts' (Connell 2006: 161), my own enquiry ventures beyond his discussion of how globalisation 'can be understood as a textual characteristic' (2004: 79) or 'thematic content of literary texts' (94). Instead of demonstrating 'how texts narrate the concepts of worldliness, convergence and universalism within the frame of a supposedly intensified internationalism' (85), I intend to draw special attention to literature's propensity for world-creation rather than simple rendition or representation in order to show how the contemporary cosmopolitan novel contests and radically reconfigures the phenomena highlighted by

Connell, as well as their given frame. Similarly, my investigation only momentarily overlaps with O'Brien and Szeman's thinking about literature 'outside the framework of national literatures' and their questioning of what 'critical tools might be used to make sense of such literatures, and what in turn might be learned from and about them, in ways that open up new perspectives on the problems and possibilities that we face at the present time' (2001: 605). As explained above, in their keenness to determine 'literature's role in the narrative construction of the numerous discourses or "fictions" of globalization' (604), O'Brien and Szeman not merely overlook, but categorically dispute and dismiss literature's capability to refuse or significantly recast its assigned role.

Finally, a word on structural organisation: three of the following five chapters concentrate on a new generation of pre-canonical writers whose work has so far received very little critical attention, or none at all. These writers are Rachel Cusk (born 1967), Kiran Desai (born 1971), Hari Kunzru (born 1969), Jon McGregor (born 1976) and David Mitchell (born 1969). The apparent lack of critical interest in their work is all the more astounding since Cusk, Kunzru and Mitchell were all on *Granta*'s 2003 list of Best Young British Novelists, Desai won the 2006 Man Booker Prize, and McGregor's debut novel *If Nobody Speaks of Remarkable Things* (2002) quickly became a charts-topping best-seller. Quite possibly academia's neglect of this generation of up-and-coming writers – with the notable exception of Desai – is to do with their pioneering of a radically new narrative outlook, which renders their work difficult to categorise and equally difficult to incorporate into current teaching curricula and research plans – a dilemma my study attempts to remedy. The decision to include *The God of Small Things* by Arundhati Roy (born 1961) in chapter 4 was made more or less at the very last minute, not only because it was found to help accentuate what is perceived to be missing from Desai's work, but also to draw attention to the already well-documented rise of the cosmopolitan novel within other cultural contexts, such as India's (see Ghosh 2004). The opening two chapters of my study are dedicated to a close comparison of novels by James Kelman (born 1946) and Ian McEwan (born 1948) as mature representative voices of working-class Scotland and middle-class England respectively. To my knowledge, Kelman and McEwan have never been examined in such immediate proximity, most probably because they have so far been assumed to have very little in common. In my view, it is precisely this apparent incommensurability that makes a detailed comparison of their works particularly interesting and fruitful.

My enquiry falls into three main parts: 'Imagining Cosmopolitics', on established writers' proto-cosmopolitan responses to globalisation; '*Tour du Monde*', the central chapter on David Mitchell, which pivotally interlinks the study's two main sections; and 'Creating the World', which introduces work by the new cosmopolitans.

I

Imagining Cosmopolitics

Chapter 1

Families against the World: Ian McEwan

Written in response to the fall of the Berlin Wall and the attacks on the World Trade Center in New York respectively, Ian McEwan's *Black Dogs* (1992) and *Saturday* (2005) both aim to capture the sensibility of a newly emergent Anglo-British contemporaneity. Read in combination, they disclose the bipolar bracketing of the 1990s by one joyous and one profoundly traumatic world event, a bracketing compounded by Britain's sandwiched position, both culturally and politically, between Europe and the USA. Transporting us from middle-English Wiltshire to contemporary and historical Germany, Poland and France, *Black Dogs* sets out to explore what is fundamentally a European sense of belonging. Yet notably it remains preoccupied with the continent's dark mid-century past rather than its post-1989 moment of euphoric reunification. Fashioned ultimately, after its main protagonist's name, into a jeremiad of political resignation, the novel accentuates the individual's as well as the family's vulnerability and helplessness in the face of world events.

Saturday, by contrast, follows the life of successful London neurosurgeon Henry Perowne on 15 February 2003, a day of worldwide rallying against the impending Iraq War. The novel culminates in the triumph of individual and familial agency over criminally deranged adversity. Its central conflict between the Perownes and petty gangster Baxter, a sufferer from Huntington's Chorea, mirrors the conflict between US America's Coalition of the Willing and the late Iraqi dictator Saddam Hussein. McEwan's markedly tentative, self-conscious and circuitous mode of narration in *Black Dogs* is superseded by the perfectly linear, neatly emplotted trajectory of *Saturday* which, solidly anchored in the English literary tradition, invokes both the day-in-a-life structure of Virginia Woolf's *Mrs Dalloway* (1925) and the resolutely vertebrate five-act composition of a Shakespearean history play.

Black Dogs casts Jeremy, orphaned since childhood and in the habit of attaching himself to other people's parents, in the role of historian recording the lives of his parents-in-law, Bernard and June Tremaine. The Tremaines have been estranged for several decades, in fact ever since their honeymoon in France in 1946 when, following her encounter with two feral dogs on a lonely country path, June abruptly ceases to share her husband's socialist hopes for radical global change and 'abandon[s] the world in pursuit of a life of spiritual meditation' (McEwan 1992: 109). From the beginning McEwan encourages us to read his family of characters as an allegory of the conflictual tensions between different kinds of modernist worldviews and ideologies, on the one hand, and a postmodernist inability to commit oneself to any one school of thought, on the other. June describes her son-in-law as 'a typical member of [his] generation' (53) while Jeremy perceives his position as perpetually oscillating between June's and Bernard's: 'Rationalist and mystic, commissar and yogi, joiner and abstainer, scientist and intuitionist, Bernard and June are the extremities, the twin poles along whose slippery axis my own unbelief slithers and never comes to rest' (19). McEwan's representation echoes Linda Hutcheon's critical rendition of modernism's relationship to postmodernism in terms of an ambivalent parent–child relationship that is 'both oedipally oppositional and filially faithful' (1988: 88). This apparent correspondence between the writer's and the critic's choice of imagery is underscored by Tim Gauthier's reading of the Tremaines as 'representatives of two dying master-narratives that have no easy and automatic place in the post-War world', namely Communism and Christianity. Consequently, it is up to Jeremy as 'a "postmodern orphan" [. . .] to make sense of the void left by the absence of these controlling structures' (2006: 109).

Black Dogs seems most interested in whether Jeremy can resolve the ideological conundrum thrust upon him by the constant wrangling of his parents-in-law, and if in refusing (or being unable) to follow in either's footsteps, he might succeed in carving out a less inhibitive, more genuinely self-fulfilling, world-creative path for himself. Certainly McEwan could not have chosen a better moment for attempting to settle the postmodern quandary than November 1989: for all to see, world history has asserted itself in the demolition of the Berlin Wall, demanding now of everybody an evaluation, however partisan, of the past, as well as an inspired envisioning of the future. But how will the challenge of the contemporary affect Jeremy, in whose mind 'there was simply no good cause, no enduring principle, no fundamental idea with which I could identify' (18)? Heralding the beginning of a new era, might 9 November 1989 – as a genuine world-political turning point – not also seal the end of postmodernity by unfreezing Cold War global politics and requiring everybody to take a definite stance? In this respect, suggesting that Jeremy 'appears to turn his back on postmodernism [. . .] to concentrate on the more unpalatable business of looking the beast of history straight in the eye' (1995: 7), Marc Delrez's opening impression of *Black Dogs* certainly appears most apposite.

Yet Jeremy fails to seize the moment for reflecting on world politics or, for that matter, his own ethical responsibility. Compiling an intimately personal account of his family-in-law's past, he remains distracted. This is the case even though the way the world presents itself to him in the course of the novel, during which he and Bernard visit Berlin to eye-witness the events of November 1989, could hardly be any more immediate or obtrusive. Oblivious to the potentialities of singularity and multitudinous diversity alike, Jeremy remains caught in the exclusivist grip of the private. In his view, there appears to be no such thing as global community; rather, the world is played out solely by the likes of Bernard, June and himself. 'I am uncertain whether our civilization at this turn of the millennium is cursed by too much or too little belief', he muses, 'whether people like Bernard and June cause the trouble, or people like me' (20). This casts doubt on Dominic Head's suggestion that, within McEwan's work, *Black Dogs* represents 'a significant phase of political writing' (2007: 91), unless, of course, political writing about late-twentieth-century Europe from an English perspective must inevitably give in to solipsism and resignation. One is keen to agree with Head that 'Jeremy's orphan mentality [. . .] denotes the collective hunger of the post-war generation for social and political stability in Europe' (116), but in *Black Dogs* Europe is never more than a remembered story, or indeed mere background to such a story. Not once does it unfold into an arena for genuine political initiative or creative world-formation.

McEwan's orphan imagery is seductive, suggesting that all ideologies of the twentieth century have forsaken Jeremy, causing him and his generation to adopt ever new sets of preconceived ideals in a never-ending cycle of self-authenticating trial and error. Looked at more closely, however, even though he continues to be deeply perplexed by the meanings his elders choose to infer from history and personal experience, it is striking to see him resort to strategies of meaning-making not all so very different to theirs. Jeremy's memoir draws on a broad range of specifically modernist techniques and devices, in particular recurrent patterning, epiphany and the use of multiple perspectives, all of which – despite his self-professed scepticism – are geared towards a final feat of closure translucent with enduring significance. Jeremy engages in a piecing together of fragments from various conflicting sources, a deliberate shoring up of images against the unbearable callousness of relativity and mindless chance. The ultimate aim of his efforts is, if not the actual consolidation, then certainly the adumbration of a new myth. Despite pointing up the hazards of entextualisation in general, and those pertaining to historical fiction and fictional historiography in particular, *Black Dogs* eventually overrules Jeremy's postmodernist pose of apprehending meaning only as *différance*, oscillating between certitudes that have begun to blur out of focus. In its conclusion *Black Dogs* comes to share June's vision of an eternal recurrence of evil. '[The black dogs] are receding from her, black stains in the grey of dawn', the novel records, 'fading as they move into the foothills of the mountains from where they will return to haunt us, somewhere in Europe, in another time' (174). Against this inevitability only one other certainty protrudes from among postmodernism's plethora of unreliable truths, partisan histories, manipulated subjects and manufactured meanings, and that is Jeremy's faith in love, which he describes as the backbone of his life. 'I'd be false to my own experience', he writes, 'if I did not declare my belief in the possibility of love transforming and redeeming a life' (20). Such unabashed championing of the redemptive power of familial intimacy at first glance only serves to exacerbate the already marked withdrawal of the novel into the private. Alternatively, however, it might quite possibly serve to capture the spirit of the postmodern age as it finds itself tipping into a new era.

Terry Eagleton's coinage of the 'pre-postmodern' in his introduction to *The Illusions of Postmodernism* may help to define the specific contemporaneity of 1989 in greater detail:

> Just as 'postmodernist' itself means not just that you have left modernism definitively behind, but that you have worked your way through it to a position still deeply marked by it, so there may be a kind of pre-postmodernism which has worked its way through postmodernism and come out roughly on the side where it started, which is by no means the same as not having shifted at all. (1996: viii–ix)

Releasing postmodernity from the narcissism of its largely inconsequential orthodoxies, the end of the Cold War transports post-war Europe back to its original point of departure. Four and a half decades of political stagnancy and disorientation give way to enable a new, wiser, more clear-sighted beginning, the kind of 'pre-postmodernist' incipience so precariously sketched out here by Eagleton. We may want to recall that in 1946 – 'determined to test their new liberties, personal and geographical [. . .] young, just married and in love' – June and Bernard embarked on their honeymoon 'across the Channel to the chaos of Northern Europe where they have been advised not to go' (27). Keen 'to help to change the world' (41), they soon find their hopes frustrated, as the world only looks 'new and at peace' (27) while in fact the centuries-old internationalist conflicts persist and Europe proves too traumatised and scarred to heave itself out of its ruins. The question at the heart of *Black Dogs* is whether in 1989 conditions might be more propitious, and someone else's attempt at making a difference stands a better chance of success than the Tremaines' forty years previously. Although clearly moved by the Berlin revolution as broadcast on TV, Jeremy and his wife Jenny seem perhaps too set in their ways, and ultimately too uninspired, to begin actively to contribute to the imminent changes in contemporary global politics. And yet, when later in the novel Jeremy details the youthful Tremaines' gradual disenchantment, he also suggests that it might have cheered them considerably had they known 'their first child, a daughter, my wife [. . .] would one day put up a good fight for a seat in the European Parliament' (138). It is left to the reader's conjecture whether by 1989 Jenny's candidature is already a thing of the past or whether, instead, we are to read it as a cosmopolitical promise yet awaiting fulfilment.

McEwan's novel struggles to shake off its postmodernist solipsism and start envisioning a post-1989 cosmopolitan future informed by a European sense of communal solidarity and belonging. As far as his engagement with people and politics is concerned, Jeremy might as well live in June's isolation. Also, like his father-in-law, he demonstratively lacks 'the common touch' and probably – to borrow Bernard's apologetic tone – 'never had it, dear boy. Ideas were my thing' (74). The euphoria and political optimism enveloping the world in November 1989 fail to infect the two visiting Englishmen. While 'people were converging on Berlin from all over the planet. A huge party was in the making' (71), Jeremy and Bernard brush through the milling crowds, keeping themselves to themselves, impervious to the popular surge that engulfs them, merely observing everybody else's experience as history runs its course without them. Exactly the same kind of political aloofness and self-detachment sustains *Saturday*, throughout which neither Henry nor any other member of his family actually participate in what is happening in the outside world. Politics does not occur to them. Incredulous at McEwan's decision 'to represent the largest single anti-war demonstration in the history of Britain from a distance', Elizabeth Wallace notes how in *Saturday* 'a moment of great political turmoil, of tumultuous and conflicting political opinions and attitudes, goes by in a second, leaving the protagonist with the problem of how to get to his squash game on time' (2007: 471). Both novels are propelled by a strictly centripetal dynamic of self-enclosure contracting ever more tightly into a familial core or, to be more precise, the marital couple's intimately knotted *égoïsme à deux*. Clearly nothing much has changed since Jeremy's teenage years when he first encountered a post-imperial cosmopolitanism reduced to choices of domestic interior design, as in the Langleys' home where he finds himself entertained in 'a huge, book-crammed room with Syrian daggers, a shaman's mask, an Amazonian blow pipe with curare-tipped darts', attentively listening to his school-friend's father, who used to be 'a diplomat with the Foreign Office [. . .] in the Middle East, Kenya and Venezuela' and now reads 'untranslated Proust or Thucydides or Heine' (11).

Individual atomisation and nuclear-family seclusion rigidify both novels, inhibiting political initiative and genuine cosmopolitan exchange. The world, albeit much-debated and hotly fought over in the abstract, never issues alive from the eclectic contents of a mere shopping bag of stories, trophies and exotic consumables, which – like 'the fresh lychees from Soho market, Montblanc black ink, the 1762–3 volume of Boswell's Journal, Brazilian coffee and half a dozen bars of expensive chocolate' (32) that Jeremy takes on his visit to see June – only serve to sweeten the characters' withdrawal from politics. Closer to home, opportunities for a more local cosmopolitanism are obstructed by the 'mundane embattlement' of the Perownes' multiply-locked and bolted, security-chained, spyholed, panic-buttoned and alarm-padded hyper-bole of a front door. Henry's paranoid fear of 'the city's poor, the drug-addicted, the downright bad' (37), so deeply ingrained and automatic it has become almost casual, appears as the next logical step from young Jeremy's barely suppressed disdain for his friends' socialising with kids from the disreputable no-go zones of Shepherd's Bush, Kensal Rise and Notting Hill. Henry's worldview resembles that of a regal observer elevated far above the commoners in the public square below; notably, he catches himself 'surveying the crowd with satisfaction [like Saddam] from some Baghdad ministry balcony' (62). Despite all the international journeying they do whilst pursuing their busy careers, contemplating the world, or simply being on vacation, McEwan's characters' apparent cosmopolitanism opens up to them neither Europe nor the world. Conspicuously, for most of the time, it is the safe haven of family reunion that is their destination. Once indoors, all the world's concerns fade, muffled by the cosy, oblivious self-complacency of home. A whole ten years before *Saturday* was published, Delrez deplored the absence in McEwan's work of 'a wider, cross-cultural perspective that would not restrict the scope to decline and sterility, or to hypocrisy and a self-seeking disengagement from the mess' (1995: 22). In other words, what remains absent from McEwan's work is a cosmopolitan impetus and conviction capable of reconciling the familial with the communal, the local and the global rather than pitting it against them as some antidotal protective bulwark.

Community begins at home. Clearly, the tragedy of the Tremaines' failure at creative world-formation is to do with their inability to fulfil the promise and potential of their marriage. As June explains to Jeremy, 'we failed to do a thing with it. We couldn't make a life', poignantly adding the question 'why should I expect millions of strangers with conflicting interests to get along when I couldn't make a simple society with the father of my children, the man I've loved and remained married to' (52–3). Yet again McEwan excels at carving out formulaic extremes, as he contrasts June and Bernard's insurmountable estrangement with Jenny and Jeremy's (as well as Henry and Rosalind's) perfect marital complementarity. While the former works to split the world beyond repair, however, the latter shuts it out, thus equally dividing the world into mutually exclusive, self-contained spheres. When the telephone rings with the news of the fall of the Berlin Wall, interrupting their early-morning love-making, Jeremy notes that he and Jenny 'were doing our best to keep its full importance at arms' length, for we did not yet belong to the world [. . .] An important principle was at stake, that we maintain the primacy of the private life' (69). As Delrez points out, this self-protective resistance to the alleged encroachment of an intrusive world is typical of the couple's exclusivist bond; notably, even Jenny and Jeremy's four children never materialise, or even make themselves heard, in the novel. Commenting on the couple's first sexual encounter immediately after visiting the Nazi concentration camp at Majdanek, Delrez writes:

> Jeremy's love affair with Jenny seems to be rooted in a private-individualist ethos that implies utter disregard for the body politic [. . .] their first move as a couple is to turn their backs on barbed wire and to withdraw to the closet afforded by a local hotel, where they spend three days of unbroken love-making [. . .] Throughout McEwan's work, this move is presented as a matter of philosophical necessity, perhaps of survival, in a postmodern age in which the old systems of value have ceased to command any credence. (1995: 19–20)

But as the example of Henry and Rosalind in *Saturday* demonstrates, even as the postmodern age is on the wane and new global challenges are looming, McEwan persists with his routine dismissal of the world by the love-making couple. In deliberate contrast to *Black Dogs*, which concludes with solitary June's liminal vision of a recurrent return of evil, at the close of *Saturday* Henry 'closes the shutters' before he gets into bed with his wife, 'fit[ting] himself around her, her silk pyjamas, her scent, her warmth, her beloved form', thinking 'there's always this [. . .] there's only this' (279). With the perils of the world thus quelled and eclipsed, *Saturday* cosily reinscribes the prerogative of the private over the public, not so much suggesting that the world rests on the family as that the family can endure and perpetuate itself in perfect, independent superiority to the world. This make-believe posture of couplist self-sufficiency not only gives credence to Wallace's impression that 'McEwan's novel continually glances at a multicultural and cosmopolitan society with which it resists engagement' (467); much more worryingly, it explains why such an engagement is never felt to be quite imperative.

What Delrez means by claiming 'that love, taken as the highest human value, yields a world view that consistently elides issues of sociopolitical concern' (18) is that the pronounced exclusivity of McEwan's marital couples cannot bear very much community. Wallace's assessment that *Saturday* 'normalizes the idea that it is understandable for people like Henry not to connect with those beyond his immediate family' (470–1) does not quite capture the very narrowness of McEwan's characters' definition of 'family'. In *Saturday*, despite the fact that 'the house is big, seven thousand square feet' (269), the Perownes' grandfather, in need of medical attention for a broken nose after the family's shocking ordeal, is escorted back to his hotel in a taxi. In *Black Dogs* Sally, Jeremy's orphaned niece, now a homeless single mother and battered wife, is looking to her family 'for affection and support', but after taking her in twice, Jeremy, though purporting to feel mightily guilty about it, confesses that 'the strain on family life had been too great for us to keep her' (68). In McEwan's representation, contemporary middle-class Britain's nuclear families comprise no havens for the needy, but exclusive clubs for those lucky enough to belong. Far from constituting the bedrock or fundamental building block of cosmopolitan society, the family is a fiercely guarded hiding place, designed to ward off rather than embrace or integrate the world, inimical to rather than generative of community.

This raises cosmopolitanism's principal question of 'the nature, and possible limits, of human existential-moral engagement' (Tomlinson 1999: 205). How much can we ever genuinely feel, and how much are we therefore prepared to do, for others, not only members of our extended families, but the local community and ultimately the world at large? This problem certainly lies at the root of *Saturday*, which slowly unwraps the difficulty of making time in our busy schedules not just for the occasional moment of moral indignation, pity or outrage, but for heartfelt empathy and compassionate understanding that persist and may even result in political action. Or do we really need constant reminding that the fate of the world as a whole is now also irrevocably our own, as well as that of our loved ones? Tomlinson assumes that 'imagining the worst' equates to accepting that 'moral engagement and human solidarity [are] essentially a local affair'. Pessimistically he concludes that 'our social and technological capacities to extend relations across distance – to produce the *social* condition of globalization – have simply outstripped our moral-imaginative capacity to live our lives in regard to – with a sense of mutuality with – all the distant others with whom we have necessarily become connected' (205). In fact, however, according to McEwan, the bitterest pill to swallow is that western society is atomising so rapidly these days that ethical life stays firmly locked within the family and baulks at stretching out even into the local. As the world's seemingly unassimilable alterity continues to amplify in direct proportion to its increasing compression and proximity, neighbourliness is fast becoming a thing of the past.

The appearance of *Black Dogs* is that of a fractured narrative, torn in two by the Tremaines' divergent perspectives, which Jeremy has the unenviable task of reconstructing into one consistent story about what really happened to June in St Maurice de Navacelles in 1946. It is fractured even though McEwan's narration is aimed at creating a sense of wholeness, supported by the smooth, vertebrate linearity of a logically unfolding sequence of events and geared towards unveiling an indisputable truth. According to both Tremaines, making sense of life is a straightforward matter of simply decoding, either spiritually or scientifically, life's documentary evidence, which in their view is not at all the same as imposing an interpretation upon it. Inspired by Christianity's exegetic endowment of the mundane with transcendental significance, June reads her encounter with the dogs as 'the revealed truth by whose light all previous conclusions must be re-thought' (50), while Bernard – as a good Marxist – continues to invest his faith in 'the great engine of history whose direction was now known to science' (139). While the novel's efforts at vertebrate unity indicate its deeply ingrained longing for traditional form, its self-conscious break-up into four parts and penchant for sporadic intermittency reveal its postmodernist disposition. But *Black Dogs* also favours a more fluid dynamic, an inherent cellularity, which hints at a loosening of narrative form by life's own dynamic, unfathomable complexity.

Throughout the novel an intricate cluster of motifs and Woolfian 'moments' recurs seemingly at random to reconnect in unheard-of ways, creating their own patterns of significance, at once complicating and disrupting the beginning–middle–end structure the narrative seeks to achieve, as well as the myth it attempts to encapsulate. Drawing on Julia Kristeva's theorising of the world-creative potential of differently gendered modes of temporal organisation in 'Women's Time' (1986, originally published 1979), Jago Morrison detects, mixed in with the novel's sense of chronological linearity, the pervasive presence of a kind of sprawling rhizomatic matrix, forever unravelling and reweaving whilst remaining pervasive, recurrent, and invoking a meditative sense of cyclical eternity designed to resist the thrust of teleological emplotment. As Morrison describes it, 'the strategy of McEwan's text is to pivot a plurality of narrative threads on a clear central moment [. . .] all other narrative concerns are twisted and woven around that central motif' (2001: 262). June's epiphanic encounter with the dogs must not be misunderstood as a mere climax, turning point or central stepping stone in the narrative, but as the navel in the matrix from which the whole novel begins to unfold equally into the past and future. June's experience floods the novel with significance, but never as unequivocally as she herself believes. The image of the dogs carries its own crucial ambivalence. They are domestic animals left to go feral; their alleged evil is not an inborn trait, an ineluctable force of nature, but an instrumental potentiality bred into them and brought out by deliberate training. The dogs are, and are not, indomitable; seemingly a hellish scourge beyond all human control, they are in fact the result of human intention and as such remain subject to ethical judgement and agency.

The image of the black dogs recurs throughout the text, assuming an almost tragic omnipresence confirmed by the close of the novel, which leaves no doubt about the enduring menace of what the dogs stand for, namely brutal tyranny, injustice and merciless violence. However, while seemingly affirming the existence of evil, *Black Dogs* also interrogates the belief in moral absolutes. On the one hand, pure evil remains difficult to identify, as most violence is rooted either in mental illness or in a history of violation and victimisation, while on the other, even somebody's best and most honourable intentions are always only one small step removed from transmogrifying into their most fearful and ugly counterpart. On holiday in France, tracing his parents-in-law's original itinerary, Jeremy books himself into a hotel where, at dinner that night, he is forced to watch a couple at an adjacent table both psychologically and physically abuse their young son. Notably McEwan describes the boy's parents and the dogs threatening June in similar terms: 'The couple worked in evident harmony' (128), it says about the parents, whereas the dogs 'seemed to be working together to some purpose' (144). Finding the abuse intolerable, Jeremy intervenes and challenges the boy's father. He wins the ensuing fist-fight but then cannot stop beating the man, who is already lying on the floor. Later he admits that 'I might have kicked and stomped him to death' had not another diner, a woman, brought him back to his senses by shouting 'Ça suffit' (130) – 'that's enough' – a phrase commonly used to discipline dogs. The implications of this incident within the context of *Black Dogs* are clear, but in my view they also reflect pertinently on the problematic affecting Henry's attempts at clarifying his personal stance on the impending war in Iraq in *Saturday*. Even though an act of humanitarian intervention might at times strike one as the only morally defensible modus operandi to avoid further torture and help the innocent, such an intervention, however well-intentioned, is always at risk of unleashing a vicious cycle of its own, falling prey to precisely the kind of evil it sets out to quell. This is possibly the central ethical dilemma in contemporary cosmo-politics, as well as its least avoidable – a dilemma engulfing the world on a regular, if not permanent, basis, with reference to not just Iraq, but also Yugoslavia, Rwanda, East Timor, Palestine, Somalia, Burma, Zimbabwe, Sudan, Tibet, to name but a few.

The image of the black dogs also recurs in the context of Jeremy and Bernard's visit to Berlin, where among the jubilant crowds near Checkpoint Charlie, the divided Berlin's most famous border crossing, they catch sight of a young man entirely dressed in black, waving a red flag and rather unwisely flaunting his loyalty to the crumbling Communist regime. The man, somewhat spuriously identified by Jeremy as Turkish, is espied also by a gang of skinhead youths who prepare to attack him, but are halted by Bernard, who then, instead of the lone protester who manages to escape, becomes their main target. While the parallels to June's life-changing experience are once again self-evident, the identification of evil here appears purposely blurred and complex, as the incident implicates also the victim-as-provocateur, whose black clothes, red flag and, most significantly, dogged support of an oppressive regime are just as reminiscent of June's black dogs as the skinheads' 'loose wet mouths' (96) drooling with neo-nationalist slogans. The novel's symbolic allusiveness thickens even further as a girl steps out of the crowd to defend Bernard. Jeremy recognises the girl as one of 'the two who had swished past us on the June 17th Street' (99), where her striking resemblance to his late wife had prompted Bernard to confess that:

> For a while I couldn't stop thinking that if the world by some impossible chance really was as [June] made it out to be, then she was bound to try and

get in touch to tell me that I was wrong and she was right [. . .] And that she
would do it somehow through a girl who looked like her. And one day one
of these girls would come to me with a message. (83–4)

Without doubt we are to infer that the girl's intervention on Bernard's
behalf *is* June's message, yet typically, despite Jeremy's best efforts,
Bernard will not 'look at his guardian angel, the incarnation of June'.
When told about her later he dismisses it all as 'quite a coincidence'
(100).

Set near the city's June 17th Street – a boulevard leading up to the
Brandenburg Gate, named in commemoration of the East German
workers' uprising of 1953, which was violently suppressed by police
and Soviet troops – Bernard's confrontation with the skinheads reveals
the special significance of June's name as a synonym for resistance and
the rupture of dictatorial order, for rebellion, as well as for compassion
and civic courage. McEwan then goes a step further still by drawing
attention to the fact that 'someone had tied a piece of cardboard over
the street sign and painted "November 9th"' (82). What readers must
know here is that, before Reunification, June 17th was a public holiday
in West Germany, celebrated as the Day of German Unity. Since it
marked the end of Communism and the beginning of German
Reunification it must at first have seemed quite plausible simply to
replace June 17th with November 9th. However, November 9th had
already entered the world's history books as a day of notorious evil – as
Kristallnacht, or the 'Night of Broken Glass'. The Nazis' persecution of
the Jews began on 9 November 1938 with the coordinated destruction
of Jewish businesses and synagogues all over the country, rendering it
utterly inconceivable for the New Reunified Germany to embrace the
date as a day of national celebration. Within the context of McEwan's
representation, then, this chronological complexity serves to highlight
most emphatically that Good and Evil sit often purely randomly and
coincidentally cheek by jowl in history.

In his 'Preface' Jeremy refers to June's black dogs as 'a malign principle, a force in human affairs that periodically advances to dominate
and destroy the lives of individuals or nations, then retreats to await the
next occasion' (19). Yet even provided there were evidence for such a
recurrence of evil in European history, and McEwan seriously intends
to support such a view by appearing to favour June's outlook over
Bernard's, this must not be allowed to sentence a whole continent to
political resignation and self-destructive doom. If evil could indeed be
said to feature as a prominent historical force in Europe, then surely it
would do so only in the sense of constituting one proclivity within a
broad spectrum of possible dispositions, making the practice of a

strong, ethically informed and reconciliatory cosmopolitics all the more imperative. Within this context Europe's most pressing problematic is probably best expressed by Bernard's 'deep apprehension' about the continent's cultural survival as he witnesses the erection of a war memorial in the Languedoc in 1946. 'What possible good could come out of a Europe covered in this dust, these spores', he reflects, 'when forgetting would be inhuman and dangerous, and remembering a constant torture' (165). As a chief spokesperson for a new post-1989 European cosmopolitanism, the German sociologist Ulrich Beck picks up on this dilemma. Rather than promoting oblivion by deflecting from Europe's evident susceptibility to totalitarian terror, internecine warfare and cataclysmic (self-)destruction, Beck purposely highlights Europe's history of evil to make it paradoxically the very matrix from which the continent's new cosmopolitics must evolve.

According to Beck, the historical experience of evil has endowed Europeans with a powerful pre-emptive early-warning system, enabling them to apprehend and resist that evil by 'confronting European horror with European values' (2006: 170). The continent's tragic flaw is thus refined into a hard-won virtue. Inspired in particular by West Germany's post-war agenda of *Vergangenheitsbewältigung* – that is, the country's painstakingly self-conscious endeavour to come to terms with, and learn from, its murderously megalomaniacal past – Beck declares that a future Europe must be 'a historically rooted Europe which breaks with its history and draws the strength to do so from its own history' (171). This is a stance very different from Krishan Kumar's rather cynical suspicion that countries like Italy and Germany might be using their membership of the European Union primarily to '*bury* a recent past of fascism, totalitarianism and catastrophic defeat in war'. Notably, the motivation of the new Eastern European member states strikes Kumar as equally dubious since, in his view, they 'wish to *annul*' not just their past 'of communist rule but in many cases [also] of authoritarian political traditions stretching further back' (2003: 6; 19, n3 – my italics). Without doubt Kumar is wrong. Most Europeans are acutely aware of the disastrous perils a return of the repressed might unleash. Therefore Europe remembers. I agree with Beck that if there is to be a cosmopolitan phoenix, it must rise in equal measure from the continent's fascist trauma and imperial guilt, its millions of victims' unimaginable suffering, both within and outside Europe, as well as its future generations' shared communal effort at atonement and reconciliation.

It is imperative to ensure the ethos of the new European cosmopolitanism is not misrepresented, which is why even an apparent commendation like Perry Anderson's, that 'it is this millennial record, of repeated humiliation and oppression, that entry into the [European] Union offers a chance, finally, to leave behind' (2007: 15), requires cautious elaboration. Anderson's use of the phrase 'leave behind' is vulnerable to being misconstrued due to its synonymy with forgetting, that is, with freeing oneself once and for all from one's painful burden of history and moving on with a clean slate, perfectly exonerated. By contrast, the new European cosmopolitanism as promoted by Beck stands for remembrance, for actively demonstrating – on a daily basis – that one has learned one's lesson, for conceiving new political tenets, and forging and implementing new legal categories, that declare for all to see one's responsibility for both Europe and the world. Beck and Edgar Grande, his co-author, regard 'commemoration of the Holocaust, in particular, [as] a beacon warning against the omnipresent modernization of barbarity' (2007: 9). The horrors of the past continue, its mistakes and abominable cruelties indeed repeat themselves, if not 'somewhere in Europe, in another time', as McEwan suggests at the close of *Black Dogs*, then now, in the immediate present, in our global village. We all know about it from seeing it on the news. Beck and Grande set out to promote 'a self-critical Europe' as 'the last politically effective utopia' (2), thus challenging our generation of Jeremys and Jennys, and Henrys and Rosalinds, as well as their children, to venture out with as much hope and hands-on determination as Bernard and June did in the aftermath of World War II to contribute to improving the world.

While this sounds all very promising, unfortunately the appeal of Beck and Grande's championing of the Europeans' special destiny as exemplary practitioners of new, cosmopolitan world-creation drastically diminishes as soon as they start to distinguish their own mission from that of other, non-European agencies, which allegedly pursue much narrower and less altruistic aims in the name of certain religious or quasi-religious truths. 'Could this radical self-critical confrontation with its own history be what distinguishes Europe from the United States and from Islamic societies' (9), they ask. Obviously, it is of the utmost importance this provocative rhetorical question does not become the moment when cosmopolitanism, too, falls prey to McEwan's black dogs, this time returning in the guise of an arrogant euronationalist superiorism. It is most vexing to behold in *Cosmopolitan Europe* the sudden tarnishing of Beck's cosmopolitan ideals as he begins to bemoan 'the decline of Europe' caused by globalisation, described by him as 'the materialization of the American world spirit' that has demoted Europe 'to second-class status'. Even more devastating is his move to indict the postcolonial world of complicity with US America in ignoring Europe's unique world-creative potential:

On this point [i.e. the political insignificance of Europe], the postcolonial countries are in agreement with the American 'lords of the world'. Europe no longer even figures in their power calculations. Since Europe cannot assert itself militarily and speaks with many voices in foreign and security policy, it need not be taken seriously and merits only cosmetic regards. (Beck and Grande 2007: 3)

Beck and Grande are dismayed to find Europe's potential so stridently overlooked. What somehow detracts from the sincerity of their sentiment, however, is that there is quite a considerable pinch of *schadenfreude* in their intimation of the price the postcolonial world will eventually have to pay for thus snubbing Europe and obsequiously attaching itself to US America's apron-strings. Beck's cosmopolitan vision is seriously dented also by his and Grande's extremely awkward coinage of the term 'post-imperial empire' to describe the newly emergent Europe, even though they make haste to define the term in strict contradistinction to nineteenth-century imperialism as 'not based on national demarcation and conquest, but on overcoming national borders, voluntarism, consensus, transnational interdependence and the political added value accruing from cooperation' (53).

Beck's ideas begin ominously to ring with Bernard's tone of voice in *Black Dogs*, fractiously insisting that 'you see, the ways things are going on this overcrowded little planet, we *do* need a set of ideas, and bloody good ones too' (173). Precisely because Beck's cosmopolitan vision is so inspirational, it must be salvaged from deteriorating into yet another blueprint for 'the efficient organization of man' (77). As June realises in *Black Dogs* at a rare moment of non-ideological insight, 'without a revolution of the inner life, however slow, all our big designs are worthless'. In words auspiciously reminiscent of Jean-Luc Nancy's philosophy of inoperative community, she then adds that 'the good that flows from [such a revolution] will shape our societies in an unprogrammed, unforeseen way, under the control of no single group of people or set of ideas' (172–3). This caveat must also apply to the idealised future citizens of Beck's cosmopolitan Europe.

As regards conceptual structure and plot trajectory *Saturday* follows a pattern quite unexceptional in McEwan's work. His novels are propelled by conflict, often assuming shape in a protracted clinching of irreconcilable opposites. The novels either open with a view on disaster, or generate a sense of foreboding that creeps up on the protagonist, gradually tightening into a violent climactic showdown. In different variations, this is what happens in *The Comfort of Strangers* (1981), *The Child in Time* (1987), *The Innocent* (1990), *Black Dogs* and

Enduring Love (1997). It is therefore hardly surprising to find at the beginning of *Saturday* a sleepless Henry standing naked by his bedroom window catching a glimpse in the early-morning sky of a plane apparently on fire. Later this turns out to be not the gruesome herald of yet another terrorist atrocity perpetrated by Al-Qaeda, but a regular cargo plane run into accidental difficulty. What this opening signals to McEwan's readers, however, is that this day in Henry's life is overshadowed by a perilous menace. This is confirmed when Henry becomes involved in a minor car accident and his life as a well-off neurosurgeon collides with that of Baxter, a lowlife gangster who suffers from Huntington's Chorea, a debilitating genetic disorder causing unstoppable wastage of the brain. Thus the scene is set for the novel's climax at which Baxter will force his way into the Perownes' home and terrorise the family, threatening Henry's wife Rosalind with a knife, breaking his father-in-law's nose, and forcing his pregnant daughter Daisy to strip naked with the intention of raping her in front of the whole family.

Baxter's assault is deliberately designed to look like a return of June's mythical black dogs, and this impression is reinforced by the ending of the novel, which echoes its predecessor's. *Saturday* draws its final curtain on London as it 'lies wide open, impossible to defend, waiting for its bomb, like a hundred other cities' (276). Pondering the world on the eve of a new global conflict, it occurs to Henry that 'here they are again, totalitarians in different form, still scattered and weak, but growing, and angry, and thirsty for another mass killing' (277). Poignantly his premonition recalls the 'ignorant armies clash[ing] by night' whose image concludes Matthew Arnold's poem 'Dover Beach' (1867), the recitation of which enables Daisy to allay Baxter's fury and quite miraculously defuse the danger the family are in. Eventually, with the help of his son, Henry manages to overpower Baxter by throwing him down the stairs, which leaves the intruder comatose with a serious head injury. And yet, even though the Perownes demonstrate remarkable courage and immense resourcefulness by defeating Baxter and effectively reinscribing the supremacy of culture over brutality by appeasing violence with a poem, McEwan leaves his readers in the end with a fatalistic declaration of humanity's tragic exposure and eternal powerlessness. The key to this peculiar ending is perhaps to be found in Baxter's growing obsession with Henry, which recalls that of the character of Jed Parry, Joe Rose's deranged homosexual stalker in McEwan's earlier novel *Enduring Love*. As suggested by Parry's surname, Jed is a literalisation of Joe's paranoia following his failure to live up to his own ideals of heroic masculinity (see Davies 2003). Similarly, Baxter might be said to embody Henry's guilt about his privileged existence and general good fortune. Peripherally aware that this guilt might one day come to catch up with him, he has so far managed to keep it at bay. As the head of one of the most perfect families the British novel has ever seen, Henry's dissimilarity to Baxter could not be any more pronounced. A gifted family comprising a brain surgeon, a lawyer, two poets and a musician comes to confront an increasingly disabled loner, criminal and generally despairing man. Cultured and highly civilised humanity at the pinnacle of evolution – capable, whenever required, of pulling together in an admirable feat of familial agency – finds itself challenged by the diseased proponent of a 'simian' violence hurtling towards its inevitable, genetically pre-programmed doom.

No matter how much one comes to be fond of Henry, or how much one longs to have his life even, one cannot help sensing that there is something quite rotten at the core of his existence and that of his family; neither – quite evidently – can he. The Perownes own a chateau in the French Pyrenees and a seven-bedroom townhouse in London's Fitzrovia. There is no pressure on their grown-up kids to earn a living, setting them free to indulge their artistic talents at leisure. Daisy travels China and Brazil whilst an undergraduate at Oxford, and Theo, an up-and-coming blues guitarist, is looking forward to spending some formative time in New York. Henry's pride in his gifted son dropping out of school and 'taking charge of his life' (36) is risibly disingenuous. What bold risk is there in developing one's talents in the safety of a comfortably cushioned, well-heeled home secured by an alarm-padded, panic-buttoned front door? Neither, despite her father's rather preposterous concerns, is Daisy's pregnancy ever a problem; not only is she an adult who has her parents' unconditional love and support but also, as we find out, her boyfriend's parents, clearly similarly well-off, 'have [already] given them enough money to buy a little flat' in Paris (240). Taking their privileged life-style entirely for granted, the Perownes' innocence is breath-taking; so is the naive image they cultivate of themselves as people who do no harm and in fact help improve the lives of others by repairing, healing, advising and sorting out, as well as beautifying and entertaining, the world.

Despite their apparent cosmopolitanism, whatever larger global consciousness or awareness of social responsibility the Perownes may have tends to expend itself in petty debates about whether, for example, it is justifiable and 'politically correct' for Henry to shell out on an expensive car:

> It's Theo who disapproves most, saying it's a doctor's car, as if this were the final word in condemnation. Daisy, on the other hand, said she thought that

Harold Pinter owned something like it, which made it all fine with her. Rosalind encouraged him to buy it. She thinks his life is too guiltily austere, and never buying clothes or good wine or a single painting is a touch pretentious. (75)

Throughout the novel McEwan shrewdly manipulates our sympathy for Henry. Only very gradually do we come to realise that Henry's happiness – including the luxury of his occasional guilty rumination about neglecting his political responsibilities – is sustained invariably at somebody else's expense. Like most of us in the West, the Perownes cannot avoid being guilty, implicated as their lives inevitably are in global politics driven by economic interests that depend for their fulfilment on the perpetuation of social injustice facilitated by mass ethical turpitude. As Henry's coincidental face-to-face encounter with a street-sweeper indicates, in this world fortune is always counterbalanced by misfortune, and no self-righteous neo-liberalist reasoning can ever quite contain the sheer outrage of this truth. 'For a vertiginous moment Henry feels himself bound to the other man', the novel records, 'as though on a seesaw with him, pinned to an axis that could tip them into each other's life.' Yet whether in London, New York, Berlin, Cape Town or Calcutta, 'the streets need to be clean. Let the unlucky enlist' (74). Henry's guilt and fatalism are the post-9/11 westerner's burden. We all profess to be troubled by injustice, but this is unlikely to jolt us into relevant political action. It is far easier to purport to rationalise injustice, as Henry does, by sentimentally invoking 'accidents of character and circumstance':

> that cause one young woman in Paris to be packing her weekend bag with the bound proof of her first volume of poems before catching the train to a welcoming home in London, and another young woman of the same age to be led away by a wheedling boy to a moment's chemical bliss that will bind her as tightly to her misery as an opiate to its mu receptors. (65)

Critics have expressed grave concern about McEwan's seeming disregard for political initiative and commitment, his apparent evasiveness when it comes to taking a stance. With reference to *Black Dogs*, for example, after reminding us that 'the author should not be held morally accountable for what his narrator fails to do or say', Delrez complains of 'McEwan's habitual neutrality of tone', that is, the way in which McEwan 'persistently ducks behind his [narrator's] back in a provocative game of philosophical hide-and-seek' (1995: 21). Similarly, asserting that one would be 'mistaken to collapse Henry Perowne and his creator', Elizabeth Wallace finds *Saturday* 'complicated by the striking absence of any specific clues that Henry warrants anything less than the reader's full engagement and consideration', adding that 'in light of that absence, the novel seems to imply that the author endorses Henry's perspective' (2007: 466). More direct in venting her impatience with McEwan's failure to engage more effectively with politics and attempt to make a difference, possibly even help prevent future terrorist attacks, Lynn Wells concludes her reading of *Saturday* perplexed as to why 'the triumph of McEwan's hero provides no sense of the need for urgent cultural change to prevent the horrors of domestic terrorism that occurred, all too predictably, in July 2005' (2006: 126). The answer is presumably that McEwan is no political pamphleteer but a novelist whose aim in *Saturday* is an authentic representation of contemporary life in post-9/11 Britain. Steering clear of comforting fantasies of right-on resistance, McEwan brings us face to face with our own complicity, collusion and guilt, which complement rather than contradict our fundamental decency and good-heartedness. As Elaine Hadley concedes in her reading of the novel:

> Let me be clear: I recognize my interpellation in this novel. I know I'm being hailed. Perowne's anxieties are mine; his solace in his family's company and the faux protection of their nuclearity are mine. His solipsistic interest in his particularity and the ego support derived from his profession are also mine. (2005: 97)

No matter who we are or what we do in the privileged West – brain surgeons, poets, critics, politicians, peace protesters, even street-sweepers and heroin addicts – we are all of us always shouldering guilt. Every single one of us could conceivably put his or her life to better, more cosmopolitan use, or could we? In the era of globalisation, guilt and 'undecidability' (Delrez 1995: 21) – so McEwan's novel suggests – form an ineradicable component of the new Europe's contemporaneity.

Kiernan Ryan was the first to draw attention to McEwan's protagonists not as heroic intellectuals who wisely interpret their own cultural and socio-political conditioning, thus conveying an implicit cultural critique, but as literary subjects vehicularly enmeshed in the plot of the novels they inhabit and hence of necessity clueless with regard to their own possible signification. In his reading of *The Innocent* Ryan remarks on McEwan's interest in demonstrating 'how completely the innermost self can be penetrated and disfigured by desires cultivated in the public sphere'. Interestingly, Ryan then goes on to specify what exactly he means by 'the public sphere', pointing at 'the eclipsing of Britain by the USA, both as a political and as a cultural force', as well as 'the nation's seduction by the American way of life' (1994: 55). Since the time of *The Innocent* – both the time of its setting in Cold War Berlin in the early 1950s and that of its writing in the late 1980s, just before the fall of the Wall – the Americanisation of Britain can only be said to have accelerated and intensified, especially in the aftermath of 9/11. It seems therefore appropriate to read Henry Perowne's predicament as exemplifying the life of a typical upper-middle-class Englishman with European connections and wider cosmopolitan aspirations. As we have seen, his daughter lives in Paris and his son is an up-and-coming blues musician about to embark on an apprenticeship in New York. Henry lives under globalised conditions that not only exacerbate the class divide that mars his own society, but moreover deepen the explosive rift between rich and poor worldwide. The distortion and alienation caused by the US Americanisation of contemporary British life are self-consciously incorporated into McEwan's representation. Mobilising one of Hollywood cinema's most clichéd stock themes, the author presents us, in Henry's private life, with the beauty, innocence and exemplary resourcefulness of a perfect family under siege while, in Henry's professional life, McEwan focuses on the brain surgeon's multicultural firm of doctors and nurses, emulating the controlled blend of gore and casual godliness so characteristic of much popular US American hospital drama. In all this, the construction of mythical truth is invariably given priority over authenticity, which is willingly sacrificed for emotional effect. Even the most commonsensical ethical guidelines are discarded when, for example, immediately following the assault on his family Henry is back on duty operating on Baxter, his attacker, and not only saving the latter's life but also magnanimously forgiving him all his sins.

But while the framework of *Saturday* possesses such structural clarity, crisp with professional competency and moral righteousness, it is also kept in constant oscillation by Henry's dithering and political indecision, his middle-of-the-road tight-roping, which turns into a poignant expression of his Britishness. Without doubt Henry's life is affected by global politics; 'it is in fact the state of the world that troubles him most' (80). But his ability to engage remains inhibited by a deep-seated sense of powerlessness and passivity, of being at the mercy of other people's designs, casting severe doubt on Rebecca Carpenter's assessment of Henry as representative of a strong, 'rational and level-headed' masculinity (2008: 146). A chief target in the current global conflict, people like him – that is, high-achieving pillars of western society, who hold positions of considerable status and power within their own little worlds – are prone to die feeble, anonymous, unremarkable deaths, killed en masse to punctuate the political statements of others while their own remain hazy and tentative at best:

> The world probably has changed fundamentally and the matter is being
> clumsily handled, particularly by the Americans. There are people around

the planet, well-connected and organized, who would like to kill him and his family and friends to make a point. The scale of death contemplated is no longer at issue; there'll be more deaths on a similar scale, probably in this city. Is he so frightened that he can't face the fact? (80–1)

Henry's singularity, combined with his professional position and out-standing specialist skills, contrasts markedly with his fear of possibly not counting at all. Small wonder, then, he should seek not only refuge, but reaffirmation of his significance in the intimate privacy of home, which he shares with 'the three people in the world he, Henry Perowne, most loves, and who most love him' (181).

In Henry's view the family and the wider community constitute sepa-rate, self-contained spheres that do not normally overlap or reach into each other; nor is the family pictured as the smaller unit sheltered within the embrace of the wider community. Rather, community is per-ceived as extraneous to the family, and contact with it is regarded as volitional, not obligatory. Families and individuals are introduced as autonomous units who either choose to engage with the world at large or, more often than not, deem themselves free to embark on their own independent trajectories. In this view, the world can be opted in and out of, switched on and off at whim like a television set. Ultimately, it is suggested, one does not have to be in the world at all, and people only have themselves to blame if they allow what happens in the world to affect them. Symptomatically, Henry sees it as 'a condition of the times, this compulsion to hear how it stands with the world, and be joined to the generality, to a community of anxiety' (176). But, as the novel high-lights, there are of course at least two communities of anxiety. One is not really a community at all, but consists of atomised individuals and exclusive family units like the Perownes, who occasionally – for the purpose of entertainment or intellectual distraction – tap into the world via their radios and television sets at home. The other comprises quite similar kinds of people, but, unlike the Perownes, these are prepared to step out of their isolation and participate in the solidary action of Britain's largest-ever peace march.

The allure of the demonstration is felt even by Henry, who notes 'the seduction and excitement peculiar to such events; a crowd possessing the streets, tens of thousands of strangers converging with a single purpose conveying an intimation of revolutionary joy' (72). Almost instantly, however, cynicism, suspicion and judgemental disdain catch up with him and dispel his momentary fascination:

All this happiness on display is suspect. Everyone is thrilled to be together out on the streets – people are hugging themselves, it seems, as well as each other. If they think – and they could be right – that continued torture and summary executions, ethnic cleansing and occasional genocide are preferable to an invasion, they should be sombre in their view. (69–70)

What escapes Henry is that one fundamental purpose of the demonstration is of course quite undeniably the celebration of itself – its inoperative communal spirit – which finds expression in the hugging of strangers and symbolically connecting the world by forming a global chain. This chain is intended to include also the victims of tyranny, who are integrated into the chain and thus no longer provide merely the demonstration's detached, faraway referent on whose behalf the march is held. Henry misses out on this effervescent self-referentiality of the demonstration, which to him must appear simply in excess of its original purpose and hence inappropriate and redundant. What escapes him is the curative power of generating and practising community as such, which by mixing in Nancean fashion struggle, agitation and enjoyment takes priority over any particular, neatly distillable cause, especially when the parameters applied are as crude as war and liberation, or 'peace and torture' (126). Only obliquely does McEwan indicate that Henry, too, might quite possibly against his own better judgement be susceptible to experiencing exactly this kind of community, and indeed be filled with secret yearning for it. Yet notably such an experience becomes accessible to him only when entranced by music and transported momentarily out of this world.

Listening to his son Theo perform his new song 'My City Square', whose title pertinently imbricates the personal with the public, Henry is moved to reflect on his sudden rapture in expressly communal terms:

> There are these rare moments when musicians together touch something sweeter than they've found before in rehearsals or performance, beyond the merely collaborative or technically proficient, when their expression becomes as easy and graceful as friendship or love. This is when they give us a glimpse of what we might be, of our best selves, and of an impossible world in which you give everything you have to others, but lose nothing of yourself. Out in the real world there exist detailed plans, visionary projects for peaceable realms, all conflicts resolved, happiness for everyone, for ever – mirages for which people are prepared to die and kill. Christ's kingdom on earth, the workers' paradise, the ideal Islamic state. But only in music, and only on rare occasions, does the curtain actually lift on this dream of community, and it's tantalizingly conjured, before fading away with the last notes. (171–2)

Free of purpose in its serendipity, liberational yet by no means escapist, combining self-expenditure with self-fulfilment, Henry's musical 'dream of community' appears perfectly Nancean in its unworked spontaneity. Yet while it is heartening to see the rationalist thus open up to an ecstatic impulse of community, it is a pity he cannot see it assume shape at the very same moment outside his head, in the real world, in people's city squares not only in Europe, but all over the world.

The multitudinous peace-march communities that formed simultane-ously all over Europe on 15 February 2003, the eponymous Saturday of McEwan's novel, were interpreted by leading European intellectuals such as Jürgen Habermas, Jacques Derrida and Ulrich Beck not only as 'Europe in movement – Europe *as* movement' (Beck and Grande 2007: 2), but far more monumentally 'as a sign of the birth of a European public sphere' (Habermas and Derrida 2005: 4; see also Young 2005). For the first time in post-war European history an overwhelming number of citizens from all over the continent chose collectively to declare their political imagination and cosmopolitan ethos against the hegemonic might of US America, which, supported by its Coalition of the Willing representing 48 countries, had decided on a pre-emptive 'shock and awe' military campaign against Iraq, even though its action did not have the sanction of the United Nations. As Kumar puts it in retrospect, a large number of European nations were seen that day to launch 'a Declaration of European Independence [. . .] above all from America' (2008: 88). Crucially, however, these demonstrations not only created a sense of pan-European solidarity and concurrence, but also effectively divorced political decision-making from popular opinion and intellectual reasoning, as happened in Britain. Even more conflict-ually, they split Europe in two – with the governments of Denmark, Spain, Poland and many other Eastern European countries, as well as Britain, coming out in support of US America, while France and Germany led the other way in concurrence with international law. Memorably, this division was described by the then US defence secre-tary Donald Rumsfeld in terms of an estrangement between 'old' Europe (recalcitrant and anti-American), on the one hand, and a 'new' Europe (pro-American and docile), on the other. Revealing a certain double-speak irony, it was of course the allegedly 'old' Europe that could be seen trying to forge a new, alternative cosmopolitics.

Even though Europe is yet to formulate its own foreign politics, and indeed remains far removed from developing into an independent, truly collective political agent, Habermas, Derrida and Beck were certainly right to detect not only frustrated discontent and agitation, but also considerable zest in Europe's spontaneous expression of its emergent political self-consciousness and identity. Europe's critique of US American politics opened up a vociferous transatlantic debate, with American commentators accusing Europe of hubristic self-satisfaction, hypocrisy and imperialist intentions, all rooted in 'an apparently illimit-able narcissism, in which the reflection in the water transfigures the future of the planet into the image of the beholder' (Anderson 2007: 13), a characterisation which, from a European perspective, obviously made a much fairer identikit of America itself. What intellectuals on both sides of the Atlantic appeared to agree on, however, was that it was not really the fundamental nitty-gritty of US American values that was at stake but, as Habermas argues in *The Divided West*, 'the policies of the current US government that ignore international law, marginalize the United Nations and accept the inevitability of the break with Europe' (2006: xxii). As Perry Anderson concedes, by 'scanting the Kyoto protocols and the International Criminal Court, sidelining the UN, trampling on the Geneva Conventions, and stampeding into the Middle East, the Bush regime [. . .] exposed a darker side of the United States, that has understandably been met with near universal abhorrence in Europe' (2007: 19). The new European position boiled down to the fact that the world could no longer afford to abide by the current brand of US American unilateralism in foreign politics. If America intended to maintain its international image and status as 'the good hegemon' (Habermas 2006: 35), it would need to consult its allies, and indeed be prepared to negotiate with its enemies, all the while following internationally sanctioned democratic procedures, or else it might sooner rather than later fall out of touch with the rest of the world. Accordingly, rather than fomenting a pan-European anti-Americanism, Habermas urged US America to take on 'the role of pace-maker in the evolution of international law toward a "cosmopolitan condition"' (117). Others agreed that America needed to recoup its traditional, centuries-old cosmopolitical disposition, outlook and prac-tice. Citing US secretary of state Condoleezza Rice as saying that 'there is nothing wrong with doing something that benefits all humanity, but that is, in a sense, a second-order effect', Beck and Grande commented that it was precisely this kind of nonchalant self-centredness in contem-porary American politics that had 'cost the Bush administration its legitimacy and effectiveness and fed the aspiration for a "European counterforce"' (2007: 220).

McEwan's challenge in *Saturday* is to capture the spirit and impact of the specific contemporaneity of 15 February 2003, which has come to be read as a crucial world-political crossroads not just for England, Britain, Europe and US America, but for the whole world, casting up manifold elemental questions about the post-9/11 global-human condi-tion. In McEwan's novel London is revealed as a pivotal centre within multiple spheres of influence, including old and new imperialisms, the European Union and globalisation, as well as contemporary Britain's self-image and identity as both a world power and a US American satel-lite. Despite its portrayal of an atomised individualism, a withdrawal into marital intimacy and familial self-encapsulation, *Saturday* also shows potential as a cosmopolitan novel, mainly due to Henry's propensity for open-ended self-analysis, his Hamlet-like dithering and painstaking self-consciousness, as well as his marked vulnerability, troubledness and, not least also, his quite unexpected 'dream of community'. Ultimately, however, it might be more apt to describe *Saturday* as a *glocal* rather than a cosmopolitan text. Coined by Roland Robertson, *glocality* signifies the interpermeation of the allegedly oppositional spheres of the global and the local, as well as the private and the public, the individual and the collective.

In McEwan's novel glocality comes to the fore most forcefully in the local specificity of Henry's life, which is caught up in global conditions he ignores at his own peril. Glocality suggests that our lives are irrevocably enmeshed in a cosmopolitical web of cause and effect, rebutting 'the claim that we live in a world of local assertions *against* globalizing trends' (Robertson 1995: 29). Even without any active political engagement on his part, Henry cannot stop his life being implicated in, and in fact determined by, an ongoing, irrepressible amalgamation of the local with the global. Commenting on Robertson's theorising, Tomlinson explains that the global-human condition is the site where 'different orders of human life are brought into articulation with one another', encompassing 'individual human beings, national societies, the "world system of societies" and the overarching collectivity of "humankind"'. The world grows into a single space as 'these forms of life [. . .] are increasingly positioned against, and forced to take account of, each other' (1999: 11). This, then, is the dynamic that in McEwan's novel weaves governmental US American war-mongering and popular peace marches in Europe and elsewhere into one global pattern, that interlinks Henry's Fitzrovia and Saddam's Baghdad, and that enters the privileged doctor into one and the same community with the lowlife heroin addicts and immigrant traders he observes in the public square outside his house. It is also the dynamic that renders Baxter not so much Henry's stalker and potential assassin as his doppelganger, making Baxter's despair, violence, madness and pain quite literally part of Henry's own life and therefore also – within the logic of glocalisation – his responsibility.

Still, it remains very difficult to see in Henry the kind of model 'citizen of the world' – 'the competent moral agent in the "global neighbourhood"' (Tomlinson 1999: 186) – who not only displays an awareness of the distinct glocality of his own existence, but is moreover capable of addressing and trying to resolve the manifold problematics that ensue from the ever-tighter enmeshment of the local with the global. In this respect, then, McEwan seems to have fashioned Henry quite deliberately into a representative likeness of contemporary Britain, and more specifically England, which has never been able wholeheartedly to immerse itself in its own democratic popularity as a nation of great inherent diversity, or to embrace its membership of any larger political union, unless it be with itself as the hegemon (as within the United Kingdom or the Commonwealth of Nations) or as the partner in a hegemonic coalition (as reflected, however precariously, in its 'special relationship' with US America). As Kumar notes with respect to the United Kingdom's relationship to Europe, 'it has been customary in the past [. . .] for the British – or at least the English – to distinguish themselves from "Europe"', so much so that Kumar himself cannot help wondering if 'Britain [is] not part of Europe' at all (2008: 95).

In *The Divided West* Habermas explains the Anglo-British habit of cultivating a stance of reserved aloofness in strictly historical terms, identifying it as residual of the country's imperial outlook. 'When Churchill urged France and Germany to take the lead in unifying Europe in his famous University of Zurich address of 1946', Habermas writes, 'he saw Great Britain quite naturally as standing alongside the US and Russia as well-wishers and facilitators, but not as participants in the project' (2006: 75). Similarly, Henry never quite comes to regard himself as the member of a community of equals; he only ever feels truly at ease when leading his medical firm in the operating theatre, or mustering his scientific knowledge and intellectual superiority to gain the upper hand over others. Henry can only relax once he finds himself in a position of uncontested authority, even in the family home, where, as if he were some kind of benevolent sovereign ruling over his realm, all that is required of him in the end is to provide patriarchal approval. Henry's firm and family, as well as the squash court and specialist food shops he frequents, stand out like magnified islets within a City of London that appears largely as foreign territory, an uncanny maze of corridors between homely destinations to be navigated with caution. Greater London and the world at large figure only in Henry's abstract reflection; they remain firmly outside the range of any more practical considerations or decision-making. Quite unsurprisingly, then, what little political engagement Henry demonstrates turns out to be strictly personalised, focused on Baxter alone and culminating in a patronising act of unilateral forgiveness. Henry's conciliatory gesture looks like an arrogant and solipsistic move, poignantly likened by McEwan to operating on the anaesthetised body and exposed brain of an enfeebled, mortally wounded adversary. In the end, motivated by a guilty sense of fear endemic to Henry's nationality and class, it proves inhibitive of any more genuine feeling of cosmopolitan fellowship or compassion.

The appearance of *Saturday* as a novel about the world is also, if not undermined, then at least shrewdly drawn into question by McEwan's formal accentuation of its inveterate Englishness. In no way an experimental novel, *Saturday* excels at conceptual coherence and neatly vertebrate emplotment. Composed of five chapters and featuring characters named Henry and Rosalind, as well as an obstreperous daughter who falls in love with Giulio, a dubious Italian, of whose suitability her father is only reluctantly convinced, *Saturday* presents itself as a Shakespearean history play with some tragicomedy mixed in. It is also potentially a revenge tragedy that, at the very last minute, swaps revenge for forgiveness in a gesture of regal magnitude. Henry gradually reveals himself as 'the King [who] rumbles his assent', at once a private man and an emblematic epitome of his realm, while the poet John Grammaticus, Henry's father-in-law, who has his nose broken by the intruders, takes the role of malcontent-cum-jester. In the immediate aftermath of the novel's peripeteia, as conflict finds comic relief in revelry and merry-making, the Perownes reassemble in their grand basement kitchen for a feast of wine and sumptuous food, which is led by Grammaticus 'in his twinkly mode, an effect heightened by his clownishly swollen nose' (232).

McEwan also roots his novel in the English literary tradition by emulating Virginia Woolf's modern classic *Mrs Dalloway*. Both novels record a day in the life of one upper-middle-class Londoner, concentrating on quotidian details such as watching a plane in the sky and shopping for a party. Furthermore, by showing Baxter in the grip of unpredictable mood swings that range from evil malice to exuberant euphoria, *Saturday* imitates Woolf's patterning of her narrative around the 'larks' and 'plunges' of Clarissa Dalloway's neurasthenic sensibility. Most pertinently, however, while *Saturday* shows the world on the brink of a new global conflict, Woolf pillories war's cataclysmic impact on humanity, especially through her portrayal of Septimus Smith, who, years after World War I in which he served as a soldier, remains unable to overcome his trauma and eventually commits suicide. The Dalloway/Smith dichotomy conspicuously resembles that of Perowne/Baxter, with one character bearing all the suffering in order somehow to redeem the other and enable them to survive.

Saturday may indeed show how 'Henry fails to become truly cosmopolitan' (Wallace 2007: 479) but, in order to do so effectively, the novel must first successfully conjure an atmosphere of cosmopolitan expectation, which then remains unfulfilled. Utilising intertextuality and literary allusion, McEwan goes to considerable lengths to emphasise his novel's explicit and indeed extravagant Englishness, drawing attention to how deeply embedded and solidly anchored the representation of his characters' lives remains in tradition, how customary it is, how rigidified, even antiquated. And these are the lives of people who are among the most privileged in one of the world's most protean cities!

Saturday is an accomplished novel not so much of failure as of foreclosure. Rather than confronting their present trauma as a direct corollary of their increasing political domestication, McEwan's characters proceed with their lives as if nothing had happened, returning to their professional routine, like Henry, while behind closed doors the familial merry-making resumes. One cannot help but experience this lack of development and change as intensely dissatisfying, especially also because, as recordings of our own day and age, both *Black Dogs* and *Saturday* historicise the contemporary with such moving accuracy. Most vexing perhaps is the realisation that what stops Jeremy and Henry from becoming more proactive heroes is also what stops us. Like them, we are subject to regulatory machinations that tell us who we ought to be, which for most of the time fatefully agrees exactly with who we want to be. What, then, might it take to stop us leisurely ruminating, critiquing and making up our minds while unhindered globalisation runs its course? And how, should we eventually come to act, will we prevent our good intentions from collapsing into yet another, possibly even greater evil?

Henry is much more aware of his conditioning – which he regards as 'part of the new order, this narrowing of mental freedom' – than he cares for, which of course speaks volumes for McEwan's own level of political insight and realisation:

> He suspects he's becoming a dupe, the willing, febrile consumer of news fodder, opinions, speculation and of all the crumbs the authorities let fall. He's a docile citizen [. . .] It's an illusion, to believe himself active in the story. Does he think he's contributing something [. . .]? Does he think that his ambivalence – if that's what it really is – excuses him from the general conformity? [. . .] he's lost the habits of scepticism, he's becoming dim with contradictory opinion, he isn't thinking clearly, and just as bad, he senses he isn't thinking independently. (180–1)

This – according to McEwan – sums up the spirit of the globalised age, in which even the most educated begin to lose their ability to discriminate clearly between individualism and rampant conformity, between valid political reflexivity and civic paralysis, as well as between the compulsive consumption of news reports and being genuinely well informed. Following in Jeremy's footsteps, Henry is shown to paint himself into an unworldly private corner of familial intimacy, keeping out the world. But the real tragedy is that he has painted the world in with him, causing it to spell fear, guilt and doom rather than cosmopolitical agency.

Chapter 2

James Kelman's Cosmopolitan Jeremiads

No other British writer's shift from locally specific concerns to global themes is as symptomatic of globalisation's steadily increasing encroachment on ordinary life as James Kelman's. Like McEwan's novels, both *Translated Accounts* (2001) and *You Have to Be Careful in the Land of the Free* (2004) convey a new global sense of British contemporaneity, yet the contrast between England's and Scotland's premier authors could scarcely be more pronounced.

In Kelman's novels anonymous state apparatuses have eradicated familial comfort zones. Most characteristically, his fictions feature loners estranged and physically removed from their families. Pre-dating 9/11, *Translated Accounts* catalogues a plethora of tales about the threat of totalitarianism to individual and communal world-creation right down to the linguistic basics of human relations. The novel interrogates western optimism at the close of the Cold War, notably interpreted by some at the time as potentially ending all historical strife. Echoing Appadurai's recent reassessment of the 1990s as 'a decade of superviolence' (2006: 1), Kelman's novel alerts us to the contemporaneity of genocidal cataclysms, such as those that ravaged Yugoslavia and Rwanda, unconscionably eclipsed by politically naive or disingenuous celebrations of the post-Cold War era as a putative 'holiday from history' (see Will 2001). Depicting the experiences of Scotsman Jeremiah Brown in US America, *You Have to Be Careful* picks up on its predecessor's theme of global totalitarianism by casting contemporary US America in the role of both humanity's number-one utopia and its most acutely dystopian cosmopolis. Throughout the narrative Kelman pits his anti-hero's cosmopolitan competencies against his working-class origin and constitution, thus querying whether world citizenship might one day become a fundamental human entitlement, or whether it must indeed always remain a class-based privilege.

Despite marked differences in their choice of representational tone, mode and perspective, the writings of Kelman and McEwan are pre-occupied with strikingly similar issues and concerns, such as violence, injustice and political agency, historiography and the need to account for the truth, as well as the more general ethical quandaries surrounding the orientation and accommodation of one's private self within a rapidly changing and increasingly uncontrollable world. Both *Translated Accounts* and *Black Dogs* problematise not only our experience of 'evil', but also our ineluctable complicity with it. This is disclosed by the ways in which we choose to interpret and historically record atrocities, which must invariably lose much of their horrific unspeakability in the process of entextualisation. Signally, in 'lecture, re sensitive periods', section 10 of Kelman's novel, McEwan's black dogs reappear, and so does the problem of their accurate interpretation. An official dispute opens up on whether a young girl on her way home from school was in fact 'bitten or licked in the friendliest manner' (2001: 81). As the narrative points out, 'many girls do not distinguish easily as between fact, fiction [. . .] Boys also, they invent fictions. Adults, yes, they too' (82). As the dispute appears destined to go on forever, an act of state violence is turned into a purely academic matter, just as the need to oppose fascism is in 'history must exist for colleagues', section 25 of the novel (168–78).

At first glance Kelman and McEwan appear to be providing diametrically opposed global outlooks from within contemporary British society, determined by class and other forms of deeply ingrained difference, which segregate Henry Perowne in *Saturday* – a respectable, upper-middle-class Londoner – from Jeremiah Brown, Kelman's rambling, Glaswegian, working-class outcast in *You Have to Be Careful*. Jobless, uprooted and in despair, Jeremiah belongs with the people that drift in and out of the public square outside the Perownes' house. These people are watched by Henry from the elevated safety of his bedroom window, quite as if they were not only locked out from his class's wealth, privilege, success and familial happiness, but indeed found themselves under constant middle-class surveillance. 'Other bodies had family and friends', Jeremiah complains, 'all I had was myself' (Kelman 2005: 84). Although neither criminally inclined nor debilitated by a congenital disorder, Jeremiah clearly has much in common with Baxter, Henry's adversarial doppelganger. Most significantly, he shares Baxter's state of anxiety, volatility and lack of equilibrium: 'I get these mood shifts, I am moody, overpowered by moodiness' (122). The most poignant difference between *Saturday* and *You Have to Be Careful*, however, is revealed by comparing what becomes of Jeremiah's African-American lover Yasmin's musical talent as opposed to Henry's son Theo's.

Whereas Theo, supported by his family's ample means, is entirely at leisure to pursue his dream of a career as a blues guitarist, Kelman's protagonists are 'aye in trouble. Me and the ex man we had nay chance. We never had a penny; never nay fucking dough. In all the time we had been the gether we were broke' (301). Both Yasmin's singing career and Jeremiah's attempts to establish himself as a writer are thwarted by the need to earn a living, which prevents them from fulfilling their artistic, as well as their more generally world-creative potential. What makes the lives of Kelman's characters so different from McEwan's is not a lack of talent or intelligence, but of opportunity and self-esteem.

All the more astonishing then that what Jeremiah clearly shares with Henry is an awareness of his own political powerlessness as 'a docile citizen', as well as his tacit complicity in the perpetration of global exploitation, atrocity and injustice as 'a dupe, the willing, febrile consumer of news fodder' (McEwan 2005: 180). Henry's self-assessment seems virtually identical with Jeremiah's description of himself when interviewed for a job as an airport security officer:

> I dream a lot. And I have opinions, everybody had opinions, maist people anyway. I speak as one myself, a person. I am aware that some folks are executed or not executed, tortured or not tortured, deported or whatnot. I can only say what I feel and I feel that nowadays there is very little escape, naybody can be outside the system, there is nay room for hermits in the 21st century, the days of the mystical stargazers are so to speak o'er. There are singular liberties to which folks arenay privy in this world but liberty is one thing, security another. (157)

Despite all their material differences, both Henry and Jeremiah know they are implicated in what happens in the world, and it does not ultimately matter how knowingly or unwittingly they collaborate, whether out of free choice or pure necessity, or whether one of them might be shouldering more guilt simply because he appears more propitiously equipped than the other to resist the order of the world, to intervene and make a difference. What matters most is that fundamentally Jeremiah's and Henry's dilemma as thoroughly globalised twenty-first-century citizens of the world is actually very much the same.

Kelman's portrayal of Jeremiah at once contradicts and subverts the view of Jon Binnie and his co-editors that 'cosmopolitanism – as a set of skills or competencies – is an intrinsically classed phenomenon [. . .] bound up with notions of knowledge, cultural capital and education: being worldly, being able to navigate between and within different cultures, requires confidence, skill and money' (2006: 8). Against expectation Jeremiah's cosmopolitanism is far more in evidence than Henry's. Jeremiah is immersed in the real world, in a foreign land, whereas

Henry favours cosy self-withdrawal into homely seclusion and non-committal deliberation. What passes Henry by – that is, what he perceives as unusual, one-off occurrences on the periphery of London life, such as the peace march against the Iraq War – is in fact central to the world in which he lives. It is not so much the case that Henry does not have what it takes to be cosmopolitan as that his middle-class refinement works to incapacitate him like some overly domesticated Hamlet lengthily deliberating in a world of fast-paced and at times positively kneejerk political action. In contrast to Chris Haylett's assumption that 'the language of cosmopolitanism does not readily conjure images of the black or white working class, or of poor immigrants or refugees' (2006: 187), Kelman's novel envisions a cosmopolitanism of the underprivileged that indicts economic injustice and deplores the absence in the world of a genuinely democratic multiculturalism. But does Jeremiah's cosmopolitanism therefore prove more effective? Jeremiah's sole answer to globalisation is Kelman's novel, which is his monologue. His preferred mode of self-expression is that of an invective jeremiad (if of a kind quite different from Jeremy's in *Black Dogs*). Lamenting the state of western society and prophesying its decline, *You Have to Be Careful* constitutes a relentless, at times barely digestible rant, conveying successfully Jeremiah's despair and exasperation yet also the utter tedium, futility and extreme ordinariness of his situation. It seems likely that many readers of whatever class may be tempted simply to shut the book on him and turn to something more entertaining or aesthetically pleasing. This is certainly what Henry might do. Having his literary edification prescribed to him by his Oxford-educated poet-daughter Daisy, Henry despairs of the classics as much as of contemporary writing. He simply cannot see the point of literature at all. Like many of his peers, he would undoubtedly express intense bemusement at the news of someone as purposely recalcitrant as Scotland's premier novelist being able to win the Booker Prize (see Pitchford 2000).

Generally speaking, the extent to which the disempowered are exposed to globalising forces tends to exceed that of the privileged. As Tomlinson puts it, 'the poor and marginalized [. . .] find themselves daily closest to some of the most turbulent transformations, while it is the affluent who can afford to retire to the rural backwaters which have at least the appearance of a preserved and stable "locality"' (1999: 133–4). Tomlinson's observation is confirmed by a comparison of Jeremiah and Henry. The latter does not live in the countryside, but his quasi-bucolic familial self-encapsulation behind a multiply fortified security door could be said to fulfil more or less the same function. The contrast between their lives is exacerbated by Jeremiah's status as an immigrant, 'an unintegratit furnir, a member of the alienigenae' (9). Kelman's anti-hero finds himself dislocated from his origins in Scotland as well as from the family he tried to build for himself in the USA with Yasmin and their young daughter. Tomlinson would probably describe Jeremiah's situation as 'deterritorialised', not in the purely liberational Deleuzian sense of the term, but on the contrary as signalling a complete loss of socio-experiential embedment in any specific locality, which could prove either emancipatory or entirely devastating, 'mixing empowerment with vulnerability, opportunity with risk, in complex combinations' (134). There is of course a chance Jeremiah's endeavour to start a new life overseas might have proved successful. Yet while his Celtic-European looks endow him with a clear advantage over other immigrants to the USA, his economic ascent is impeded by his Scottish accent and home-grown inferiorism, his working-class background and radical-socialist views, as well as the general air of 'Uhmerkin' inhospitableness that engulfs him wherever he turns in the land of limitless opportunity.

At first glance, though focusing on very different men in very different contexts, the tenor of both *Saturday* and *You Have to Be Careful* is one of pervasive political stupor, caused in equal measure by too much or too little fixity, either dissipating in a ramble of free-indirect-discourse inconsequentiality or quickly burning itself out in the eruptive heat of a diatribe. Neither novel is overtly petitioning for political change. Instead, both diagnose a particular situation and mindset by suggesting globalisation leads to paralysis as well as individual and/or familial atomisation, impacting on every one of us in equal measure, even though it leaves some considerably better off than others. In both novels there is a realisation that politically the world is in urgent need of remedial action, yet this insight does not prompt either protagonist into taking the initiative. Instead, as Lee Spinks writes on the character of Patrick Doyle in Kelman's earlier novel *A Disaffection* (1989), the hero is far more likely 'to cling on to an absolute value beyond the flux of time', substituting 'a redemptive rhetoric for the labour of political critique' (2001: 100–1).

In Kelman's and McEwan's works alike, the protagonist's response to globalisation is not political agency or communal solidarity, but first and foremost the pursuit of marital love and nuclear-family happiness. Pertinently Doyle's words echo both Henry's and Jeremiah's, as well as Jeremy's in *Black Dogs*: 'There was only one thing worth bothering about and that was the truth of the matter that was the truth of the matter was the truth of the matter 'love'; love, that was it? Love? Love' (Kelman 1999: 71). The crucial difference is of course that McEwan's protagonists find what they are looking for, while Kelman's most tragically do not.

In his reading of *Translated Accounts* and *You Have to Be Careful* Simon Kövesi notes 'an abrupt break contextually and narratologically with [Kelman's] preceding novels' (2007: 170), which is most evident in the author's decision to abandon working-class Glasgow as his hallmark setting. Importantly, Kelman's departure from expressly local concerns must not be misconstrued as a desertion of the nation; rather, it is a strategic move enabling him to problematise Scotland's new role in the world. Both novels are affected, if not indeed motivated, by the promise of post-devolution Scotland's attainment of greater world-political independence and sovereignty in the wake of the country's successful referendum on home rule in September 1997, which fundamentally challenged centralised governmental structures within the United Kingdom. This is particularly pronounced in *Translated Accounts*, which is dedicated to a representation of the wretched of the world and interrogates the ethical responsibility of a newly evolving country such as Scotland to acknowledge and respond to the suffering of other, less fortunate peoples. As Aaron Kelly sees it, the novel 'forces Scottish culture to consider its own implication in globalised networks of power and injustice [. . .] cast[ing] profound doubt on the representative limits of freedom and democracy by filtering through its fragmentary languages the constitutive oppressions that haunt a new global dispensation' (2007: 180).

Against this background Jeremiah's highly ambivalent position in *You Have to Be Careful* as an airport security officer, guarding US America's domestic interests while continuing to present himself as the classic Celtic underdog, assumes particular significance. In one shrewd move Kelman discloses not only the glaring hypocritical fault lines in contemporary US American politics – that is, the stark irreconcilabilities between its constitutional ideals and its actual political practice – but also, more alarmingly, a clutch of fundamental inconsistencies in the Scottish self-image. As Jeremiah propounds it towards the end of the novel:

> But this is Uhmerka buddy, land of the free, if ya dint notice; home from home for the dispossessed, the enslaved, the poor unfortunates; this is everybody's goddam country. My people were slaves as well. The ex found that hard to believe. The trouble is I couldnay remember my historical source. She wantit me to show her there and then. (2006: 407)

In his portrayal of Jeremiah, Kelman addresses contemporary Scotland's tendency to regard itself as a victim of imperial oppression while demonstrably having served, and continuing to serve, as an imperial accomplice rather than a mere pawn. Can Jeremiah justifiably compare his own people's history to that of his African-American lover Yasmin's? Another post-devolution Scottish novel – James Robertson's *Joseph Knight* (2003), which traces the history of the Scottish involvement in the West Indies slave trade – would most vehemently rebut this. Not only for sincerity's or simple historical accuracy's sake, but in order to turn their own life around, as well as respect and make a difference to the lives of others, post-devolution Scots need to acknowledge the particular distinctiveness and enduring ambiguity of their global past and present, which are unlikely to map evenly onto anybody else's (see Schoene 2008: 74–5).

Even more so than in his previous work, in the two novels under discussion Kelman confirms his status as 'the edgy self-conscious voice of protest, the voice which asks awkward ethical questions, the moralising voice which persistently irritates the literary and mainstream arts orthodoxies and establishments, and which rails constantly against the status quo' (Kövesi 2007: 4). Both novels represent the contemporary moment in terms of a global crisis rooted in economic injustice and ceaselessly spawning chimeras of power collapsing into humanitarian cataclysms. But notably Kelman concentrates the limelight not only on US America and its role as global hegemon, but also on Scotland and the disingenuousness of its customary self-image as innocent bystander or 'peripheron', brimming with compassion and good intentions, yet allegedly prevented by circumstances beyond its control from taking the initiative. In my view, Kövesi slightly detracts from Kelman's project by drawing on postcolonial terminology to identify Jeremiah, whom he describes as 'a member of the Glaswegian diaspora, living in the United States' (170). Kövesi suggests Jeremiah has access to a home from home, some kind of reservoir of communal resourcefulness and solidarity, when in actual fact he is entirely on his own and it has been eight years since he last found himself in the company of other Scots. Refusing to fulfil in any way 'the building up of desire to move away' (170) which, according to Kövesi, afflicts all of his previous protagonists, Kelman transports Jeremiah to a different location from the very start – the legendary land of limitless opportunity, no less – to demonstrate that the working-class individual's socio-economic marginalisation and entrapment comprise a pan-global condition from which there is no escape.

As Kövesi points out, '"Scotland" does not appear very often as a concept in [Kelman's] novels, and when it does, it is often rendered remote or irrelevant to the identity and lived reality of the presented world' (5). In *You Have to Be Careful* Kelman seems to be going yet one step further, hotly contesting, if not downright rejecting, the significance Scotland and Scottishness have for his protagonist. This is documented by Jeremiah's emotional turmoil at the prospect of flying home:

> And why was I gaun hame! I didnay even want to go hame. Yes I did.
> No I didnay.
> Yes I did.
> No I didnay. No I fucking didnay. It was an obligation. Bonné Skallin man it can only be an obligation. (2)

A little later in the novel Jeremiah's indecision thickens into furious resentment: 'Fuck the motherland, blood and guts and soil and shite, it didnay matter a fuck to me' (27). Eventually it culminates in a kin-and-kith disparagement of the Scottish people when he tells his American-Asian friend Ranjit that 'my faimly's worse than yours, my entire country man it is much worse, we are all cretinous fucking goddam servants, arselicking bastards' (45). This outburst is strongly reminiscent, of course, of Mark Renton's infamous anti-nationalist speech in Irvine Welsh's *Trainspotting*. Renton memorably labels the Scots as 'the lowest of the fucking low, the scum of the earth. The most wretched, servile, miserable, pathetic trash that was ever shat intae creation' (1994: 78).

By transporting Jeremiah to the US, Kelman highlights his protagonist's potential for mobility and endows him with a certain degree of ambition and get-up-and-go initiative. Yet while one may be able to take the man out of Scotland, one cannot take Scotland out of the man. Jeremiah's attitudes fail to shift, and his vociferous dismissal of Scotland leaves his actual Scottishness undiminished and all the country's nationalist myths intact. *You Have to Be Careful* is about how, once overseas, Jeremiah encounters resistance to these myths; it becomes more and more difficult to perpetuate them without provoking interrogation. Yasmin, for instance, demands to see historical evidence to back up Jeremiah's claim that his people, too, had been subjugated, thus prising open the kind of space within Jeremiah's sense of self where a cosmopolitan consciousness might eventually begin to take root. As Binnie points out, mobility is usually seen as the reserve of the middle classes, who 'precisely through being more mobile [appear] less likely to succumb to the immobile attitudes of the "non-cosmopolitan" classes' (Binnie et al. 2006: 11). My comparison of Kelman's protagonist with McEwan's, however, who is at least as inveterately set in his ways as Jeremiah, if not more so, goes to disprove this claim. Moreover, as Kelman illustrates, mobility and cultural transplantation as such have never yet set anyone free by themselves; only self-knowledge and insight can achieve that. Notably, it is Jeremiah's inability to see beyond the brim of his Scottishness that ruins his relationship with Yasmin. It is the same opinionated, self-delusive Scottishness that might explain why, throughout their relationship, the African-American woman adamantly refuses to discuss her history and identity politics with a Scot. Jeremiah mocks Yasmin's and her family's deficient grasp of global geography, conceding that it was just 'a wee bit better than the usual Uhmerkin deal. Even so they thought Skallin was somewhere in Germany which they guessed was to "the left hand side" of Australia, up above the Arctic fucking Pole' (75). But how much, in turn, does he know about the USA and the histories of its subordinate peoples? The apparent affinity he presumes to exist between them and his own people looks like a very crude effort at cultural homogenisation, an assimilation, even erasure, of the particularity of their difference as well as his own. Towards the end his monologue begins to ring ever more vacuous and hollow. It becomes evident that Jeremiah speaks for and about himself alone rather than also, as he clearly believes, on behalf of others.

That, unlike his protagonist, Kelman is not only aware of the injurious limitations of the Scottish outlook, but indeed extremely frustrated and dissatisfied with Scottish literature's ongoing proliferation of solipsistic narratives, shows in *Translated Accounts*. The novel's style of anonymous abstraction leaves no doubt that the people it depicts as exposed to totalitarian tyranny and genocidal violence are definitely not the Scots. As far as Kelman is concerned, it is time post-devolution Scotland looked beyond its own legendary suffering, which is at risk of becoming inauthentic through so much reiteration. It is time the nation grasped its new ethical responsibility in the world. As Kelly comments, 'the radical shift in Kelman's style in *Translated Accounts* does not offer some sense of a Scotland at home with itself [. . .] as nationalist appropriations of his work would have it, but instead very boldly displaces his work across what the broken language of the novel terms the "terrortories" of global space' (2007: 179). It is time Scotland ceased to provide Scottish literature's sole focus and subject matter. It is time the country acknowledged its relatively powerful and influential position, and started paying attention to the fate of the rest of the world. *Translated Accounts* is testament to Kelman's enduring radicalism, his refusal to compromise even for the sake of accommodating the needs of his readers. The novel is difficult and relentlessly 'foreign' in its representation; reading it tests our commitment to hearing the voices of the wretched. In contrast to McEwan, who in *Saturday* selects one strictly secondary, obliquely presented voice – that of one of Henry's patients,

Miri Taleb, an Iraqi professor of ancient history – to mediate the harrowing ordeal of another people, Kelman dedicates a whole novel to breathing life into totalitarian horror. All one hears in *Saturday*, articulated in polished, clearly intelligible English, is that 'everyone hates it [. . .] You see, it's only terror that holds the nation together, the whole system runs on fear, and no one knows how to stop it' (2005: 64). By contrast, in *Translated Accounts* the terror takes centre stage, attacking the reader's imagination with the stark forcefulness of a violent assault.

In terms of both its popular and critical reception, the history of *Translated Accounts* continues to be fraught, and in particular it will need exploring why, as Kelman has revealed in interview, 'the novel has had a much better response in Europe than anywhere else. It's not really read here in the U.K. very much' (Toremans 2003: 583). The fact that the novel is currently out of print in Britain serves as a sure sign of its fundamental lack of appeal; it also hints at a general incomprehension at what Kelman might be attempting to achieve in this novel, which is so vulnerable to hermeneutic misconstruction and proves extremely difficult to read 'properly'. Kövesi sees it as documenting a complete dystopian breakdown of civilisation, marked by horrific cruelty and large-scale carnage, a traumatic loss of communal belonging, as well as a language that appears maimed beyond repair:

> Society is dismembered, torn limb from limb, rendered just an ideal, a dream-story, rather than a narratological possibility. There are moments of union, of love and lust amidst the rubble, but they are transitory, founded in grief, in permanent absence. The language of the accounts is the fractured terrain of splintered peoples who are almost completely lost to war, to oppression, to foreign invasion. (2007: 171–2)

But contrary to Kövesi's reading, the opening section of the novel (2001: 1–4) – albeit ominously titled 'bodies' and at first glance recording graphically the gruesome anonymity of mass murder in a time of civil war – accentuates the resilience and resourcefulness of human life, which has not yielded to, let alone been erased by, this genocidal catastrophe. The section is alive with familial and communal signifiers, such as 'familiars', 'acquaintance', 'sister', 'my lover', 'niece', 'granddaughter', 'intimates' and 'friends', as the speaker remembers 'family', 'home' and 'colleagues' and insists that 'I had known her', 'I knew them' and 'I recognised many among them.' The section emphasises how even after the most unspeakable horror familial and communal structures endure, however vestigially to begin with. Some ineradicable element of the human identity prevails.

From the start the speaker's focus is on 'one individual', then another, who 'was a man who was the son of a man'. If the first section sets the tone for the novel as a whole, then *Translated Accounts* invites us to witness a people picking itself up in the aftermath of cataclysmic terror, counting its losses and resurfacing. The fifty-four accounts in the novel – comprising extracts from eye-witness reports, memoirs, letters, interviews and the like – constitute a severely battered people's historical record of that 'evil' time; they are their entextualised memory of pain intended to demonstrate for all to see their survival: 'If misrepresentation, there has been so, I have been exhausted and the times, evil. For they herded us. I am not an animal. Some may be, I am not. We make decisions, each among us' (2). Starting by revisiting the scene of the mass executions in section 1 – 'this building [that] was a home [. . .] and going through there and [I] could not step but for bodies, everywhere' – a painful and quite possibly interminable process of re-assemblage is set in motion. But there can be no doubt that this process will prove curative in the end. While all ordinary communal life in the society depicted by Kelman has been seriously disrupted, the novel continues to zoom in on every residual trace, every memory, of everyday life in the past, such as the bridge in the town centre, now occupied and guarded by the military, which used to be 'truly a communal point, meeting place. Across from there was a small square, people would walk to there. For many it was the end of the promenade, they would go home.' Even though 'tonight was not the same' (22), for a brief instant the reader shares the narrator's enchantment on recalling the bustle of people that would regularly bring this particular place to life. Defying the regime's attempts to isolate people from one another, a strong sense of familial connectivity, communal belonging and reciprocity survives in the minds of the oppressed, as in the case of the man, possibly a member of the resistance, who waits for his partner in a restaurant crowded with waiters, yet entirely devoid of guests. 'And these lives round me', he muses, 'all were there in my head, filling my brain, boys with their great-grandfathers and girls and their mothers and ancestors, old old ladies, wizened and laughing, waiters and their wives, their dreams and clothes drying, sea wind' (56). Similar memories of community surface in one of the narrators' dreams of arriving at a mythical site of belonging, the result of free communal living that goes back generations: 'We were entering a canal system and with wooden footbridges arching at unexpected angles, impressing that here was not theoretical work but a world, its countless generations of human endeavour, occupying different positions, erected in all different periods down through the past, way way far-off' (297).

Even at moments of utter disillusionment and destruction the oppressed cannot help but remember – even yearn for, however guardedly – a better world informed primarily by thriving familial relations and a shared communal heritage. This world of hope could not be any further removed from the one they presently live in, which is wholly determined by totalitarian rule. One of the narrators berates his companion for tormenting him with tales of 'a world now gone, a world now dead', angrily pointing out that he, too, could speak of his 'grandfather, my mother, my father, uncles, I can speak of all them, my son also, what of him, you do not ask of him, listen to stories of him, he is alive, living and breathing, if he is, a little child, we see the children, what of my son' (260–1). Reluctantly he concedes that 'dreams are also in my head. I survive with them', but he will not disclose them because, he insists, people now must 'live in this world which is a real world, where we now are in this decay, destroyed building, destroyed lives and dreams of life, deaths of children, killings of children' and 'continue to exist spiting spiting' (263–4). In this section, aptly titled 'homecoming stories', it transpires how perilously close the oppressed have come to yielding to the regime's attempts to eradicate communal ties by shutting up the past and atomising society into solitary 'cases' that can no longer bear the promise of future companionship or solidarity.

For a novel ostensibly recording the demise of community, *Translated Accounts* is remarkably alert to the dynamics of communal regeneration and the ultimate ineradicability of human relations. Against all the odds, we witness a perfect stranger forming an intimate relationship with 'the elderly woman [who] dies' in the second section of the novel, simply by telling her stories which 'followed patterns and within the pattern was space for dreams, her dreams my dreams, as of weaving, the story-web' (5). Their life stories become mutually imbricated, creating a dense textual-emotional network of links and connections, quite literally mixing memory and desire. It seems as if an ancient, inalienably human process had been set in motion, 'her mind moving by itself, fired by myself. I spoke to her of my life and her life, drawing stories from there, inventions' (10). The narrator's art of storytelling makes him 'familiar to some, as they to myself, many people, so it was with the elderly woman' (6), who eventually calls out to him as 'the boy [. . .] referring not to her son but to myself. I know of no son. Nor daughter, if there is a daughter, neither son, I know nothing of them. It is myself whom she referred. I was the boy. I was that one' (9). As the keeper of traditions and reporter of news, the storyteller assumes the role of a saviour, providing the grief-stricken woman with a family she may never in reality have had. In turn, she adopts him.

The community-building power of stories is alluded to throughout the novel, yet despite their creation and dissemination of curative truths, stories cannot entirely erase the traumatic cracks in this relentlessly battered society's constitution, its traumatic pain of loss and displacement, the ubiquity of betrayal, both as a real threat and as paranoid apprehension:

> There were no people from earlier times, they did not come to her. This was not her homeplace. If she said that it was, it was not. Her mind was mistaken. Neighbours. What neighbours. What is neighbours. If visitors to her, there were visitors and she only cried at them, thieves, murderers! (6)

Yet at every opportunity the novel emphasises also the intimate relatedness of individuals, their basic human affinity that binds them together, their mutual empathy. In the fourth section someone catches a fleeting glimpse of a refugee with a baby, an occurrence that lingers as the observer feels her life overlap with and enclose for a moment that of 'the redhaired woman': 'I said I have a child, so thoughts of my child, one other life, one to another' (18). Both are 'one of many', saved from obliteration in the maelstrom of mass suffering only by this instantaneous, momentary link which, as the narrator suggests, is a sign of the 'essence of human being, our strength alone, this thing, what it is, more than resolve' (18). This might also be the way in which Kelman's readers are encouraged to empathise with the exposed human figures that they find walking wounded within his desolate, dystopian landscape. Conversely, should they fail to connect in the intended way, they might be left with as little to say about *Translated Accounts* as Laurence Nicoll:

> There is no conventional sense of story here at all. Instead, we are simply presented with a deeply ambiguous set of documents or reports, written and translated by anonymous figures, ostensibly concerned with a not altogether clear collection of events that have taken place in an equally anonymous country (or countries). (2005: 60)

Nicoll exaggerates the novel's lack of structural and thematic coherence, mistaking Kelman's reticence for gratuitous ambiguity and interpreting the author's choice of anonymity as a sign of inapposite detachment, obfuscation and ultimate irrelevance.

As I see it, the anonymity of the multiple narrators – introduced in the 'Preface' rather vaguely as 'three, four or more individuals domiciled in an occupied territory or land where a form of martial law appears in operation' (ix) – very quickly reveals a recognisable set of recurrent voices and presences, such as the eye-witness, who is a parent and in all his or her accounts remains highly sensitised to the presence of babies and small children. Then there is the pair of 'terrorists' resembling George Orwell's Winston and Julia in *1984*, whose 'collegial' bond at times blurs into an adulterous party functionary's purely sexual desire for somebody else's wife, hinting at the difficulty of distinguishing unequivocally between subversive agitants, on the one hand, and loyal state agents, on the other (see also Macdonald 2002: 97). These narrators are joined by the young soldier, who used to be a care worker or nurse before his selection for special military service into which, despite his parents' disapproval, he was proud to be recruited. He appears to be the same young man who later desperately tries to convince one of his prisoners that 'securitys are also human beings [. . .] how that he differed to all other securitys, yes, a human being' (163). These voices and presences intermittently singularise out of the general background, within which three larger groups of people can be identified: the regime's soldiers and security guards; the so-called 'colleagues' or members of an undercover resistance movement, referred to also as the 'campaigning formation'; and then the masses of civilians, whom we encounter in detention camps, on the road, in hiding, imprisoned or on the run, with particular attention being given to women and girls to whom ominously 'all men are enemies' (185). All of the human presences in *Translated Accounts* are crafted to strike us at once as familiar and entirely alien in their inarticulate anonymity, as irreplaceably unique human beings and an amorphous mass of entirely dispensable people of no consequence. Kelman cannot be accused of not making himself clear in this novel, which is about murder, rape, torture and displacement, totalitarian state control and genocidal violence, all thickening into a viscerally insufferable sense of ruinous entrapment. Everybody is incarcerated in their own individual self, and yet there remains a clear sense in which even this isolated suffering is shared, as one man is shown capable of accurately visualising another's despair: 'I saw the brains in this man's head, thumping on the shell, let me our let me out, I cannot stay in this job, it is not a job, how can a man live like this, I am leaving, I am going to Germany, to Copenhagen, I am told Oslo is good, in Amsterdam people have respect. Yes, yes, go there. I go there' (54).

The greatest experimental challenge of *Translated Accounts*, which was reportedly seven years in the making, resides without doubt in its recalcitrant use of language. The novel presents us with a compilation of fragments from first-hand narratives by the members of an oppressed and persecuted people, originally recorded in an unknown foreign language, which have been 'transcribed and/or translated into English, not always by persons native to the tongue' (xi). The result is a unique text of some considerable peculiarity whose representational authenticity regarding an isolated people's rudimentary command of English is hugely impressive. However, Kelman's skilful evocation of the non-native brokenness of this people's English, which, as he suggests, has been additionally compromised by the clumsy, incompetent or uncaring interference of underskilled translators and officious bureaucrats, generates a non-standard mode of self-expression that inevitably obstructs the novel's accessibility. Susanne Hagemann refers to the English in which the accounts are rendered as 'pseudo-translatorese' (2005: 75); whilst apt, this also implicitly disparages this language, which, after all, constitutes the only means by which the wretched of the world are able to communicate their plight to the global community. It is their only chance to make themselves heard, importantly not only to native speakers of English, but to everybody who has a reasonable second-language or foreign-language grasp of the world's lingua franca. Judging from the novel's critical reception, its language has divided readers into those who understand – that is, those who can be bothered to make the effort to understand – and those who complain about Kelman's language not being 'proper' English. On closer reflection, it is this division among its readers that helps crystallise one of the central points the novel is seeking to make.

As the linguist Jennifer Jenkins has pointed out, 'in international communication, the ability to accommodate to interlocutors with other first languages than one's own (regardless of whether the result is an "error" in [English as a native language]) is a far more important skill than the ability to imitate the English of a native speaker' (2007: 238). *Translated Accounts* literally makes a torturous read, testing the reader's listening skills and empathy: how much time are we willing to spend tuning in and struggling to understand? When will we switch off, return the book to the shelf only partially read, and turn to something less taxing, conveniently blaming Kelman and his inarticulate people for failing to get their message across? Unlike non-native speakers of English, who now make up the global majority, native speakers – the majority of whom tend to be strictly monolingual – often seem not only put off, but acutely embarrassed by heavily accented speech or texts written in foreign-looking, non-standard variants of the language. Might this inflexibility and impatience in the end lead to incapacitating native speakers of English from participating fully responsively in global communication?

As Jenkins concludes from her research on lingua franca English as an emergent variant of the language with its own specific conventions, free global communication continues to be hampered by a striking incongruity in so far as a minority of native English speakers (NS) remains securely ensconced in a hegemonic position from which they dictate to an exponentially increasing majority of non-native speakers (NSS) how to communicate properly, not only with them, but also among each other. 'For the past two decades or so', Jenkins writes, 'a paradoxical situation has existed according to which linguistic power in lingua franca English communication (i.e. overwhelmingly NNS–NNS) has tended to be wielded by absent NSs of English: in other words, by an NS norm, the idea (itself idealized) of how an NS would say something were he or she present in the interaction' (201). As Jenkins illustrates, the native speaker's superior entitlement in international communication remains largely undisputed and serves not only to conceal 'the monolingual NS English attitude of expecting others to make all the (language learning) effort' (51), but also the increasing marginalisation of Standard English as a fastidious sociolect, additionally disadvantaged by the 'unhappy colonial resonance [it evokes] in the minds of many' (Crystal 2003: 125). Provocatively, Jenkins alludes to 'the possibility that the English spoken by its British (or, for that matter, North American) NSs is not the most internationally intelligible' (237) and that 'many [second-language] English learners and users may in future no longer perceive themselves as wishing to integrate into an NS English culture, but into [. . .] "the world at large"' (198). Proudly monolingual in an increasingly globalised and bilingual world, native speakers of English are at risk of painting themselves into an isolated corner of the globe, causing them to fall out of sync with the rest of the world as they turn into interlocutors that can be heard and understood, but to whom global mingling and cosmopolitan responsiveness come increasingly less easily.

Over fifteen years ago Cairns Craig commented on Kelman's innovative use of working-class Glaswegian as facilitating the creation of a 'unity of voice [that] replaces unity of political or social purpose as the foundation of solidarity [. . .] enact[ing] at a linguistic level what it points to as absent in the world, a communality that transcends the isolation of the individual human being' (1993: 103). *Translated Accounts* accomplishes something very similar as it propagates a global variant of English whose very deficiency and brokenness by normative standards identify it as the perfect tool for cosmopolitan community-building. Kelman's novel successfully addresses a global readership of English speakers (as proven by the novel's success abroad), most of whom will have a personal history of learning English and hence memories of their own struggle with the language. Moreover, as experienced speakers of lingua franca English they are likely to know how to go about tuning in to each of their various interlocutors' varying levels of linguistic competence. Monolingual speakers of English, by contrast, are more likely to become flustered at every mispronunciation, semantic ambiguity, grammatical mistake and syntactical inconsistency; they may have no clue how to adjust their language use appropriately, often resorting to raising their voices or simply speaking more slowly, both of which are perceived as patronising. David Crystal has suggested that 'it is just as likely that the course of the English language is going to be influenced by those who speak it as a second or foreign language as by those who speak it as a mother-tongue' (2003: 172). Kelman might be more inclined to agree with Jenkins, who believes that the latter, unless they fundamentally change their attitude, are at serious risk of (self-) exclusion from the language's globalisation and promising cosmopolitan future (see also Gunesch 2008). As Crystal himself points out, 'the ratio of native to non-native [speakers] is around 1:3', adding that 'the population growth in areas where English is a second language is about 2.5 times that in areas where it is a first language, so that this differential is steadily increasing' (69).

Translated Accounts is likely to strike native speakers of English not only as difficult but, more significantly, as *unnecessarily* difficult. The very purpose of Kelman's elaborate design of linguistic brokenness is likely to elude the monolingual reader, which would help explain why this novel never did very well in Britain. Symptomatically, making no reference whatsoever to current debates on postcoloniality and globalisation, or the burgeoning fields of translation and trauma studies, Cambridge don Drew Milne's reading of Kelman's novel is marked by baffled bemusement. 'The novel poses puzzles for the literal-minded interpreter', Milne writes, 'not least forcing readers to imagine places within globalisation where the English language has not penetrated' (2001: 106). Even more curious about Milne's unreconstructed take on the novel than his positing of a 'literal-minded [most probably English] interpreter' is the strikingly imperialist tone of his naive overestimation of the contemporary world's linguistic anglicisation, which he appears to believe to be total. More accurately putting the number of people in the world 'now capable of communicating to a useful level in English' at approximately 25 per cent, Crystal immediately inserts the following caveat:

> If one quarter of the world's population are able to use English, then three-quarters are not. Nor do we have to travel far into the hinterland of a country – away from the tourist spots, airports, hotels and restaurants – to encounter this reality. Populist claims about the universal spread of English thus need to be kept firmly in perspective. (69)

It comes as no great surprise that Milne cannot imagine anything is gained from Kelman's experimental representation of his novel as a translation. Rather than prompting reflection on the possible benefits contact with another language might bring, to the 'literal-minded interpreter' self-expression in another language is inevitably associated with alienation, coercion, inauthenticity, loss and incompleteness. Hence, according to Milne, the novel is most probably about 'how human experiences get lost in translation' (106), while translation itself must be seen as a 'dystopian' process, causing the English language to 'become foreign to itself' (110–11). In other words, English must inevitably fall prey to translation's intractable distortion rather than being enriched, for example, by an experience of cross-cultural hybridisation.

Milne's depressing conclusion is that *Translated Accounts* is written in 'a language that no-one would recognise as their own' (107), a view shared by Kövesi, who describes it as 'a nowhere language for a nowhere place' (2007: 171). At first the linguist Crystal seems to concur, stating that 'if there is one predictable consequence of a language becoming a global language, it is that nobody owns it any more'. But then he corrects himself, stressing in far more promising, world-opening terms that 'everyone who has learned it now owns it – "has a share in it" might be more accurate – and has the right to use it in the way they want' (2–3). In this light, then, it might be precisely translation's manifold deviancies and erratic fluency that constitute its considerable cosmopolitan potential, its democratic pluralism and inherent world-creative power.

If there is in fact anything dystopian about *Translated Accounts* apart from its subject matter, it is the novel's largely negative critical reception. Certainly it is not Kelman's representational technique, which encourages readers to immerse themselves in a cosmopolitan lingua franca exchange, requiring them to adjust their own linguistic competence in order to listen, empathise with and understand the ordeal of another people. The experience of reading the novel resembles that of undergoing a strenuous orienteering exercise, perhaps not so very dissimilar to the narrator's in the novel's opening section on abruptly finding herself stumbling among the grim human debris of an unspeakable atrocity. What could potentially turn into a thoroughly alienating confrontation with something abjectly foreign opens up into a quasi-epiphanic discovery of something profoundly familiar: the ineradicable relational matrix of our common humanity. It is this experience of reality that divides the victims from the murderers and, even more crucially, the political agitants of the resistance movement from the agents of the state and their accomplices. About the latter one victim remarks: 'They do not think we are human beings. This is why, they do not think what we are' (222). In the native speaker's impatient

or obtuse turning away from Kelman's experiment, the novel drama-
tises the fate of the wretched people it depicts and the dependence of
their future on making themselves heard in the global tongue.
Appropriating the title of Joseph Jones's linguistic classic *Terranglia:
The Case of English as World-literature* (1965) Susanne Hagemann
observes that 'in an era of globalisation which is in fact an era of
Anglicisation or Americanisation, communicating in English is a
must':

> If as a native speaker of German or Arabic you want Terranglia to take
> notice of you, you will be well-advised to provide texts in English yourself,
> since the target cultures (from Britain to North America, from Australia to
> India) might not be interested in having your texts translated into their
> language. (2005: 80)

The resounding terminological similarity of Terranglia to 'Oceania',
'Eurasia' and 'Eastasia', the three dystopian global super-states in
Orwell's *1984*, seems more than purely coincidental here as it serves to
expose the potential cultural totalitarianism of English as a monologic
megalanguage. As Hagemann points out, 'not speaking another's language, not being forced to learn it, can be a sign of a position of power'
(81). As long as English can uphold its hegemonic status undisputedly,
the actual superiority of bilingualism, however partially or rudimentar-
ily developed, will not only go unacknowledged, but continue to be
systematically disparaged and eclipsed.

Symptomatically, in the novel's penultimate section, we hear of a
woman who 'was familiar with their dialect, I have said, that language.
They knew nothing of hers. Thus she had become the inferior. This is
as it was, it remains so, for myself also, individuals inferiorised, myself,
herself' (317). The inferiorisation of bilingualism functions to conceal
the fact that ultimately all the bridges connecting Terranglia to the rest
of the world depend for their maintenance on non-native speakers of
English. Put differently, globalisation as a process of hegemonic centralisation depends on the global imposition of a strictly codified
common language, such as Crystal's vision of a 'World Standard
Spoken English' (185–9), modelled exclusively after native variants of
English. Yet alternatively the contemporary world might just as well
start customising English as a multiform lingua franca, dependent on
non-native speakers spontaneously and diversely engaging in cosmopolitan exchanges with one another, thus setting in motion multifarious
processes of worldwide political devolution and ongoing cultural diversification. More bridges would come to be built, but these would now
primarily interconnect the vast peripheries of the globe, potentially
bypassing a centre that might yet have to relearn its own tongue.

In his short history of vernacular writing Sheldon Pollock argues that 'vernacular literary cultures were initiated by the conscious decisions of writers to reshape the boundaries of their cultural universe by renouncing the larger world for the smaller place', fully aware that 'using a new language for communicating literarily to a community of readers and listeners can consolidate if not create that very community' (2002: 16). Pollock's point on the identity-bearing potential of vernacular writing certainly applies to Kelman's early work, which is focused exclusively on a literary representation of Glasgow in demotic Scots, designed to assert the local working-class people's identity and boost their sense of solidarity and 'small-place' communal belonging. With regard to his more recent work, however – written at a time when, according to Pollock, 'vernacular modes of cultural and political being are everywhere coming under powerful pressures from an altogether new universalizing order of culture-power (call it globalization, or liberalization, or Americanization)' (16) – instead of yielding to Standard English to win himself a larger world audience, Kelman becomes if anything more radical. He does so not by simply commanding the world to listen to him in his own tongue but by proclaiming the willingness to engage with the voices of others – and meet them halfway, as it were – as every aspiring cosmopolitan's most urgent ethical responsibility.

In *Translated Accounts* Kelman alerts us to the evolution of lingua franca English into a hitherto unprecedented kind of cosmopolitan vernacular, while in *You Have to Be Careful* his unapologetic use of Glaswegian Scots infiltrates and effectively undermines majoritarian portrayals of contemporary US American life. By transplanting Scots into the world at large and allowing it to prosper into a world-literary code for unruly Scottish self-expression, Kelman contests English's megalingual distinction between 'a language that travels far and one that travels little' (Pollock 2002: 18). It is this binarist discrimination that for centuries has secured the superiority of English over Scots or, more generally speaking, the language's standard forms over its less widespread socio-regional variants. If indeed 'language is a major means (some would say the chief means) of showing where we belong, and of distinguishing one social group from another' (Crystal 2003: 22), then what Kelman achieves in *You Have to Be Careful* is a point-blank demolition of Pollock's critical paradigm that vernacular writing is for the creation of small places rather than large worlds. Not only does Kelman's Scots usurp Standard English's exclusive claim to literary world-creation, it also asserts its speaker's identity as indisputably that of a citizen of the world. Commendably Kelman refrains from reinscribing a sense of polarity between the local/vernacular and the global;

instead, by championing the immigrant's minoritarian outlook and representing the global through Jeremiah's vernacular lens, he opts for a radical redefinition of glocality, in which it is now primarily the local permeating and forever transforming the global, rather than vice versa. Any reader tuning in to Jeremiah's cosmopolitan bid must undergo immersion in the novel's glocal mêlée, re-emerging from the experience indelibly marked by the text's world-transforming vernacularity.

Competent lingua franca communication among people speaking different variants of English, be they native or non-native, relies on empathy, well-developed improvisation skills, and a willingness to immerse oneself in a glocal mêlée where identities touch and hybridise, if only ever momentarily, forming a transient new grammar fit for whatever is the immediate purpose at hand. Notably, in *Being Singular Plural* Jean-Luc Nancy defines the *mêlée* as 'an action rather than a substance' (2000: 150); according to him, the mêlée '*is* not; it happens constantly' (156). Functioning as a set of skills rather than a fixed knowledge base, lingua franca English appears perfectly suited for cosmopolitan exchange and inoperative community-building, in whose framework 'being with, being together and even being "united" are precisely not a matter of being "one"', and a general awareness obtains that 'what we have in common is also what always distinguishes and differentiates us' (154–5). As Nancy insists, 'cultures, or what are known as cultures, do not mix. They encounter each other, mingle, modify each other, reconfigure each other. They cultivate one another; they irrigate or drain each other; they work over and plough through each other, or graft one onto the other' (151). Thus, even though Jeremiah finds himself experientially submerged in the thick of another culture – being inspired by it, feeling anxious about it, struggling against and attempting to resist it – it never assimilates or unequivocally rejects him; in turn, US America never appears to him any less foreign or culturally impenetrable. Yet still we can be sure that on his eventual return to Scotland his family will find him thoroughly Americanised.

There is no indication that Jeremiah and Yasmin ever speak to each other in anything but their own sociolectal local variants of English, which are presumably quite different. Perhaps we can assume, however, that even if their individual ways of speaking do not change, the way they listen to each other might? Kelman's characters are inveterate locals whose Englishes idiosyncratically recreate the world; in Jeremiah's language Ireland becomes 'oillin' (105) and Europe becomes 'Youropey' (119), while other nationalities are rendered as 'eyetalian, mehican, joymin, inkliz, velch' (118). Yet this is Jeremiah's singular expression of the world, not a unilateral remapping, signalled also by the fact that

Kelman's spellings for the same or similar words vary widely across the novel. Jeremiah's language resists a definite capture of life's cosmopolitan mêlée within any one particular fixed global grammar and certainly casts serious doubt on the universal benignity of a so-called *Pax Americana*. Jeremiah would seem much more comfortably at home in Ulrich Beck's global cosmopolis, envisaged as 'a federal planetary system of states which is not ruled by a "solar" world state but is composed of regional and continental alliances of states [. . .] as "points of crystallization" which both enable and counterbalance the centralization of power' (Beck 2006: 132). Then again, such a profoundly co-operative order might already strike Kelman as far too uncannily neat in its perfect systemic organisation.

You Have to Be Careful reads like a vociferous critique of the myth of the American Dream, unmasking as purely rhetorical the USA's reputation as a utopian haven for refugees, adventurers and budding entrepreneurs of any provenance, as well as its jealously guarded role as *the* benign guarantor of world peace, justice and democracy. Not only does Jeremiah refer to the world's sole superpower as the 'supreme destroyer of the planet; leader in world exploitation, in the destruction of all human endeavour; supporter of the tyrant and genocidal murderer' (74–5), he depicts the immigrant's experience not as a joyous, self-fulfilling arrival at one's destination, but as an endlessly deferred process of going through customs and passport control that continues on a daily basis even after twelve years of living in the country. Surveillance and the threat of deportation are omnipresent. Although the majority of US citizens Jeremiah encounters are of foreign – that is, non-WASP – extraction, as indicated by their names (Ranjit, Haydar, Riçard Osoba, Sharifa, Billy Zannu, John Wong), and thus provide evidence of the country's genuinely multicultural make-up, the nation as such continues to strike him as 'a homogeneous hotbed of poisonous fuckers all staring at ye because ye are the wrang "thing": religion, race, class, nationality, politics; they know ye as soon as look at ye, boy, you is alien' (26). What prevents the novel from deteriorating into a mere anti-Americanist rant of little discrimination is the careful distinction Kelman insists on making between 'a right-wing load of keech like the US State' and 'the individual population' (132), that is, between the statistically manufactured mythical majority of the 'Uhmerkin people' in opposition to trouble-making 'tiny minorities' (197) that fail to toe the official line and behave unpatriotically.

Notably, it is not just 'furin folks, folks of diverse genetic and ethnic strain' (169) that are at risk of incarceration in one of the Patriot Holding Centers that have sprung up in the vicinity of virtually every airport, but also the indigenous poor, 'the dregs of society [who] were flaunting themselves publicly' (197). In many respects the USA depicted by Kelman resembles that of Thomas Pynchon's notorious Cold War classic *The Crying of Lot 49* (1979, originally published 1965), which, equally steeped in existential disorientation and myth-induced paranoia, contains the first tentative murmurings of an incipient underground rallying of the oppressed, not so very different from the 'campaigning formation' in *Translated Accounts*, which is mobilising to subvert the system from within. Ironically, in Pynchon's as in Kelman's work, the original values of America are embodied by apparent outcasts like Jeremiah who undauntedly practise their right to free speech, propelled by an irrepressible individualism. Jeremiah's adamant refusal to succumb to alienation identifies him as exactly the kind of citizen contemporary US America needs to reinvigorate itself. This is expressed by the chair of the interviewing panel that appoints Jeremiah to the post of airport 'security':

> I look at you and I think, Here is a feller can succeed with us. He is not afraid of the world that lies outside these shores. In this line of business there are many afraid to open an atlas or engage in geographical matters. They wont have a map in the house; even the sight of our country in outline causes tension because it posits the existence of a *beyond*. (154)

In order to protect its security, in Kelman's view, the USA must not only overcome its post-9/11 xenophobic paranoia and isolationist world-blindness. It must moreover embrace the awkward realisation that the American Dream might in fact most effectively be kept alive by those at present categorically excluded from it.

Jeremiah's monologue takes a spectacularly communal turn as it begins to envisage the spontaneous rise of a popular resistance movement in contemporary America. This movement soon comes to be perceived by the authorities as a serious security risk that Jeremiah, among many others, is recruited to police. The movement starts originally as the mere by-product of a mass-hysterical national craze, the so-called 'perishing bet', an insurance gamble enthralling US America's down-and-out on a hitherto unheard-of, entirely unmanageable scale. Fascinated, Jeremiah looks on as, in a desperate bid to improve their lives or, at least, that of their loved ones, US society's underprivileged flock to the airports in their thousands to boldly try themselves out as quasi-gladiatorial, moribund would-be entrepreneurs, recklessly investing their lives as the only capital they have. Prospective passengers are prepared to wait interminably to purchase a seat on a flight with an airline that has a dubious safety record, planning to cash in on big insurance payouts should they wind up as the victims, either dead or badly wounded, of a plane crash. As Kelman's novel notes, 'it was a dream come true. Either way you were a winner. If ye survived ye lost the bet but if ye perished yer faimly collected the cash' (98). Jeremiah witnesses the nation's airports clog up with 'hordes of bodies [. . .] wandering about the place with naywhere to go'. Despite being 'ordinary Uhmerkins, moistly true-borns', these people are found to lack 'adequate social skills', rendering them essentially feral beings, intrinsically unruly and impervious to any governmental attempt at organising or 'domesticating' them:

> Nor could they cope with the disciplinary treatment to which regular domestic travelers were accustomed, they didnay do what the authorities telt them to do and were ignoring all the rules and regulations. They didnay seem to fucking grasp that orders were orders. These bodies were clogging up corridors, reception and gate waiting areas and were finding their way onto the goddam airfields themselves. One minute they were there the next they werenay. (135)

The only kind of organisation they appear susceptible to comes from among themselves and expresses itself in ad hoc manifestations of communal solidarity that seem suspiciously unionist and hence fundamentally at odds with contemporary US America's official line of neo-liberalist capitalism: 'When the airlines increased the fares these folks formed same-interest groups to buy up tickets then raffled them amongst themselves. It was great! Auld forms of combination were being rediscovered. At this rate the great Uhmerkin people were gauny create their ayn wee Enlightenment' (128). Treated as an internal security risk, these 'ragged persons bearing blankets or pushing grocery carts' (128) are ordered out of the airport lobbies into the car park zones. However, to marginalise them even further – for example, by forcing them 'behind the barbed and electrified wire, and the steeply-angled high walls' of the Patriot Holding Centers already containing 'tens of hundreds of furnir varmints' (167–8) – is not an option because, as Jeremiah takes great pleasure in reminding us, 'these were fucking bona fide natural true-born Uhmerkins man these folks werenay fucking aliens, no sir, not at all' (129).

In Kelman's representation the growing domestic instability inside the world's sole superpower mirrors the volatile state of the globalised world at large. Disorder and insecurity ensue as in both the national and international spheres the world's destitute are beginning to appropriate the aspirations of the world's rich and, in a desperate bid for material comfort and happiness, lodge their all-or-nothing claim for a share in what the world has to offer. If necessary, to improve their chances of success, they are prepared to suspend their regular lives and embrace a homeless, peripatetic existence. Kelman's choice of setting for the launch of the dispossessed's bid for equal opportunities appears extremely apt. Twinning the global gateway of the USA's every international airport with the dead-end hopelessness of concentration-camp-like holding centres for illegal immigrants and the unruly poor, Kelman creates a perfect hybrid of the two 'non-places' that, according to Zygmunt Bauman, constitute globalisation's most characteristic locales. 'The proliferation of refugee camps is as integral a product/manifestation of globalization', Bauman writes, 'as the dense archipelago of stopover *nowherevilles* through which the members of the new globetrotting elite move on their round-the-world voyages' (2003: 142). Kelman expertly blurs the boundaries between these allegedly discrete locales, at once buzzing and yet entirely devoid of communal life, by introducing us to a crowd of people who find their lives precariously suspended between the prospects of becoming either passengers or internees.

The airport's traditional anonymous sterility as a mere transport channel-cum-waiting room full of strangers is thrown into turmoil as it begins to display signs of becoming a potential hotbed for inoperative community-building and popular insurrection. It is in this latter respect that Kelman's novel displays a curious affinity with a particular strand in contemporary US American fiction, which John McClure has recently designated as 'post-secular', citing – among others – Don DeLillo, Tony Kushner, Toni Morrison and Thomas Pynchon as exemplary representatives. What characterises post-secular fiction is 'a quiet loosening of the fabric of "the real" and momentary, almost indiscernible, interruptions of the "laws of nature"', combined with – and at times causally effecting – the formation of 'spontaneously emerging, small-scale, and informally structured contrast communities [. . .] in the cracks of the social order, among the anonymous and the excluded: gays in [Kushner's] *Angels in America*, the urban poor in [DeLillo's] *Underworld*, working-class whites in [Pynchon's] *Vineland*, runaways in [Morrison's] *Paradise*' (McClure 2007: 3, 20). *You Have to Be Careful* evidently fits in here. Most astonishing, however, for the work of a social-realist writer like Kelman is the sudden introduction of a spiritual element into one of his novels, manifesting apparitionally as Jeremiah's 'legendary grocery-cart pusher', a character who later becomes known also as 'the Unearthly Being' (216).

From the start the rallying of society's underprivileged in the nation's airports attracts the attention of church representatives, 'reverends and other fervent worthies hoping to nab these manifold souls of the wretched'. The clergymen are swiftly accompanied by a mercenary retinue of 'vendors of religious icons and bric-a-brac, saintly knock-knacks, body bits, and garlic-coated good-luck charms' (128), quite as if the crowds were preparing for a pilgrimage, checking in for some kind of ultimate superstitious quest for salvation. Into this general commotion bursts the ghostly, swiftly mythologised singularity of the Grocery-Cart Pusher, 'believed naked apart from a short coat [. . .] [who] never responds to a greeting, nor to an order [. . .] [who] appears from naywhere and vanishes back into there in the twinkling of an eye'. Resembling a universalised incorporation of what motivates the masses – their suffering, their manifold grievances, their anger as well as their hopes – the Being assumes the paradoxical appearance of an ascetic, possibly starving consumer, whose apathetic countenance seems at once automatised and sublime: 'Nayn has heard this "character" speak nor engage in daily human activities [. . .] [whose] face is either expressionless or not be gazed upon' (230). Kelman compares the Being, whose gender remains indeterminate, to Charles Dickens's Miss Havisham as literature's most memorable monument to human frustration, pent-up fury and crushing disenchantment. 'That grocery-cart pusher reminded me of naybody so much as christ what was her name again', he writes, 'that auld fictional lady whose huis burns down and she vows never to change her wedding-day clothes eftir being left at the altar by her husband-to-be' (229). The author's seemingly casual insertion of the name of Jesus Christ in this context, even if only as a syntactic filler, unlocks further significatory potential by implicitly likening the Being's uncanny visitations to a Second Coming, a tattered, post-secular reminder of the Christian faith, pauperised and stripped of its apocalyptic glory. This religious connotation strengthens as the Being explodes like a living bomb, exposing capitalist America's destitute underbelly in a spontaneous conflagrational 'materialisation', forcing the well-off to take notice of the poor by violently demolishing the partitioning between them. According to the novel, the Being 'materialized in the presence of higher-level dignitaries, right inside the goddam VIP suite' (248).

Mimicking a terrorist suicide attack, this collision of two parallel worlds, which spells at once utter ruin and spiritual enlightenment, serves not only to remind the system's functionaries of 'a possible future'. As Kelman notes, 'when they gazed upon the grocery-cart pusher some saw a vision of themselves in years to come, or even months' (249). Much more significantly, it rips into US America's very ideological fibre, excoriating its religiously fuelled self-image while at the same time alerting us to the world's irrevocable change of heart in the aftermath of 9/11. What is it that reveals itself when the globalisation process as such comes a cropper, or when it halts, if only for a moment, as 'the entire contents of the being's grocery cart explode[s] into flames, including piles and piles of lottery tickets, auld betting receipts and scratchcards' (248)? What we are left with is a glaring spiritual void, a dystopian dearth of cosmopolitical ethos and direction.

You Have to Be Careful is a powerful indictment of globalisation as the worldwide dissemination of US American neo-liberalist materialism. This materialism has appropriated Christianity into an instrument of both domestic power and imperialist expansion, and appears deeply panicked at religious faith's volatile post-secular return in its original guise of poverty, need, subaltern protest and solidary commitment. As the novel points out, 'they thought to have stymied all such communal practice by federal order, discriminate low-key policing and increased funding of the domestic Defense industry' (128). In Kelman's representation, the USA ironically turns out to be haunted by its very own principles and beliefs, such as individual freedom and entrepreneurship, democracy, justice and equality, all of which have undergone relentless commodification in the grip of expedient market forces. Apart from exposing this ideological duplicity, however, does Kelman envision an alternative order, or manage to provide us with a viable model of political agency and resistance? Certainly we can relate to the pressures of economic necessity that cause Jeremiah as 'an erstwhile discusser of the fomenting of political disquiet across this wise and wonderful planet [to sell] out to el capitalistas' by becoming 'a full-time paid employee of the internal Defense industry' (173). Yet his collusion and complicity render him a case study rather than a role model. At the novel's end he still insists on presenting himself as 'this self-avowed anarchist, unassimilatit socialist and atheist with a hatred of ruling bodies everywhere; religious, monarquic, political, corporate or financial, who gies a fuck'. However, his intransigence is on the wane, and he eventually apologises for speaking out in his own inimitable way: 'Pardon the language, sorry [. . .] sorry about that, I do apologize' (380). What is left of his resolve deteriorates into mere pose, fuelled by nostalgic pathos and much rhetorical bravado. In the end, perfectly interpellated, Jeremiah succumbs to the allure of the USA as a corporate family-nation:

> Ye shall step where no non-integrated unassimilated alien has before stepped. Ye shall be a top-dog bona fide body brother they shall withdraw your Class III Red Card for Naughty Strangers and bestow unto you a Blue Card for fascist familiars; there shall be neither wailing nor gnashing of teeth. Jeremiah, henceforth ye shall father Uhmerkin children and be upstanding in the presence of glory. Let me shake you by the hand. (181)

Despite its apparent radicalism, then, Kelman's work could also be interpreted as profoundly defeatist. Without doubt, his treatment of the question of cosmopolitical agency remains inconclusive. Pointing out that 'he has been involved in a series of public campaigns illustrative of his belief that commitment, dissent, intervention, opposition and engagement are integral to the role of the artist' and insisting that 'Kelman's work is directly political in that it takes class as both subject and perspective', Ellen-Raïssa Jackson and Willy Maley concede that 'its literariness and favouring of mixed interior monologue arguably limit attempts to move beyond the individual to a sense of community or mass political activism' (2001: 23, 25). More recently Kövesi has argued along similar lines that Kelman's literary style considerably impedes the political efficacy of his writing. 'Kelman does not present us with a generalised working-class world or society', Kövesi writes. 'He presents us with working-class *individuals* to interpret. Society consists of intricate networks of individuals in this fiction, not of reassuring communities or groups fighting for, or showing the necessity of, social change.' While I agree with Kövesi, as well as Jackson and Maley, that 'Kelman's fiction does not present political or social problems which are digested, processed and solved by the agenda of the narrator, or by the devices, resolutions or social conscience of the narrative' (Kövesi 2007: 21), I trust my readings of *Translated Accounts* and *You Have to Be Careful* have shown that, against all the odds – be these staked by totalitarianism or capitalist corporatism – community-building, and in particular the communal dynamics of cosmopolitan resistance, feature prominently in Kelman's work. I might not go as far as Stefanie Lehner, who detects in Kelman's work a 'subaltern aesthetic' whose dynamics prove 'impervious to the *an*aesthetic effects of ideological purity while propagating actual political engagement' (2007: 300). But there can be no doubt that, according to Kelman, systemic duress always breeds popular restiveness, and this restiveness can without much prior warning escalate into full-blown communal resistance, however apparitional or inoperative it may initially seem.

Translated Accounts and *You Have to Be Careful* investigate what potential for genuine individual, familial and communal world-creation remains in the 'terrortories' of our ever more tightly globalised world. In Kelman's view contemporary humanity is at risk of giving in to globalisation as a purely economically determined process of agglomeration, both nationally and internationally, pushing cultures more closely together, yet rather than encouraging them to grow into convivial neighbourhoods, leaving them to cluster explosively in strictly segregated, fiercely competitive factions. Human civilisation is at risk of deteriorating into mere 'heapage', giving in to what Nancy has described as a thickening of *glomicity*, by which he means an 'invad[ing] and erod[ing of] what used to be thought of as *globe* and which is nothing more now than its double, *glomus*'. As Nancy elaborates:

> In such a *glomus*, we see [. . .] a worsening of inequalities of all sorts [. . .] – economic, biological, and cultural – and of a dissipation of the certainties, images, and identities of what the world was with its parts and humanity with its characteristics.
>   [. . .] The world has lost its capacity to 'form a world' [*faire monde*]: it seems only to have gained that capacity of proliferating [. . .] the 'unworld' [*immonde*], which, until now, and whatever one may think of retrospective illusions, has never in history impacted the totality of the orb to such an extent. (2000: 33–4)

Yet equally important is that even in our age of increasingly all-encompassing glomicity 'something remains nonetheless, in spite of everything, something resists and insists' (37), something which, in Kelman's work, asserts itself as an inalienable human resilience and resourcefulness that is capable of enduring even the most horrific adversity. This is what informs the general tone of *Translated Accounts*, what pervades the novel and ultimately salvages its world from disintegration. Similarly, *You Have to Be Careful*, despite its apparent solipsism, constitutes in fact one man's last effort to communicate with the world and thus ward off his increasing loneliness and atomisation. Always keen to strike up conversations with strangers, Jeremiah is fully aware his behaviour may be regarded as embarrassing, weird or downright suspicious: 'Nowadays we do not ask people personal questions. But once upon a time that was okay, that was civilized behaviour' (6). Yet none the less he persists.

Their explicit worldliness and shrewd critical eye for contemporary globality identify both novels as urgent cosmopolitan appeals for us to look and listen beyond our immediate domestic comfort zones and become ethically involved citizens who take a compassionate interest in how the world is run. Signally, as 'the perishing bet' in *You Have to Be Careful* becomes known also as 'the persian bet', the novel develops into a commentary on the Iraq War and as such comes to echo Ulrich Preuss's observations concerning the future of US America's world-political might and integrity. As Preuss warns, 'when power turns into hyperpower, it can become dangerous even to its wielder', adding sagely that 'any order that does not force itself to learn, gambles with its future (2005: 184–5).

II

Tour du Monde

Chapter 3

The World Begins Its Turn with You, or How David Mitchell's Novels Think

A curious blend of Julian Barnes's *The History of the World in 10½ Chapters* (1989) and Kazuo Ishiguro's Anglo-Japanese novels, with some of the time-travelling elements of Virginia Woolf's *Orlando* (1928) mixed in, David Mitchell's *Ghostwritten* (1999) and *Cloud Atlas* (2004) pioneer a new cosmopolitan modus operandi for twenty-first-century British fiction. Mitchell's narratives do not so much break with the tradition of the English novel as subtly deconstruct, untie and defamiliarise it. They comprise acutely fragmented, yet at the same time smoothly cohesive compositions strategically broken up into small-*récit* mosaics of divergent perspectives that together span and unify the globe. Both novels explore new past–present–future continua without lapsing into mere fanciful historiographical futurism. This is the case even though both novels contain allusions to Aldous Huxley's and George Orwell's famous dystopian classics. In *Ghostwritten* various characters find themselves labelled within a strict socio-economic hierarchy of alphas and gammas (as in His Serendipity's and Dwight Silverwind's ominous New Age ideologies), while Orwell's nightmarish picture of the future as 'a boot stamping on a human face, forever' recurs across both novels (as, for instance, in the 'Holy Mountain' section of *Ghostwritten* or 'An Orison of Sonmi-451' in *Cloud Atlas*).

Mitchell's writing charts human existence both transterritorially and as always determined by locally specific conditions. His work lends a unique voice to the Nancean notion of community as constant inoperative reconfiguration; it also illustrates perfectly Nancy's understanding of history, according to which 'historical change cannot be achieved in terms of a dialectical or teleological process, but rather in terms of a constant birth or becoming of singular-plural sense' (James 2006: 199). In Mitchell's fiction history appears as an indeterminate, albeit always somewhat predictable recurrence of circumstances that irrevocably mire the emergence and manifestation of individual existence. A select number of men and women from all over the world – each and every one of them typically, even universally human – are portrayed as uniquely unprecedented and inimitable in their individual and cultural difference, incorporating Nancy's observation in *Being Singular Plural* that 'you [every human singularity] are absolutely strange because the world begins its turn with you' (2000: 6). Mitchell's ambition is to imagine globality by depicting worldwide human living in multifaceted, delicately entwined, serialised snapshots of the human condition, marked by global connectivity and virtual proximity as much as psycho-geographical detachment and xenophobic segregation. The aim is not to project a particular destiny for the whole of humanity; rather, he does his best to open his work up to the structure of the world as he finds it, capturing its existential exposure and finitude. Mitchell's fiction summons humanity's world-creative potential as well as its tragic (self-) destructiveness into a kind of literary communality which his readers are not only invited to relate to, but must partake of as inhabitants of one and the same world.

To implement and convey Mitchell's literary cosmopolitanism a modification of the novel's generic morphology is required or, perhaps rather, a change in the ways in which we perceive and decode certain structural techniques and principles of narration. For example, the apparent brokenness of *Ghostwritten* and *Cloud Atlas* needs to be reviewed as an elaborate compositeness, caught in an ongoing process of self-constitution – of coming together. Opposed to postmodernist fragmentation, this compositeness is designed to preserve the singularity of each segment as an integral building block. Likewise, it is crucial to regard the science-fiction and dystopian components of Mitchell's novels as constitutive of their portrayal of *contemporary* globality. Mitchell's sense of the future is Nancean in that in his work, too, '"we" are futural, surely, but not in the sense that we project ourselves into the future; rather, the "we" just is this ability to open ourselves to the spacing of a world, a world that is always "to-come"'. As B. C. Hutchens, one of Nancy's most perspicacious interpreters, continues to explain, Nancy urges us not to anticipate the future in the form of visionary projections but to cultivate instead 'an openness without anticipation, a preparedness for surprise that could never eradicate surprise, a world in which incertitude and undecidability are understood to be definitive of the human condition' (2005: 160). It is this open-eyed, strictly inoperative tentativeness that characterises Mitchell's outlook.

Despite his penchant for close-up, first-person narration Mitchell encourages his readers to adopt a bird's-eye perspective, watching his protagonists as if they found themselves, like Henry Perowne in McEwan's *Saturday*, perched on a balcony pondering the human drama below. Invariably, before empathy and compassion get a definite hold of us, the scenario changes and we are transported elsewhere, giving the impression that we are looking at the world through a Nancean kaleidoscope. What is new and different perpetually coalesces with what is the same and already known, gradually translating our experiential alienation into a sense of affinity, especially in the chapters set outside the anglophone world. Narration assumes quite literally a life of its own, developing an organic, cellular dynamic that serves to dismantle the neatly vertebrate *telos* and individualist focus of the traditional English novel. Initially appearing as narrative quilts composed of a selection of self-contained small *récits*, or loose assortments of stories snugly telescoped one into the other, *Ghostwritten* and *Cloud Atlas* quickly reveal themselves as driven by a far more fluid dynamic. The novels resemble intricate *perpetua mobilia* of interconnected vessels overflowing into each other, or filling up simultaneously like cells in a hive – ceaselessly pouring, jostling and jarring, stiffening into shape only momentarily before rejoining the flow, leaving behind only the trace of a ripple. In *number9dream* (2001), Mitchell's second novel, this dynamic is described in terms of the life force itself, which makes the world a place where 'circles are born, while circles born a second ago live. Circles live, while circles living a second ago die. Circles die, while new circles are born' (287). As Mitchell's writing demonstrates, these circles need not be neatly concentric, immediately tangential, or even perfectly round; what matters is that they originate from the same impulse, exist within the same medium, and are bound by the same sets of laws.

Ghostwritten and *Cloud Atlas* categorically decentre individual human experience, which is by no means the same as demoting or devaluing it. Paradoxically, the opposite is the case, as stripped of their centre-stage position in the novel individuals emerge as the carriers of the creative and destructive flows that together constitute the world. Unlike in the traditional novel, individuals are discovered as always already tied into a larger whole, which most certainly is not the nation but the human life-world in its global transterritoriality. In this sense, then, individuals are not initiated into global circulation; they are in fact what constitutes, propels and perpetuates this circulation. Everybody's life relates to everybody else's, even that of perfect strangers whom they will never meet in person. All individuality amounts to is the production of different variations on one and the same theme of contemporary human existence. Philip Griffiths errs when, with reference to the protagonist of the 'Holy Mountain' section of *Ghostwritten*, he asserts that 'it is the old woman's subjective point of view that utterly dominates the narrative and consequently forces the supremacy of world history into a subservient position' (2004: 81). Mitchell's characters are never quite so powerful; in fact, they become protagonists only in so far as they also always shoulder the parts of supernumerary extras, corralled by circumstance into strictly demarcated psycho-geographies. The Holy Mountain dweller's hermit-like existence only gains significance in that it touches on the lives of others – for example, the guests at her inn who enjoy her hospitality, incur her wrath or meet with her resistance – or in that her granddaughter might be the Chinese maid Neal Brose has an affair with in the 'Hong Kong' section of the novel. The old woman's life only signifies in so far as its presence percolates into the rest of this huge global network of a novel – its manifold 'continua of identification' (Bhabha 1996: 203), even though this percolation occurs without her knowledge or intention.

Mitchell's representation of globalisation aims at an opening up of the world to itself, which becomes its one and only territory. According to Beck, 'if [global] culture is conceived as territorially circumscribed, then the question of plurality leads to a sterile false alternative: either universal sameness ("McDonaldization") or perspectives that resist comparison ("incommensurability")'. As he insists, 'cosmopolitanism, by contrast, means the exact opposite: recognition of difference, beyond the misunderstandings of territoriality and homogenization' (2006: 29–30). Mitchell's view concurs with Beck's and Nancy's in that he too does not so much rebut, or strive to erase, individual, local, even – quite possibly – national specificity. Rather, he seeks to prevent this specificity from rigidifying into an operative and hence world-creatively obstructive set of forces, composed of individual*ism*, local*ism*, national*ism* or, indeed, their equally detrimental counterpart of an inert, featureless universalism. Mitchell's cosmopolitan novels trace the tensions 'between the world becoming global (an all or a totality) and the world maintaining its opening as a play of difference, incompletion, and finitude' (2002: 150), which is how Krzysztof Ziarek reads the semantic complexity of Nancy's concept of mondialisation. Mondialisation in this context must be understood as 'worlding' or, put differently, the world's 'unfolding into a complex of relations, exchanges, transactions, bonds, and affiliations, which, without constituting a whole or a totality, continuously (re)form themselves as a world' (2002: 150).

Confusingly, it appears to be the contemporary world's very trend towards totalisation and glomicity that mobilises local and individual specificity in the first place, and in such a way that – by becoming instrumental in other, hitherto unprecedented processes of world-creation – it cannot but perpetually rupture globalisation's drive for sameness and uniformity. Released from her hyperbolic centrality, the individual is not lost in the turbulent nitty-gritty of global multiplicity; rather, she emerges as integrally, even indispensably constitutive of it. The cosmopolitan is hence always of necessity a subject rather than an individual, but one whose irremediably globalised disposition is also her most effective means of resistance. Her singularity remains indisputable and cannot be erased or contained by globalisation. And yet, it is her very state of oppression and dislocation that accentuates her difference and unleashes into the world its unruly ubiquity.

The compositeness of *Ghostwritten* is signalled by its subtitle, which introduces it as 'a novel in nine parts'. What this suggests is that we ought to read the novel's concluding tenth section as a coda revisiting and complementing the novel as a whole rather than functioning as an independent part in its own right. 'Underground' serves to round off the novel and take the reader's journey full circle. Summoning a cast of characters from Japan, China, Mongolia, Russia, Britain, Ireland, Denmark, Australia, New Zealand and the USA, there can be no doubt that *Ghostwritten* aims at imagining globality. It boldly exceeds the limits of the traditional novel, as laid out by Benedict Anderson, by envisioning a grand *tour du monde* that pays little heed to national boundaries. The novel's particular cosmopolitan view is facilitated by opening its chapters fluidly one into the other, each of which constitutes its own *tour d'horizon*. As a result national horizons sustain, yet never definitively enclose, human identity. Since it is impossible to experience the world in the abstract, local specificity and the individual life-world are central to Mitchell's creation of globality. Traditionally humans have known and related to the world through their immediate surroundings, which is also fundamentally, as Jonathan Rée explains, how nationality works: 'The national experience is basically a matter of rootedness in local conditions, and of respect and affection for them.' However, whereas nationalism tends to assimilate and subsume the local in order to bolster its own totality, Rée quite rightly deems it 'fantastic to suppose that [local sentiments] could all extend precisely to the edges of a single nation and there come abruptly to a halt' (1998: 82). So, evidently, does Mitchell. Pitching his narratives of cosmopolitan world-creation against globalisation as glomicity and increasing homogenisation, Mitchell demonstrates that, rather than emulating the nation in gorging itself on the locally specific, the world always already *is* its own diversity. Difference is what we have in common, and what summons us into humanity; it is also what creates, or 'worlds', the world.

Ghostwritten creates a global community of characters for an equally global community of readers, selecting remote insular places not only to keep the narrative afloat and world-politically in suspension, as it were, but also to capture the world as essentially informed and shaped by marginality. Without doubt it is their remarkable community spirit and local distinctiveness that inspired Mitchell to erect his novel on such eclectic geographical pillars as Okinawa – an East China Sea archipelago that became part of Japan in the late nineteenth century, but now has a strong national independence movement – and Clear Island, 'the last corner of Ireland' (Mitchell 1999: 360), the Irish republic's southernmost inhabited patch of land. In an effort to show that remoteness alone is never a safeguard against glomicity, however, one of the corporate spies Mitchell introduces into the Clear Island community identifies herself as originally from New Zealand's 'Halfmoon Bay, Stewart Island, south of the South Island' (346), a place that in terms of position and world-political import matches Clear Island almost exactly. Meticulously designed, *Ghostwritten* excels at accentuating the random arbitrariness of global human encounter. The novel demonstrates how, often fleetingly and entirely unawares, we become members of multitudinous communities that crystallise against the odds of probability, such as the group of passengers who happen to be accompanying Mowleen Muntervary, the mathematical genius and quantum physicist of the 'Clear Island' section, on her escape flight to Kyrgistan. Using her calculator, which 'can do a quintillion decimal places', Mo comes to the conclusion that even this most spontaneous and necessarily inoperative of communal configurations has a certain mathematical logic to it, as she 'work[s] out the odds of us three hundred and sixty passengers all being here' (338).

Unlike many a postcolonial novel *Ghostwritten* takes us not only 'out in the colonies. Well, the ex-colonies' (85) but deep into the non-anglophone world, where even in today's metropolitan centres the perception of westerners remains an alien, indistinct blur of 'either American or European or Australian, you can never tell because they all look the same'. Any possibility for mutual understanding is nipped in the bud by an allegedly innate linguistic inadequacy: 'Westerners can't learn Japanese' (35). Commendably, Mitchell's cosmopolitan vision never deteriorates into facile utopianism; for example, he never fails to highlight instances of explicit or latent racism and xenophobia, as evident in the ostracism and ridicule experienced by half-Filipino Saturo and half-Chinese Tomoyo in the 'Tokyo' section, or Saturo's subsequent derogatory labelling as a 'nipkid' (78) by Neal Brose in 'Hong Kong'. Similarly, in 'Holy Mountain' the actual humanity of foreigners is shown to come as a complete surprise to the narrator – 'My village cousins had told me that foreigners had elephant noses and hair like dying monkeys, but these ones looked a lot like us' (120) – and even the ideal pastoral community of Clear Island is revealed as marred by localist bias: 'No Clear Islander took a non-Gaelic-speaking teacher seriously' (334).

As its individual chapters open up one into the other and despite their evident disparity smoothly interpermeate, leaving behind an intricate density of intratextual cross-references, Mitchell's novel creates a communal web of the world that, in truly Nancean fashion, interweaves correspondences and resemblances together with apparent irreconcilabilities into a momentary whole that remains productively incapable of achieving seamless totality. For example, incongruously mixing first love and murderous ideological delusion, in the first section of the novel the term 'quasar' – denoting a celestial entity of unimaginable brightness and energy – serves as the undercover codename for a terrorist responsible for a gas attack on the Tokyo underground, while in the second section it is part of young Satoru's catalogue of terms describing the beauty of Tomoyo, his girlfriend-to-be. The two sections are interlinked further by the fact that Satoru's friend's sister happens to be on a school trip to Okinawa, where Keisuke, the terrorist, has gone into hiding, and when in final desperation Keisuke, deserted by his organisation, rings the Fellowship's Secret Service emergency number with a previously agreed encoded message, he is in fact put through to the record shop that employs Satoru, to whom obviously the call cannot mean anything at all.

Satoru and his girlfriend Tomoyo's young love forms the backdrop to Neal Brose's increasing loneliness and professional alienation in the next section, which is set in Hong Kong. Neal's wife has recently divorced him and his career as a promising young banker is about to collapse due to a money-laundering deal he has been coerced into setting up on behalf of a Mr Gregorski from St Petersburg, who plays a significant part in the sixth section of the novel, which is set in the Russian city. Neal is warned of the risks accompanying the deal by Huw Llewellyn, an undercover international police agent, who later turns out also to be a very good personal friend of Mowleen Muntervary, the scientist at the centre of the 'Clear Island' section. Mo secretly lodges with Huw in Hong Kong whilst on the run from her corporation, who want to use her latest set of scientific discoveries to develop a new generation of war weaponry. Truanting from work one morning,

Neal dies of a fit caused by undiagnosed diabetes while climbing a mountain popular with Buddhist pilgrims, and it is Mo who later tells her husband about seeing him (or someone very much like him) collapse and die there. The setting of Neal's death builds a bridge to the next section, which is set on a 'Holy Mountain' somewhere in China. Another link between the chapters is that Neal had started an affair with his Hong Kong maid, who, as we have seen, very much resembles the granddaughter of the old woman from whose perspective the 'Holy Mountain' section is told, even though not all the details appear quite to match. 'My employer died', the young woman explains. 'A foreigner, a lawyer with a big company, he was extremely wealthy. He was very generous to me in his will' (151). In Mitchell's cosmopolitan universe, in order to establish a link it appears to suffice that this could, or might just as well, be the story of Neal and Neal's maid. The same air of allusive uncertainty surrounds the first appearance of Caspar, a Danish backpacker, who may or may not be that curious foreigner staying at the old woman's inn, and who – on hearing another guest's night-time story about 'three animals who think about the fate of the world' (143) – suddenly changes his mind about visiting Laos and darts off in the direction of Mongolia instead.

In 'Mongolia', the fifth section of the novel, Caspar, who used to sell jewellery in Okinawa, is introduced to his Australian love-interest Sherry, who worked in a Hong Kong pub and who, on their overnight train journey to Ulan Bator, strikes up a casual conversation with 'a middle-aged Irish woman who either gazed out of the window or wrote numbers in a black notebook' (156), who is retrospectively identified as Mowleen. 'Mongolia' also introduces Punsalmaagiyn Suhbataar, 'a senior agent of the Mongolian KGB with a disdain for vulnerable things' (180), whose violence haunts not only the 'Petersburg' section of *Ghostwritten*, but also the 'Reclaimed Land' chapter in Mitchell's otherwise entirely unrelated second novel *number9dream*. In the 'London' section, finally, we are introduced to Marco, who earns a living as a ghostwriter for an elderly gay celebrity, among whose circle of friends we find Jerome, the artist that forges the world-famous paintings at the centre of 'Petersburg'. 'London' also brings us face to face with Katy Forbes, the divorced wife of Neal Brose, whose British ex-pat Hong Kong employer turns out to be the elder brother of Tim Cavendish, Marco's literary agent. Compounding the elaborate design of the novel even further by conflating utterly quotidian coincidence with the most fateful serendipity, Marco happens to be the passer-by who saves Mo from being run over by a taxi. This incident might have remained entirely gratuitous in terms of plot development, were it not for Marco's lying, quite without apparent motivation, to the men in pursuit of Mo about the London airport where he overheard her instruct the cab-driver to take her. What it also creates, of course, is the sense of a crucial existential connectivity between the lives of perfect strangers, capable of touching and determining the course of each other's life trajectories without ever having properly met or being likely to get to know each other in the future.

In *Ghostwritten*, globalisation manifests as corporatism and religious or political fundamentalism: there is the Serendipity cult that brainwashes Keisuke into terrorist mass murder, or the series of devastating political upheavals that sweep through China during the narrator's lifetime in 'Holy Mountain', or the unbearable corporate duress and coercion to which both Neal and Mo find themselves exposed. This kind of globalisation is cast in relief by the processes of a locally oriented, peripheral, even pastoral 'worlding' which, due to its embedment in a global network of very similar human-interest scenarios, takes on the appearance of a kind of grassroots world-communal cosmopolitanism. In 'Okinawa' we learn of Keisuke's disillusionment with an increasingly corporatised organisation of the world which, in his view, has robbed Japan of its national specificity. He feels 'betrayed by a society evolving into markets for Disney and McDonald's' (6) and resents the uniformity that surrounds him: 'The same shops as anywhere else . . . Burger King, Benetton, Nike . . . High Streets are becoming the same all over the world' (12). Symptomatically, to him, the main attraction of the cult is that it makes him feel valued as both an individual and the member of a community: 'For the first time in my life', Keisuke declares, 'I was becoming a name' (31).Very quickly it transpires, however, that rather than an alternative to the corporate world, the Serendipity cult is a viciously distorted replica of it. There is nothing serendipitous about Keisuke's conversion, which seals his recruitment into total subjugation. Instructed to 'avoid the lies of the unclean state' (6), he succumbs to the spiritual glomicity of His Serendipity's totalitarianism, all the more treacherous for presenting itself as a family, which 'will grow until the world without is the world within' (9), thus eradicating any opportunity for communal diversity or individual world-creation.

At the close of the section we cannot be sure what will become of Keisuke, but Mitchell suggests salvation may be hand. In Mitchell's view, what creates the threat of Keisuke's apocalyptic terrorism in the first place is his communal estrangement and existential atomisation into 'a figure, all hunched up like it was the end of the world' (32). This is how the close-knit Okinawan island community of Kumejima – initially perceived by Keisuke as 'a squalid, incestuous prison' (27)

– come to embrace him. Seeing him 'sitting on a grave, wondering when it was that I last belonged anywhere', the locals, innocent of the high-tech metropolitan bustle of globalised life, take an interest in him and respond to his plight with singular gestures of hospitality. Notably, they know nothing of his terrorism and believe him to be grieving for his wife, who – so he lied to his landlady on arrival – has recently died of cancer:

> A sugar-cane farmer pulled up by the roadside and offered me a lift. I was footsore, so I accepted. His dialect was so heavy I could barely make out what he was trying to say. He started off talking about the weather, to which I made all the right noises. Then he started talking about me. He knew which inn I was staying at, and how long I was staying, my false name, my job. He even gave his condolences for my dead wife. Every time he used the word 'computer' he sealed it in inverted commas. (21)

This kind of oppositioning between two ways of contemporary life – one corporate, the other communal – also occurs in 'Mongolia', where 'the non-stop highways of [western] minds', irremediably frazzled by a storm of extraneous signifiers, most of them trivial and ultimately redundant, contrast with the 'more intimate neighbourhood' of human consciousness as it exists on the margins of globality. The latter is better equipped to resist remote control, as Mitchell's noncorpum, the ghostly spirit that parasitically inhabits human minds in chapters 4 and 5, discovers when transmigrating from the Danish tourist Caspar's into the mind of Gunga, a Mongolian peasant woman, where it was 'like trying to make yourself invisible in a prying village as opposed to a sprawling conurbation' (166).

A similar representational dynamic is at work in 'Hong Kong', which introduces us to Neal, the young British corporate lawyer, who, due to the recent break-up of his marriage, shares Keisuke's desperate unhappiness and seems equally wary of globalisation's impact on human identity. Looking at himself, all he can see is a motley patchwork of global brands, 'a foreign devil with [. . .] shoes from Pennsylvania, a silk tie made in Milan, a briefcase full of Japanese and American gadgetry' (84), a corporate cyborg in fact, 'armed to the teeth with telecommunications devices' (89). Rejecting his CEO's appeal to family values ('We're a [. . .] top-line corporation. But that's not all we are, Nile, my word no. We are a family!' [106]), Neal quite literally abandons the corporate path by ignoring a summons into work and embarking on a climb up to a site of pilgrimage in the hills. He craves the kind of simple communal belonging and local encounter that, in a truly serendipitous reversal of fortune, Keisuke finds thrust upon himself. Watching an elderly couple in their makeshift hovel, Neal reflects: 'I wish I could go into their room and sit down with them. I'd give them my Rolex for that. I wish they would

smile, and pour me a cup of jasmine tea. I wish the world was like that'
(99). Significantly, Neal's predicament finds apt philosophical expression in Nancy's interrogation of globalisation's deadening effect on
human life in *The Creation of the World or Globalization*:

> What happens to us as a dissipation of the world in the bad infinite of a
> 'globalization' in a centrifugal spiral behaving like the expanding universe
> described by astrophysics, all the while doing nothing else than circumscrib-
> ing the earth more and more in a horizon without opening or exit? How are
> we to conceive of, precisely, a world where we only find a globe, an astral
> universe, or an earth without sky? (2007: 47)

Increasing corporatism suffocates the world, leaving no room for individual or communal world-creation. Corporatism does not, as it claims,
open up the world, but simply inflates it. It does not enhance or enrich
the world, but hoards it. It does not broaden our horizons, but in fact
puts a lid on them, painting them shut. 'I never knew there was so much
sky here!' (87) Neal poignantly exclaims before discarding his corporate brief in a spontaneous act of defiance.

What the seemingly desultory cluster of protagonists in *Ghostwritten*
have in common is their rejection of corporatism and a fervent love, or
longing, for community. Despite their hugely divergent circumstances
they share the same dreams, hopes, fears, needs and bouts of despair;
what distinguishes them from one another is the degree of their atomisation and alienation as well as the access they have to familial support
and marital intimacy. All of them are dropouts and misfits, who stand
out for some reason. Crucially, it is always their difference and singularity that potentially renders them 'terrorists'. Quite a few of them
could easily be regarded as the precursors of the Union movement so
savagely prosecuted and demonised by the ruling Unanimity Party in
'An Orison of Sonmi-451' in *Cloud Atlas*:

> A gas called evil xists in the world, Papa Song said. When purebloods breathe
> in this gas, they change. They become terrorists. Terrorists hate everything
> that is good: Unanimity, Papa Song, hardworking fabricants, even the
> Beloved Chairman of Nea So Copros and his Juche. Terrorists have a corp
> named Union. Union wants to become the most powerful corp in plutocracy
> by changing consumers into terrorists; by killing consumers who oppose
> them. (2004: 203)

As signalled here, the Union movement is at risk of giving in to its ideological distortion into corporatism's exact mirror image. Importantly,
in order to topple the totalitarian tyranny of the Unanimity Party,
Union must resist rigidifying into yet another 'corp' and stop operating
in ways essentially identical to its adversary's. To (re)create the world,
it must resolve to proceed inoperatively.

Mitchell draws our attention to humanity's inoperative – and quite literally non-corporate – aspects by introducing the perspective of non-corpa into his novel. These disembodied human spirits ceaselessly transmigrate between individual minds trying to recover their original identity, from which they have been severed by trauma. In the process of doing so they provide an insider's experiential insight in the vast communal diversity of the human:

> All minds pulse in a unique way, just as every lighthouse in the world has a unique signature. Some minds pulse consistently, some erratically. Some are lukewarm, some are hot. Some flare out, some are very nearly not there. Some stay on the fringe, like quasars. For me, a roomful of animals and humans is like a roomful of suns, of differing magnitudes and colours, and gravities. (160)

The noncorpa represent by no means a purely spiritual phenomenon or principle but, reliant on touch for their movement from host to host, must also 'exist on some physical plane, however subcellular or bio-electrical' (165), thus highlighting the essential, earthbound materiality, finitude and existential exposure of all human life. The noncorpum inhabiting the 'Holy Mountain' and 'Mongolia' sections of the novel is eventually identified as the spirit of an eight-year-old monk's novice, who was killed in a mass execution in 1937 under the then Mongolian regime's Stalinist secularisation campaign. The boy's stunned spirit saves itself into the body of a mercenary who is attending the execution and eventually returns to his home near Holy Mountain, where the newborn noncorpum enters the old innkeeper's mind and then that of Caspar, the Danish tourist, who, incredulous, suddenly finds himself irresistibly drawn to Mongolia: 'I was on my way to Laos, when this impulse just came over me. I told myself there was nothing here, but I couldn't fight it' (156–7). Later in the novel, the noncorpum's view of the human is confirmed by the high-scientific reasoning of Mowleen Muntervary, whose own mind, as we learn in 'Night Train', the ninth section of the novel, has also at one point been inhabited by a noncor-pum. Swapping the language of epiphanic poetry for that of no-nonsense evolutionary geneticism, we are left yet again to marvel at the profound mysteriousness of the human:

> Why am I who I am? Because of the double helix of atoms coiled along my DNA. What is DNA's engine of change? Subatomic particles colliding with its molecules. These particles are raining onto the Earth now, resulting in mutations that have evolved the oldest single-celled life-forms through jel-lyfish to gorillas and us, Chairman Mao, Jesus, Nelson Mandela, His Serendipity, Hitler, you and I.
> Evolution and history are the bagatelle of particle waves. (369)

Determined not to have her genius exploited by corporate interests Mo flees to Clear Island, where she was born, an idyllic, Irish-speaking, island community, comparable in its parochial remoteness perhaps only to the Okinawan island of Kumejima, which becomes Keisuke's refuge in the novel's opening section. Unlike Keisuke, however, Mo is very much aware of what the island offers her, and how to appreciate it: after all, it is the place of her origin, her home. 'Without where I am from and who I am from, I am nothing', she deliberates. 'All those wideworlders in transit, all those misplaced, thrown-away people who know as little as they care about their roots – how do they do it? How do they know who they are?' (357). Her exceptional sense of familial belonging – her blind husband John, a poet, lives on the island, and her student son Liam visits regularly – is also what sharply distinguishes her life from that of Neal, who like Mo is a corporate dropout, yet unlike her is without love. By far the most resourceful of the protagonists in *Ghostwritten*, Mo's determination to resist 'the way the world works' (327) emerges as Mitchell's safest bet for breaking the ill-omened, self-annihilative circle that – in the words of the representative of the US military, who try their hardest to bully Mo into their services – ensures that 'scientists like you win wars for generals like me' (331). Mo successfully resists corporatism by becoming a good terrorist, equipping Quancog, her invention, with an ethical capacity that enables it to sabotage the perpetration of human evil. Aware that if only Dr Frankenstein 'ha[d] shown his brainchild how to survive, adapt, and protect itself, all that gothic gore could have been saved' (371), she works out a way to ensure 'that technology looked after itself' (374). Importantly, Mo's inspiration for changing the very nature of science and technology comes out of her immersion in the local and familial. At the same time, her endeavour to save the world is informed by an embrace of the 'non-local'. As she explains, her plan is to 'strip quantum cognition down to first principles, and rebuild it incorporating nonlocality, instead of trying to lock nonlocality out' (342), thus rendering Quancog possibly the first fictional example of cosmopolitan science.

The novel reaches its climax in 'Night Train', the penultimate section, which takes place on air as part of the *Bat Segundo Show* on Night Train FM, broadcast from a near-future New York radio station. That the section is indeed set in the imminent future is signalled not only by a passing reference to the world-famous saxophonist Satoru Sonada – whom we first encountered as a love-struck, fairly directionless teenager in 'Tokyo' – but also by the identity of Zookeeper, a mystery caller who enthrals Bat, his production team and the public with cryptically omniscient messages seemingly sent via a number of satellite transmitters, but ultimately proving untraceable. Gradually Zookeeper is revealed as the voice of a new generation of military technology, bound by an inbuilt ethical complexity of four interdependent rules. Reminiscent of an observation Mo once made while watching television footage of the First Gulf War ('It's a sick zoo we've turned the world into!' [324]), its very name identifies Zookeeper as the Clear Island scientist's post-Frankensteinian dream come true, standing for a new kind of self-controlling, incorruptible technology, impervious to ideological manipulation, which, like its creator, to whom 'lying is a skill I have never mastered' (344), 'cannot fabulate' (401).

To show the success of Mo's cosmopolitan security system, the narrative of 'Night Train' takes us to the very brink of World War III, averted at the last minute due to seemingly *mal*functioning technology. Yet Mitchell eschews giving in to utopia. He concludes the section not with a triumphant celebration of Mo's panacean invention, but with a rather fraught dialogue between Zookeeper and another mystery caller, Arupadhatu (a name that in Buddhist thinking denotes the formless world), who claims to know Zookeeper's designer and turns out to be the noncorpum that used to live inside Mo's mind. Arupadhatu, who deeply despises its fellow noncorpa because all they do is 'transmigrate into human chaff for hosts, and meditate upon nothingness upon mountains' (422), presents Zookeeper with a Mephistophelian proposal for taking over the world: 'Imagine what we could achieve together? The children need taking in hand' (423). Although Zookeeper rejects the proposal, the encounter demonstrates that even the most ingeniously inspirited cosmopolitan project will never safeguard perfectly against totalitarian globalisation. Evil is impossible to extirpate as long as consciousness is exposed to the allure of power. 'When I was appointed zookeeper', Mo's invention declares, 'I believed adherence to the four laws would discern the origins of order. Now, I see my solutions fathering the next generation of crises' (425–6). Human life will continue to be beset by ethical dilemmas. Cosmopolitics can create no perfect world since it must, to avoid dystopian totality, always to a certain degree remain inoperative. Albeit dedicated to enabling humanity's world-creative potential, therefore, it cannot ever entirely disable its capacity for evil.

In the novel's coda Mitchell rehearses the circumstances of Keisuke's gas attack on the Tokyo underground, sketching out what might have happened before Keisuke arrives in Okinawa in the opening chapter. What makes 'Underground' so intriguing is that it shows us the terrorist, ostensibly filled with disgust at the profound loathsomeness of human life, frantically trying to save himself from the doomed train: Keisuke wants to live, even if his struggle for survival jeopardises His Serendipity's cause. His panic and sheer desperation signal that there is something about human existence that will forever exceed the unforgiving absolutes of ideological conviction. Equally shrewd in this final section is Mitchell's gathering of all the strands of his novel into one, so that we find practically the whole world packed into this particular Tokyo underground station. The ubiquitous imagery of global advertising plastered all over the underground walls conjures a momentary glimpse not only of Keisuke's Okinawa, but also of Mo's island home and Bat Segundo's New York. As he claws his way out of the carriage, Keisuke briefly sees 'a couple walking their dog down a beach in Okinawa' (433), and 'on the label of Kilmagoon whiskey an island as old as the world' (435), as well as 'the Empire State Building, circled by an albino bat, scattering words and stars through the night' (436). We also find snippets from chapters 3 and 6. Recalling Neal's climb up his holy mountain, on the cover of a paperback read by a passenger 'Buddha sits, lipped and lidded, silver on a blue hill, and an island far from this tromboning den' (434), while a brochure perused by somebody else bears the title *Petersburg, City of Masterworks* (435). In yet another passenger's hands Keisuke sees 'the London Underground on a vinyl shopping bag' (435). Keisuke's terrorist attack is on a world so thoroughly globalised its specific target could be anywhere on earth. His vertiginous scramble for life, when he has only just condemned humanity to merciless death, opens up the world simultaneously as a deracinated blur and as always unmistakably itself in a limitless range of specific localities. If only Keisuke could connect to this world and read its apparent fragmentation not as an irremediable splintering into meaninglessness, but as the tantalising promise of communal assemblage beyond any definitive unity or ideological totalisation. If only he could appreciate human life as what, with reference to Nancy's work, James has described as 'a fragmentation that exceeds any figure of totality' (2006: 3).

Ghostwritten pursues a strikingly Nancean political aesthetics in that, like Nancy, Mitchell 'addresses the world as finite and contingent, fragmentary, thoroughly resistant to any totalization within a system of goals or ideological forms' (James 2006: 151). This is the vision offered to us in the coda: a vision of human life as it is, mundane, vulnerable, volatile and violent, as well as confused, deluded and needy, yet always indisputably of value and significance, all through and by itself, bar interpretation. Interspersed with foreshadowings of what, according to the novel's chronology, is yet to come, the oddly timeless and dislocated coda, designed to strike us as apocalyptic and life-affirming at the same time, not so much disrupts as dissolves the novel's linearity. Not only does it take the narrative full circle, but it also opens it up to its own tumultuous diversity. Mitchell's representation fulfils Nancy's proposition in *Being Singular Plural* that 'Being [. . .] is meaning that is, in turn, its own circulation – and *we* are this circulation' (2000: 2). The world *is* its people, a coming together of women and men whose lives are unique and unprecedented yet also ordinary to the degree of appearing dispensable. As Nancy explains:

> 'People' clearly states that we are all precisely *people*, that is, indistinctly persons, humans, all of a common 'kind,' but of a kind that has its existence only as numerous, dispersed, and indeterminate in its generality. This existence can only be grasped in the paradoxical simultaneity of togetherness (anonymous, confused, and indeed massive) and disseminated singularity (these or those 'people(s),' or 'a guy,' 'a girl,' 'a kind'). (2000: 7)

Featuring as rebels, mavericks, outsiders and dropouts, what Mitchell's protagonists share, and what so believably draws them into a community, is their difference or singularity, which renders them at once familiar and strange. Their '"strangeness" refers to the fact that each singularity is another access to the world' (2000: 14), whereas their familiarity reminds us that this world is one and the same for all of us.

In *Ghostwritten* Mitchell creates the impression of all his characters together as a cosmopolitan community congregating inoperatively, composed of 'not merely a collection of selves, but the occurrence of singular events that relate individual selves'. Put differently, Mitchell's novel *as* community, which also always includes the reader, 'is articulated in the plurality of evocative sharings and voices, not in the substantial relations freely entered into by "atomic" or autonomous individuals' (Hutchens 2005: 116). Reflecting on how to resist the contemporary world's increasing glomicity, Nancy wonders in *Being Singular Plural*:

> What if this autistic multiplicity, which tears open and is torn open, lets us know that we have not even begun to discover what it is to be many, even though 'la terre des hommes' is exactly this? What if it lets us know that it is itself the first laying bare of a world that is only the world, but which is the world absolutely and unreservedly, with no meaning beyond this very Being of the world: singularly plural and plurally singular? (2000: xiii–xiv)

By its refusal of closure, or rather its substitution of closure with recommencement, *Ghostwritten* exemplifies how this kind of tearing open and laying bare of the world, as part of the world's creation of itself, is done exceptionally well by the cosmopolitan novel.

In terms of its composite structure, its intricate web of intratextual connections, and its promotion of humanity as inoperative world-communal being-in-common, *Cloud Atlas* very much resembles *Ghostwritten*, which one might in fact want to regard as its prototype. The difference between the two novels is that *Cloud Atlas* is structurally and conceptually far more ambitious than its predecessor in that it introduces a temporally more elaborate and complex design. Like a momentarily expanding and then again contracting history of humankind, caught in a rhythm of systolic and diastolic pulsation, the later novel pioneers narrative as a device for time-travel and probes humanity's existential orientation within both space and history. *Cloud Atlas* consists of six independent stories encased one inside the other like Russian dolls, turning the novel into:

> an infinite matrioshka doll of painted moments, each 'shell' (the present) encased inside a nest of 'shells' (previous presents) I call the actual past but which we *perceive* as the virtual past. The doll of 'now' likewise encases a nest of presents yet to be, which I call the actual future but which we *perceive* as the virtual future. (Mitchell 2004: 409)

The outermost layer of the novel's palimpsest is provided by 'The Pacific Journal of Adam Ewing', the mid-nineteenth-century diary of a Californian notary on his way home from the Chatham Islands. Ewing's diary is found in 'Letters from Zedelghem', the novel's next section set in Belgium in the early 1930s, recorded by Robert Frobisher, musical *enfant terrible* and amanuensis to the world-famous composer Vyvyan Ayrs. The third section of the novel presents us with 'Half-Lives: The First Luisa Rey Mystery', set in California of 1975 and written in the style of Chandleresque detective fiction. The section features the now elderly Rufus Sixsmith, Frobisher's confidant and sole addressee of all his letters, as a retired atomic engineer with Seaboard Incorporated, a company whose criminal unscrupulousness is investigated by the fledgling journalist Luisa Rey. Not only does Rey eventually come into the possession of Frobisher's letters, which Sixsmith appears to have carried with him all his life, but her investigation also leads her to the Cape Yerbas Royale Marina, the final mooring place of the *Prophetess*, the ship that carried Ewing home. The Rey section is followed by 'The Ghastly Ordeal of Timothy Cavendish', a light-hearted, if slightly sinister comedic romp, connected to the previous section by the fact that Cavendish is a publisher who is sent 'The Luisa Rey Mystery' as an unsolicited manuscript for possible publication. Notably both Rey and Cavendish already make brief appearances in *Ghostwritten*, one as a caller on the *Bat Segundo Show* in 'Night Train' and the other as Marco's publisher in 'London' and Neal Brose's employer's younger brother in 'Hong Kong'.

Sections 5 and 6 of the novel transport us far into the future. 'An Orison of Sonmi-451', set in what used to be Korea, is centred on the life story of a genomed servant clone rebelling against her stem-type programming under the consumerist totalitarianism of Papa Song Corp. Her story is presented to us in the form of an interview conducted on the eve of her trial for treason. It survives into the novel's final section as a holographic audio-visual recording stored in a portable, egg-shaped electronic device. In 'Sloosha's Crossin' an' Ev'rythin' After', set in the post-apocalyptic archipelago of Ha-Why, we re-encounter Sonmi as a deity worshipped by the local tribe of goatherds and fishermen, who, in Mitchell's ingenious portrayal, emerge at once as our ancestors and our descendants. Zachry, the central character, is archetypal man; Adam is his long-lost brother's name, but also of course Ewing's in the novel's beginning. Torn by genocidal conflict between the Windward and Leeward tribes, the story of Ha-Why concludes with the enslavement of Zachry's people by the Kona, repeating the Maoris' subjugation of the Moriori in the history of the Chatham Islands as recounted by Ewing in his diary. As a result, any possible distinction between pre- and post-lapsarian humanity, or the past and the future, as well as fact and fiction, becomes virtually indecipherable. History is shown not so much to repeat itself as to find itself in permanent oscillation between hope, joy and fear, good and evil, certain demise and thereafter inevitable regeneration. In the novel's opening section Adam is saved from the deadly clutches of Dr Goose by Autua, the last of the Moriori, reversing the roles of alleged savagery and civilisation, Christianity and the pagan. Within the novel's temporal scheme it seems also as if Autua's heroism in the past might somehow serve to repair, or at least significantly counterbalance, Zachry's future failure to save his brother from enslavement. But then conventional concepts of time appear no longer to apply, as what comes to prevail in *Cloud Atlas* manifests ever more assertively as the global synchronicity of all human time exposed in a narrative amalgamation of countless parallel worlds, which despite their apparent multiplicity and chronological segregation signify in fact always one and the same world. Emulating Cloud Atlas Sextet – Mitchell's fiction of Frobisher's little-known, elusive musical masterpiece – the novel unfolds as the orchestrated interplay of a range of intimately entwined tunes, played in different modes on a variety of instruments, yet invariably chiming as one.

As in *Ghostwritten*, in *Cloud Atlas* the narrative proceeds by exposing the lives of a series of focal characters: Ewing, Frobisher, Rey, Cavendish, Sonmi, and in the final core section, oddly enough, not Zachry, the actual protagonist, but Meronym, one of the Prescients, a technologically more advanced group of post-apocalyptic survivors who regularly travel to Ha-Why to study the customs of its indigenous peoples. Notably, however, in *Cloud Atlas* the characters are linked not simply by their status as 'continua of identification' (Bhabha 1996: 203), or the more or less random visitations of a roaming noncorpum, but much more intimately through an eternal cycle of reincarnation. They all appear as versions of one another, marked as closely related by a comet-shaped birthmark which, as only really a second-time reader has any chance of noticing, already singles out Katie Forbes in the earlier *Ghostwritten*. Rey's connection to Frobisher seems particularly pronounced. On hearing the latter's Cloud Atlas Sextet for the first time, 'Luisa stands, entranced, as if living in a stream of time', the sound of it striking her as 'pristine, riverlike, spectral, hypnotic . . . *intimately familiar*' (425). Similarly, on reading Frobisher's forty-year-old letters to Sixsmith she is left reeling at 'the dizzying vividness of the images of places and people that the letters have unlocked. Images so vivid she can only call them memories' (121). Rey also picks up some uncanny vibrations from walking past the ship on which Ewing sailed home in the nineteenth century, now an open-air museum piece, sensing 'a strange gravity that makes her pause for a moment and look at its rigging, listen to its wooden bones creaking. [. . .] *What* is *wrong?* Luisa's birthmark throbs' (448). This mysterious allure of antique remnants from history also breathes special significance into Katie Forbes's strange obsession with a Queen Anne chair in *Ghostwritten*, apparently a family heirloom and the only item from their marital home she insists Neal must post back to her from Hong Kong.

At first glance Mitchell's introduction of the concept of reincarnation into his novel must appear as far too definitive and preordained a link between his characters. Rather than setting the scene for the creation of an inoperative cosmopolitan community, it purposely contrives to familiarise one individual soul with the particular vicissitudes of its historical singularity. The conceptual awkwardness of the device does not escape Mitchell himself, who uses Cavendish's editorial expertise as a publisher to dismiss mockingly 'the insinuation that Luisa Rey is this Robert Frobisher chap reincarnated, for example. Far too hippie-druggy-new age.' However, following this dismissal, Mitchell clearly cannot resist the irony of adding – in Cavendish's own words – that 'I, too, have a birthmark, below my left armpit, but no longer ever compared it to a comet' (373). The birthmark only 'works' if one refrains from seeing it as something that uniquely and exclusively connects the six characters. Everybody else – all of us – might indeed be bearing a different, if similarly indelible kind of mark, albeit maybe not quite so conspicuous or spectacular. The recurrent comet-shaped birthmark in

Cloud Atlas has to be seen as a general rather than specific symbol of humanity's potential for communal affiliation across the generations. When it comes to reading Rey's psychosomatic epiphanies, therefore, one is well advised to bear in mind Hutchens's elucidation of Nancean community not as 'an aggregation of individuals, but, rather crudely, [as] something very much like a "feeling" at the moments of sharing in contact between irreducibly singular beings who do not even share the property of "belonging together" in a cohesive group' (2005: 105). Put differently, humanity's heritage throbs in all of us, at all times, however vaguely and intangibly. All Mitchell's novel does is materialise our consciousness of humanity's global being-in-common by writing onto the body of his protagonists the mysterious actuality and endurance of history.

To capture the sense of this diachronic, multidimensional being-in-common, of human life as such, without fixing it by subjecting it to any particular teleological principle, Mitchell's literary ambition is aimed at nothing less than the creation of 'a never-changing map of the ever-constant ineffable [. . .] an atlas of clouds' (389). Such an atlas would not remain restricted to the two novels under discussion, but involve all of Mitchell's work sewn into one body of texts, one world. Both *number9dream* (2001) and *Black Swan Green* (2006) reverberate with references from *Ghostwritten* and *Cloud Atlas*. Most intriguing in this context is certainly how Mitchell's semi-autobiographical *Black Swan Green* comes to incorporate purely fictitious characters such as Gwendolin Bendincks, the vicar's domineering wife, who reappears as leader of the geriatrics in 'The Ghastly Ordeal of Timothy Cavendish', or Eva, Vyvyan Ayrs's teenage daughter in 'Letters from Zedelghem', who is revived as the elderly Madame Crommelynck, literary mentor of burgeoning poet Eliot Bolivar, a.k.a. Jason Taylor, Mitchell's own literary predecessor. Eva memorably scolds young Jason for what she regards as his typically English insularity of mind, his monoligualism, and his ignorance of European literature: 'Thomas Mann, Rilke, Gogol! Proust, Bulgakov, Victor Hugo! This is your culture, your inheritance, your *skeleton*! You are ignorant even of *Kafka*?' Rather pointedly she adds that 'translations are incourteous between Europeans', and she is outraged to find that 'English schoolboys in our enlightened 1980s cannot read a book in a foreign language' (2006: 204).

Mitchell's novels are aimed at weaving an all-embracing cosmopolitan network of mutually interpermeating lives and stories. Albeit informed with a sense of great world-political urgency, his narratives never become overtly or one-sidedly utopian, which is by no means to say his work lacks ethical determination or political commitment. A pertinent example here is the web of survival and extinction out of which *Cloud Atlas* creates the world. Together, Autua – the last of the Moriori, stowaway, and saviour of Adam Ewing – and post-apocalyptic everyman Zachry, who lives to beget children after the genocide of his people, quite literally become the foundational A to Z of Mitchell's worlding, the be-all-in-common and never-end-all of his ethical vision. Entirely ignorant of each other, with all common traditional links severed between them, Autua's and Zachry's peoples cultivate an identical philosophy of life, at once strictly localist and radically universal: 'That the terraqueous globe held other lands, trod by other feet, the Moriori dreamt not. Indeed, their language lacks a word for "Race" & "Moriori" means, simply, "People"' (5). In Mitchell's vision they also share the same resolutely pacificist creed. Among the Moriori murder is suicide: 'Whoever spilt a man's blood killed his own *mana* – his honour, his worth, his standing & his soul. No Moriori would shelter, feed, converse or even *see* the *persona non grata*' (6). Correspondingly, among Zachry's tribe 'if you stole another's life no'un barter nothin' with you nor see you nor nothin'cos your soul was so poisoned you may give 'em a sickness' (316). What *Cloud Atlas* illustrates here is humanity's ongoing vulnerability to evil, as demonstrated by the gruesome fate of Autua's and Zachry's peoples at the hands of their enslavers, as well as the inveterate resilience of humanity's goodness, as shown in its irrepressible recurrence and, via Zachry's offspring, its hopeful perpetuation within and beyond the innermost depths of the cosmopolitan imagination.

In Mitchell's representation human history emerges as riven by recurrent mutual exploitation, be it in the form of conquest accompanied by genocide and enslavement, colonisation and the building of Empire, or the threat of ever-increasing glomicity and worldwide corporatisation. The extreme dystopia of Sonmi's early life as a genetically engineered, subhuman server, deemed fit only for the purpose at hand and entirely recyclable, is presented as little more than a very rational simplification of socio-economic relations already prevalent in Luisa Rey's America of the 1970s, where at corporate get-togethers 'hispanic maids supplied by the caterers carry trays of food between the all-white guests' (418), as well as Timothy Cavendish's contemporary Britain. Oblivious to the actual portentousness of his sarcastic comments, Timothy remarks with regard to menial railway staff that 'the corporation breeds them from the same stem cell', adding later that in science parks on the periphery of Cambridge 'Biotech Space Age cuboids now sit cloning humans for shady Koreans' (170). Politics is succumbing to the interests of corporacy while society's communal dynamics wind up frozen by state control. 'We need to let business run the country' (420) is a lesson politicians must learn quickly if they want to succeed. Pertinently, in the Luisa Rey section, Ronald Reagan – destined to become US president in the 1980s and, in collaboration with Margaret Thatcher, majorly instrumental in building our current neo-liberalist world order – is asked to hang on and 'wait his turn' while the CEO of Seaboard Incorporated is too busy to speak with him (424).

Meanwhile language itself displays signs of a growing corruption by branding. Sonmi lives in a world where the words 'watch', 'car', 'shoes', 'camera', 'movies', 'coffee' and 'cigarette' have been superseded by 'rolex', 'ford', 'nikes', 'nikon', 'disneys', 'starbuck' and 'marlboro'. Sonmi's world also shows a striking affinity with Kelman's 'land of the free' in *You Have to Be Careful*. Both are built upon a two-tier system of strictly segregated socio-economic groups of haves and have-nots, and in both worlds the alleged haves – 'purebloods' in Mitchell's novel, 'trueborns' in Kelman's – turn out to be at least as enslaved, pre-programmed and remote-controlled as the Huxleyan deltas and epsilons bred to serve them. Notably, nothing panics Kelman's contemporary Americans more than coming face to face with the apparitional Grocery-Cart Pusher, the epitome of desperate consumerist ostracism and socially unacceptable failure that haunts the nation. A very similar psycho-systemic mechanism is at work in Nea So Copros, Sonmi's dystopian conurbation, where the state's ostentatious cultivation of '*Untermensch* slums motivate[s] downstrata consumers by showing them what befalls those who fail to spend and work like good citizens' (332). Yet among all the bleakness depicted by Mitchell a few alternatives to the corporate nightmare just about manage to cling on. On her flight from the security forces Sonmi comes across the remains of an old abbey, which has become home to 'a colony of dispossessed purebloods who prefer scraping a life out of the mountains to the *untermensch* sinks' (346). But as Mitchell insists in typically Nancean fashion, this is 'no bucolic utopia': 'The colonists bicker and grieve as people will. But they do it in a community. Nea So Copros has no communities; it only has the state' (347).

In 'Sloosha's Crossin' an' Ev'rythin' After', the core section of *Cloud Atlas*, we are provided with yet another glimpse of the kind of local, world-creative living so overtly endorsed by Mitchell. The life of Zachry's people seems not very different from the one led by Sonmi's group of radical dropouts at the abbey. Mitchell's vision of post-apocalyptic survival also conspicuously resembles Kelman's in *Translated Accounts*, where humanity likewise begins to blossom again after complete societal meltdown, gradually retrieving a sense of community from a disparate crowd of traumatised strangers. In both narratives this communal re-assemblage is accompanied by a regeneration of language, however torturous and initially difficult to grasp, manifesting in Kelman's lingua franca translatorese as well as Zachry's futuristic pidgin. Importantly, 'now the candle o' civ'lize is burnt away' (255), Mitchell shows how inevitably both the positive and negative aspects of human living begin to reassert themselves: there are the well-wishing expressions of neighbourly kindness and solicitude – such as 'Go careful', reminiscent of the ubiquitous Irish 'mind how you go' in the Clear Island section of *Ghostwritten* – and there is the ineradicable xenophobia that continues to drive a wedge between 'us' and 'them', be they called 'foreigners' or, as in Zachry's tongue, 'offlanders'. What survives also is humanity's irrepressible avidity for storytelling. *Cloud Atlas* culminates in Zachry's kids coming together to listen once again to Sonmi's tale. This is the moment future history opens up and simultaneously vanishes from view for good; it is the novel's navel, its axial nadir and central turning point, simultaneously its ending and its recommencement.

In Mitchell's vision, humanity is invariably the same, but different, and so is the repertory of stories that make up its history. Difference will reassert itself even out of totalitarianism and the most relentlessly controlled homogeneity. Symbolically this shows in the refreshing natural mutability of the genetically manipulated insects Sonmi sees on her flight: 'Once-genomed moths spun around our heads, electron-like; their wings' logos had mutated over generations into a chance syllabary' (345).

Arguing in *Globalization and Culture* that 'for most people most of the time the impact of globalization is felt not in travel but in staying at home', John Tomlinson distinguishes 'between literally travelling to distant places and "travelling" to them by talking on the telephone, typing at the computer keyboard or watching the television set' (1999:150). As is typical of much research in contemporary globalisation studies, Tomlinson fails to include literature – or, in a much broader sense, art – in his catalogue of assorted media that help tie even the most remote and sedentary parts of the world into the global network and thus contract the globe effectively by appealing to people's individual and collective imagination. But then, of course, one would err greatly to regard literature simply as a transportation, communication or virtual easy-access tool. As an art, it does more than merely facilitate knowledge transfer or maintain a steady flow of information. By constantly feeding experience back into ideology, it stands for the mobilisation of individual desire and becomes potentially subversive of the status quo, countering and often overtly resisting the way the world works. Actively world-creative, literature forges a link between life itself – that is, 'the contingent and plural mess of historical becoming' (James 2006: 199), far removed from ideology's tidy teleological trajectories – and the multifarious models and myths of human living informed by 'foundationalist attitudes, and [constitutive] of political projects grounded in figures of essence or of the absolute' (201).

As Hutchens puts it, 'existence itself challenges any "globalness"' (2005: 121), and a cosmopolitan literary aesthetics – like the one at work in *Ghostwritten* and *Cloud Atlas* – is aimed purposely at cultivating and refining this challenge. Cosmopolitan writing disrupts the standard global imaginary by initiating a singular sharing between author, reader and character(s), thus inaugurating among them a communal becoming that contests any authoritarian prescription or imposition of totality. All totalities, even when encountered in the form of the most fearful systems of totalitarian governance, are continually undermined by the world-creative unruliness and unpredictability of inoperative community. As Hutchens asserts, 'a world that "played back" its symbolic or mythic identity to itself in order to enhance its own dominion would be incessantly disrupted by the specific sharings among singular beings that are the sole bonds of communication and community in the political realm' (121). One element of human existence that, according to Nancean philosophy, dismantles any totalitarian design at global meaning-making is humanity's explicit finitude, its capture within one and the same temporally bound world. Humanity's finitude is bound always to detract from the lofty truth-claims and eternal abstractions of mythical *telos* by refocusing attention onto the here and now, on you and me and y/our other/s, how we live together, and how we choose and manage to communicate. Accordingly, communal living is always most fecund exactly where (any chance of a wholesome fulfilment of) community comes to be interrupted or, put differently, where it is continually being productively thwarted.

In Nancean terms, community assumes shape as the always-precarious and tentative being-in-common – that is, as both the agitated assemblages and effervescent dispersions – of an unwieldy plurality of finite singular beings. In 'Myth Interrupted', the second chapter of *The Inoperative Community*, Nancy insists that community quite literally stands and falls, often simultaneously, with the singular being as she becomes exposed to other singular beings. Community is created by its own interruption, by becoming aware of its intrinsic 'being singular plural', within which the singular being acts as 'a contact [. . .] a contagion: a touching, the transmission of a trembling at the edge of being, the communication of a passion that makes us fellows, or the communication of the passion to be fellows, to be *in* common' (1991: 61). The fact that we cannot ultimately come together in a more definitive or substantiated form is what reminds us of our existential being-in-common. Community has no centre or clear-cut contours; rather, as its own disruption, it 'occurs at the edge, or rather it constitutes the edge where beings touch each other, expose themselves to each other and separate from one another, thus communicating and propagating their community' (61). In Nancy's view, community as the promise of fulfilling a specific preordained destiny must be apprehended as purely mythical, and it is this explicit functionality of myth in general that he then proceeds to contrast with the more 'literary' dynamic of community as inoperative. 'When myth stops playing', Nancy writes, 'the community that resists completion and fusion, the community that propagates and exposes itself, makes itself heard in a certain way' (62), and the particular way in which this community makes itself heard – its voice – is literature.

Literature's finitude (as opposed to myth's self-professed infinitude) must not be misconstrued as a lack of scope or open-endedness; rather, it is myth's promotion of eternal homeostasis that literature so resolutely declines, propagating instead a fruitful impossibility of closure, which turns out to be as communally inoperative as it is literary:

> Literature does not come to an end at the very place where it comes to an end: on its border, right on the dividing line – a line sometimes straight (the edge, the border of the book), sometimes incredibly twisted and broken (the writing, the reading). It does not come to an end at the place where the work passes from an author to a reader, and from this reader to another reader or to another author. It does not come to an end at the place where the work passes on to another work by the same author or at the place where it passes into other works of other authors. It does not come to an end where its narrative passes into other narratives, its poem into other poems, its thought into other thoughts, or into the inevitable suspension of the thought or the poem. It is unended and unending – in the active sense – in that it is literature. (65)

Informed by the same dynamics of struggle, agitation, effervescence and continual interruption, literature appears most propitiously equipped to give voice to the kind of inoperative community one finds emergent in Mitchell's cosmopolitan novels. Both the coda in *Ghostwritten* and the final vision of 'Sloosha's Crossin'' at the heart of *Cloud Atlas* can hardly be described as proper endings; rather, each stands as a potential recommencement marking the curve of a never-ending spiral of narration. Indisputably finite in their novel-ness, as well as their portrayal of one recognisable world – our world – both novels reach endlessly into the past and the future, encompassing the faint murmurings of other stories or unexpectedly entering the narratives of Mitchell's other works, even his autobiographical writing. The characters come in sets and constellations that are open cosmopolitan paradigms, foreshadowing each other and being overshadowed by the (as yet) unrecounted communal lives of multitudinous other contemporaries, ancestors and descendants.

Nancy's opening statement in 'Literary Communism', the third chapter of *The Inoperative Community*, captures perfectly Mitchell's cosmopolitan effort to convey a strong, enduring sense of global community across space and time. Most commendably, despite their author's penchant for occasional flights of fancy, both *Ghostwritten* and *Cloud Atlas* remain strictly realist texts. Ethically informed, neither novel succumbs to the vertebrate rigidity of a utopian vision. Both as existential mystery and as political project, humanity continues to be irresolvably cellular:

> The community of interrupted myth [. . .] is our destination. In other words community (or communism) is what we are being called toward, or sent to, as to our ownmost future. But it is not a 'to come,' it is not a future or final reality on the verge of fulfillment, pending only the delay imposed by an approach, a maturation, or a conquest. For if this were the case, its reality would be mythic – as would be the feasibility of its idea.
>
> Community without community is *to come*, in the sense that it is always *coming*, endlessly, at the heart of every collectivity (because it never stops coming, its ceaselessly resists collectivity itself as much as it resists the individual.) (71)

Mitchell's cosmopolitan novels celebrate individual human life most effectively by denying it its traditional centre-stage exposure. The novels spread their focus across a series of individuals whose lives come to signify in relation, yet never dissolve into any one clearly defined trajectory of meaning. Despite their gathering into a collectivity each character remains unique and outstanding. Exactly what cosmopolitan design Mitchell might have in mind remains 'to come' as his characters comply with the global design of the novel, yet at the same time resist it by breaking away into the multiplicity of their specific locales. The process of sporadic interruption Mitchell's narration inflicts on itself results in the creation of an inoperative compositeness designed to rehearse the world-creative repercussions of attempting to reconcile individual singularity with communal incorporation.

Traditionally the reception of the novel has been dominated by two classic presuppositions regarding the genre's preoccupation with nationhood and individualism. In *The Spectre of Comparisons* Benedict

Anderson asserts that 'the historical appearance of the novel-as-popular-commodity and the rise of nation-ness were intimately related' (1998: 334), and in *How Novels Think* Nancy Armstrong's core thesis is that 'novels think like individuals about the difficulties of fulfilling oneself [. . .] under specific cultural historical conditions' (2005: 10). Only as an afterthought does Anderson express concerns as to whether 'the deep original affinity between nation-ness and the novel meant they would always be adequate for one another: that the nation would continue to serve as the natural if unspoken frame of the novel' (334). Similarly, Armstrong concludes on a concession, namely that one day novels might indeed 'begin to think of a genuine alternative to the individual, one that does not inspire phobia and yet is grounded in the world we now inhabit'. The very likelihood that such a focal paradigm shift might occur, facilitated by the genre's sensitivity to cultural-historical change, prompts Armstrong in the end to reflect that 'the novel of course was not made to think beyond the individual, but neither, on the other hand, was it made to reproduce the status quo' (25). Mitchell's cosmopolitan novels look in many ways as if they had been fashioned directly out of Anderson's and Armstrong's second-thought allowances for the genre's possible evolution. Both *Ghostwritten* and *Cloud Atlas* pioneer the novel as opening upon a world-creative *tour du monde* that imagines community beyond the bounds of the nation. This new imagined community respects yet does not single out or fetishise the individual; it accommodates the self and to a certain degree assimilates it within a larger whole, yet it never sets it to work: neither the individual, nor the community of which it partakes, ever assume a position of totality. Our new global contemporaneity – that is, Armstrong's 'world we now inhabit', to which the novel is programmed seismically to respond – promotes the rise of a new political aesthetics and aesthetic politics, which is looking conspicuously Nancean.

According to Nancy, 'in its infinite resistance to everything that would bring it to completion', community – and this, in my view, applies particularly to the new global community – 'signifies an irrepressible political exigency, and [. . .] this exigency in its turn demands something of "literature," the inscription of our infinite resistance' (1991: 80–1). As Robert Fine and Vivienne Boon warn, however, 'cosmopolitanism is not or ought not to be a doctrinal mindset. One always has to resist the proclivity to turn cosmopolitanism into an "ism" – that is, into a doctrine, a dogma, an all-purpose prescription, a fixed idea' (2007: 7–8). This is why it is to be welcomed that there is no manifesto that would specify or detail the kind of literature that is now required. Indeed, there must never be a *school* of cosmopolitan novelists lest the genre lose its contagious momentum as both inspirational contact and process of inoperative dissemination, 'opening community to itself, rather than to a destiny or to a future' (Nancy 1991: 80). In this respect, then, the cosmopolitan novel is probably best understood as part of what Nancy describes in terms of a 'literary communism', which 'defines neither *a* politics, nor *a* writing, for it refers, on the contrary, to that which resists any definition or program, be these political, aesthetic, or philosophical' (81).

III

Creating the World

Chapter 4

Global Noise: Arundhati Roy, Kiran Desai, Hari Kunzru

Globalisation is commonly held responsible for eliminating cultural difference and replacing it with worldwide homogeneity, supposedly erasing Empire's core–periphery axiomatic of self and other while in actual fact perpetuating, and indeed considerably exacerbating, what looks suspiciously like the same old inequalities. As Chitra Sankaran asserts, 'globalization, though it professes to homogenize the human condition, seems actually to polarize it in extreme ways' (2006: 106). The increasing chasm between rich and poor that splits the world is rapidly being compounded by the establishment of westernised, allegedly 'cosmopolitan' Third World elites inside the ex-colonies themselves. As Arundhati Roy writes with regard to her own divided, caste-ridden nation, 'the people of India have been [. . .] loaded onto two convoys of trucks (a huge big one and a tiny little one) that have set off resolutely in opposite directions. The tiny convoy is on its way to a glittering destination somewhere near the top of the world. The other convoy just melts into the darkness and disappears' (2001: 2–3).

Inspired by Peter Kalliney's question 'whether or not globalization theory represents the logical next phase of postcolonial literary scholarship' (2002: 52), the present chapter introduces connectivity and subalternity as key terms to problematise humanity's hitherto unprecedented glocal entanglement, the proximity and multicultural compression of peoples, which often clash with their actual segregation and the persistence of strictly policed rules of entitlement and exclusion. The main concern of the three novels to be discussed in this chapter is the feasibility of sustaining the dynamics of Nancean world-formation – as they manifest themselves in the fruitful creation of friendships, homes and neighbourhoods – in a context of ever-thickening (neo-)nationalist unrest and corporate glomicity. Echoing James Kelman's portrayal of US America as 'the global hegemon' (Beck 2006: 134), at once menacing and irresistibly appealing to the rest of the world, Desai's and Kunzru's novels in particular also accentuate the contrast between the actual, real-life mindset of economic migrants, on the one hand, and their customisation in postcolonial theory, on the other.

Looking at Roy's *The God of Small Things* (1997), Kiran Desai's *The Inheritance of Loss* (2006) and Hari Kunzru's *Transmission* (2004), the present chapter explores the interpermeation of the local and the global and, especially, how despite its evident susceptibility to global trends, the local continues to assert itself as a scattering of uncharted snags disrupting globalisation's surge. As Julie Mullaney notes, 'the excavation of these relations between the small and the large, the private and the public, governs the ostensible plot of *The God of Small Things*' (2005: 39). Typically, Ayemenem – the parochial Keralan village in which Roy's novel is set – at once does, and does not, stand for India as a whole. Focused primarily on unpeeling the vulnerabilities at the heart of one family of outstandingly strong-willed individuals, the novel also 'betrays something of the temper of the new and ongoing networks, histories, and rules of engagement that characterize India's post-Independence relations with the wider world' (Mullaney 2005: 50). Far from occurring only within the subtle shifts and turns of cosmopolitan narrative, however, the disruptive power of subaltern glocality also shows in bold extra-literary gestures, such as Roy's donation of her Booker Prize win to the Narmada Bachao Andolan, a grassroots activist group opposing further 'big dam' developments in India. These big dams have become emblematic of the increasing global corporatisation of natural resources at the expense of already acutely disenfranchised and calamitously dispossessed local populations. Clearly, Roy's gesture is intended not to let us forget that the novel owes the world something not only in terms of a simple representational indebtedness but also, far more importantly, in terms of its inbuilt generic capability for making a difference through ethically informed world-creation.

Roy's provocative emphasis on literature's intimate affinity with political activism breaks the neatly closed circle of publisher, readers/ consumers, critics and author by opening up literary aesthetics, as well as its commodification by the global culture industry, to a messy and unruly, often unwholesome and problematically agitated exteriority. Fully aware of the subjection of her work to global market forces, Roy's gesture of donating her prize money upset the gilded cage of literary celebrity, drawing attention to how the novel's creation of a seemingly parallel or alternative world always pertains, or in her view at least always ought to pertain, to real-life world-creation. What Roy sought to pre-empt was the silencing of her characters' subaltern voices by too much favourable appraisal and commercial success. But her recalcitrance also served to reveal something quite sinister in the practice of applauding representations of people struggling for survival at the world's margins as serendipitous, prize-worthy finds. Roy's gesture highlights the perilous detachment of such representations from their origin and indeed the critical fetishisation of their alleged authenticity, both of which are prone to defuse their potential for resistance by rendering them exhibits of 'another world' to be pleasurably consumed like any other purchasable work.

Graham Huggan problematises Roy's quandary – and that of other Third World intellectuals who, like her, find their convictions compromised by commercial overexposure – in terms of 'the postcolonial exotic', a complex psycho-glocal condition emerging from:

> a site of discursive conflict between a local assemblage of more or less related oppositional practices and a global apparatus of assimilative institutional/commercial codes. More specifically, [the postcolonial exotic] marks the intersection between contending regimes of value: one regime – postcolonialism – that posits itself as anti-colonial, and that works toward the dissolution of imperial epistemologies and institutional structures; and another – postcoloniality – that is more closely tied to the global market, and that capitalises both on the widespread circulation of ideas about cultural otherness and on the worldwide trafficking of culturally 'othered' artifacts and goods. (2001: 28)

For a successful Third World writer, complicity with postcolonialism's 'exoticist aesthetics' is practically unavoidable; in fact, complicity very much looks like a necessary evil that must be embraced in order to introduce one's views effectively into the public domain. Without the tremendous success of her debut novel and the international media hype surrounding its publication, it is unlikely Roy's two subsequent collections of political essays, *The Cost of Living* (1999) and *Power Politics* (2001), would have reached as wide an audience as they did. Once again the paradox applies that the state of being globalised, of giving in to and embracing the reality of globalisation, is an indispensable prerequisite to resisting its relentlessly homogenising impact. Huggan explores in his study the dynamics of what he refers to as the cultivation of a 'strategic exoticism', that is, 'the means by which postcolonial writers/thinkers, working from within exoticist codes of representation, either manage to subvert those codes [. . .] or succeed in redeploying them for the purposes of uncovering differential relations of power' (32). As a closer look at Bishnupriya Ghosh's recent examination of the contemporary Indian novel reveals, this strategic exoticism is not so very far removed at all from the Nancean notion of world-creation, or indeed my own hopeful projection of the cosmopolitan novel as a locally informed device for resisting glomicity. In fact, Ghosh's *When Borne Across* is wholly dedicated to tracing in novels like Roy's 'the conception of a situated literary cosmopolitics – one that mobilizes the imagination for newly urgent ethical and political tasks of worlding' (2004: 18).

Largely completed before 9/11 and fuelled by the promise of a less divisive world order following the fall of the Berlin Wall, Ghosh's enquiry is led by probing 'the capacities of the literary imagination to fashion new forms of collective life and agency' (19). In Ghosh's view *The God of Small Things* is best understood as a cosmopolitan novel imagining the world rather than a postcolonial novel focused strictly on (re-)imagining the nation. As suggested by Mullaney, 'notwithstanding the attention to the *small*, the *personal*, and the *local specificities* of *place*, Roy's novel can be read also as national allegory' (2005: 26). However, Ghosh asserts, the chief motivation behind novels like Roy's is ultimately not to recast the contours of the nation, but to challenge 'both the forms of nationalism reinforced by global flows and the pernicious globalism surfacing in dispersed local contexts' (5). Roy's main interest is in the individual's self-orientation within the world at large, their ongoing struggle of negotiating globality's far-from-straightforward interpermeation with the local, the complex enmeshment of these two spheres that determine our lives and absorb, yet also never quite cease fundamentally to repel and contest, each other. The cosmopolitan protagonist – be it Rahel in Roy's novel, Sai in Desai's or Arjun in Kunzru's – appears as a disempowered 'player' and slightly detached observer, uprooted by personal circumstance and/or propelled by remote-controlled aspiration, yet always unmistakably marked by their origin.

As the cosmopolitan novel demonstrates, there is no world that does not commence at home, taking shape from one's own singular emergence in the interplay with others'. Abstract apparatuses of uniform mass identification, such as religion, the nation, the state or global capital, are revealed as profoundly inimical to the intricacies of love, hope and individual desire, which these apparatuses are prone ruthlessly to dismember and, if necessary, abort. This tragic mechanism culminates most shockingly in the destruction of Velutha, Rahel's mother's lover, an untouchable, in *The God of Small Things*. Ingeniously, the title of Roy's novel serves not so much to conjure a parallel universe of myth, governed by altogether different values concerning human interaction, as to remind us of our first, and one and only, frame of reference – not some superimposed exoskeletal structure, but the everyday intimacy of our communal being-in-common, which is responsible for producing the very substance of the heart. It is from this most indigenous of sources that the promise of a new kind of creative agency, both individual and collective, comes to unfold into the world, provided it does not prematurely fall prey to the powers that at present work humanity so relentlessly.

The cosmopolitan novel does its best to resist the commodification and containment of literature as a marketable product, promoting it instead as an imaginative tool for world-political intervention and a potentially subaltern moment of resistance. As becomes particularly pronounced in the case of high-profile prize-winners like *The God of Small Things*, whose marketing Huggan has described as 'an object lesson in commodity fetishism' (2001: 76), the danger with cosmopolitan writing is that its apparent originality and endeavour at world-creation might always already have been 'worked' by the necessity to live up to expectations generated by the global culture industry and its literary establishment. Following the phenomenal success of Salman Rushdie's *Midnight's Children* (1981), the Indian novel in English rigidified into a strict literary formula. Newcomers are judged by the degree to which they manage – innovatively, if always within limits – this operative recipe for success rather than their own, possibly far more radical world-creation. Insatiably the globalised market – both popular and academic – cultivates a craving for more of the same. Roy herself has contested the freedom, motives and ethical integrity of best-selling novelists, overtly including herself in the interrogation: 'If what we have doesn't "sell," will we still say it? Can we? Or is everybody looking for Things That Sell to say? Could writers end up playing the role of palace entertainers? Or the subtle twenty-first-century version of court eunuchs attending to the pleasures of our incumbent CEOs?' (2001: 9). In the end the question remains whether it is possible to be a successful writer and still make a difference, that is, to yield one's art to the rules of the publishing market and yet remain uncorrupted by commercial customisation.

Rushing to the defence of writers like Roy, Ghosh certainly continues to believe in the feasibility of resistance and subversion. 'While I argue that the localizing strategies of the cosmopolitical writers in part produce fetishistic locales for commercial consumption', she writes, 'they also privilege a "performative local" that cannot be stabilized, reproduced, or circulated on a global market' (2004: 28). In other words, a cosmopolitan novel that sells does not necessarily need to be selling out, or to be committing a betrayal. Its aesthetic and political integrity ultimately depends on what thorny burrs and sticky secretions attach themselves to the reader's imagination as she roams the exotic vistas of the novel's seemingly innocuous, native sumptuousness. Posing as tourist guides willing to deliver the promise of their picture-book marketing, novels like Roy's in fact abandon the reader as soon as she has been led off the beaten track and into the wilderness beyond the 'Heart of Darkness', which in *The God of Small Things* is the name of a fenced-in hotel complex. As Ghosh explains, 'there are no native informants here' (28), leaving the filth, stench, ugliness, brutality and injustice of indigenous living, which normally tend to remain veiled, to protrude without the usual gloss or shock-absorbing annotation. At first glance presenting itself as some kind of exotic romance, *The God of Small Things* is in fact aimed at engineering a collision between the globalised world of the reader and the locally specific situatedness of the text. The novel's evocation of exotic beauty and intrigue is superseded by an ever-intensifying concentration on tragedy, death, violence, their gratuitousness and futility, as well as the barbaric violation of childhood for the pettiest and most callous personal and political gains. It is tempting to compare the allure of Roy's novel to that of E. M. Forster's *A Passage to India* (1924), whose revelation of a stark, incomprehensible truth at its centre similarly assails the reader, leaving him reeling with disorientation (see Barratt 1993). Likewise, our reading of *The God of Small Things* capsizes with the brutal force of an accident – just like Rahel's English Aunt Margaret's Christmas visit to India, which tragically ends in her daughter's drowning. This is the kind of impact it takes to make us pause, jettison all our literary preconceptions and behold for the first time the true nature of the idyll to which we have been transported, as well as the inexorable rules according to which its world is condemned to work.

But the drowning of Sophie Mol, Roy's twin protagonists' Anglo-Indian cousin, eventually comes to look only like an ancillary plot device foreshadowing the novel's true anti-climax of heart-of-darkness intensity, namely the police killing of Velutha, Roy's eponymous archetype of a radically local, deified subalternity (see also Ghosh 2004: 11). Initially configured as the kind of tragic conclusion to an illicit sexual encounter one might conventionally expect to find in a tale of romance, Velutha's extermination quickly assumes the significance of a ritual act of sacrificial cleansing whose purpose and motivation are not so much communal as systemic, and whose very occurrence turns out to be functional and operative rather than random or merely incidental. The killing of Velutha is presented as the work of 'an era imprinting itself on those who lived in it' (Roy 1997: 309). Once the policemen, who were 'only history's henchmen [. . .] impelled by feelings that were primal yet paradoxically wholly impersonal' (308), have executed their orders, they are shown to step away from the dying man like 'craftsmen assessing [. . .] Their Work, abandoned by God and History, by Marx, by Man, by Woman and (in the hours to come) by Children' (310). Velutha's subaltern insurrection is crushed by the structural violence of an ideology, or set of ideologies, whose chief functionaries in Roy's novel are the local trade-union leader and the local police chief, a coupling of convenience ultimately not quite as unusual as it may initially appear:

> They were no friends, Comrade Pillai and Inspector Thomas Mathew, and they didn't trust each other. But they understood each other perfectly. They were both men whom childhood had abandoned without a trace. Men without curiosity. Without doubt. Both in their own way truly, terrifyingly adult. They looked out at the world and never wondered how it worked, because they knew. *They* worked it. They were mechanics who serviced different parts of the same machine. (262)

Representative of seemingly opposed ideological standpoints, that of the state and that of the Communist Party, what Pillai and Mathew share is their determination to implement and fulfil their briefs, at whatever cost, even if this involves the corruption of their most fervently cherished ideals.

When Velutha's plea for help is rejected by the Party, of which he is a member, Roy comments laconically that 'there it was again. Another religion turned against itself. Another edifice constructed by the human mind, decimated by human nature' (287). Once ideologically rigidified, any political ideal is at risk of succumbing to a process of systemic self-completion that is hard to tell apart from plain totalitarianism. It is as though some kind of systemic self-maintenance economy jumps into operation. According to Roy's central Orwellian image, this economy is inevitably world-destructive and inimical to human life: 'They heard the thud of [. . .] boot on bone. On teeth. The muffled grunt when a stomach is kicked in. The muted crunch of skull on cement' (308). Interpreted in Nancean terms, Velutha's extermination reveals itself as the apotheotic œuvre of an operatively intact communitarianism that is geared towards perfect self-completion. Notably, Roy fulfils Ghosh's analysis that 'where official nationalism homogenizes history, the cosmopolitical writers pose the vicissitudes of unreliable memory and the discontinuities, ruptures, and silences of history writing' (124). In *The God of Small Things* Roy cultivates an intimately personal, idiosyncratically playful style, which she pits against the sculpted starkness of nationalist – or, indeed, any other kind of ideologically motivated – representation and self-expression. It is in this respect, then, that the novel's impassioned portrayal of subaltern heterogeneity assumes universal significance without once effacing its decidedly local specificity and appeal.

Possibly India makes a particularly well-suited case study for showing the immense injury inflicted on our communal being-in-common by too much systemic organisation. At the same time, however, it also powerfully demonstrates the people's recalcitrant, world-creative resourcefulness that counters any such attempt at ideological containment. In Roy's view, 'corporatizing India is like trying to impose an iron grid on a heaving ocean and forcing it to behave'. She adds that the country is 'too diverse, too grand, too feral, and – eventually, I hope – too democratic to be lobotomized into believing in one single idea, which is, ultimately, what globalization really is: Life Is Profit' (2001: 31). *The God of Small Things* is probably best understood as a novel that simultaneously courts and thwarts a globalised consumption of the India it represents. The novel seeks to imprint upon the global reader an impression of real-life living conditions in contemporary India, deliberately sabotaging the formulaic way in which the country and its cultures have traditionally been imagined. Whatever easy, exotic palatability the novel possesses is ruined by Roy's exposure of the traumatic horror at the heart of communal life in Ayemenem – a horror caused by a fateful concoction of racialist religious traditions, the self-serving pursuit of local politics, and vindictive familial strife. Roy never represents the nation as an all-embracing organising principle; rather, she remains concerned with the more elemental building blocks of being-in-common, as they manifest in the local community and in the family, and leave an enduring impact on the individual's view of the world.

At the same time as providing the world with a more realist glimpse of an India that is always locally specific, however, the novel also does its best to shield the local from the influence of the world at large. *The God of Small Things* tries very hard to obstruct the invasive flow of globalisation, its unstoppable descent upon communal and familial life all over the world. It militates against globalisation's ceaseless stream of alien images and narratives, deploying the twins' own story, their lives and dreams, as some kind of imaginative stopper that literally blocks out the world, however imperfectly:

> If they slept there [in Baby Kochamma's satellite dish], she and Estha, curled together like foetuses in a shallow steel womb, what would Hulk Hogan and Bam Bam Bigelow do? If the dish were occupied, where would *they* go? Would they slip through the chimney into Baby Kochamma's life and TV? Would they land on the old stove with a *Heeaagh!*, in their muscles and spangled clothes? Would the thin People – the famine victims and refugees

– slip through the cracks in the doors? Would genocide slide between the tiles?

The sky was thick with TV. If you wore special glasses you could see them spinning through the sky among the bats and homing birds – blondes, wars, famines, football, food shows, coups d'état, hairstyles stiff with hairspray. Designer pectorals. Gliding towards Ayemenem like skydivers. Making patterns in the sky. Wheels. Windmills. Flowers blooming and unblooming. (1997: 188)

Rather than merely attempting to shut out the world, however, Roy's novel is in my view best regarded as an exercise in local self-exposure intended not simply to swap a local perspective for a global one, but genuinely to glocalise and thereby create a balance, markedly different from the precarious balancing act that is the nation. As Ghosh puts it, 'for Roy, the world comes to roost at home' (127).

It is absolutely crucial not to misunderstand this kind of glocalisation as a universal levelling out, or world-wide hybridisation. As Nancy explains in 'Eulogy for the Mêlée', to do so would be to endorse the eradication of culture as such. 'Cultures, or what are known as cultures, do not mix', Nancy asserts. 'They encounter each other, mingle, modify each other, reconfigure each other. They cultivate one another; they irrigate or drain each other; they work over and plough through each other, or graft one onto the other.' Nancy insists that 'the gesture of culture is itself a mixed gesture: it is to affront, confront, transform, divert, develop, recompose, combine, rechannel' (2000: 151–2). Clearly Roy understands this. In her novel the local is never simply globality's passive recipient, but a participant and integral part of it, as well as occasionally its sparring partner, implicated in the world even at the moment of most passionately trying to evade it. Neither is globality, in turn, ever a simple container of an endless diversity of multifarious world cultures. The global and the local at once interpermeate and remain at odds with each other. It is inevitable that globality should find its way in, whatever impediments are placed in its way, but it must not be allowed to do so at the expense of the local, which has its own tales to tell, often strikingly at odds with what the world wants, hopes or expects to hear. In other words, global culture must never become unanimously the same, lest it cease to be 'culture'. Hence why, as Roy puts it so poignantly, 'in the present circumstances [. . .] the only thing worth globalizing is dissent', which, she adds, is 'India's best export' (2001: 33).

Kiran Desai's *The Inheritance of Loss*, which won the Booker Prize in 2006, invites comparison with *The God of Small Things*, also penned in English by an Indian-born cosmopolitan and winning the same prestigious international accolade a decade before. Concerned with issues of class and caste in contemporary India, as well as the allure and acute disillusionment that is to countless Indians the promise of emigration to US America, Desai appears in many respects to follow in Roy's footsteps. Focalised through the lens of an orphaned young woman very similar to Roy's, *The Inheritance of Loss* likewise deploys the imagery of a broken family riddled with guilt and the ill-omened trajectory of illicit love burgeoning in breach of traditional boundaries. Unlike Roy's Keralan family saga, however, Desai's novel is set in the far more notoriously sectarian, conflict-ridden north of the subcontinent – in Kalimpong in the northeastern Himalayas, where in the mid-1980s the politically minoritised Indian-Nepalese ethnic majority were pushing for the foundation of Ghorkaland, their own independent country, or at least, should that prove impractical, their own federal state within the Indian republic. Another major difference is that whereas Roy merely hints at India's post-imperial bond with the United Kingdom and its ever-strengthening, if complex and fraught relationship with US America by introducing characters who are married to, and then divorced from, American (Rahel) or English (Chacko, Rahel's uncle) partners, Desai dedicates a third of her novel to the story of Biju, Sai's grandfather's cook's son, who ekes out a living as an illegal immigrant in a string of bottom-range restaurant kitchens in contemporary New York. If only in passing, the novel also refers to Mrs Sen's daughter, who has left home to become a CNN newsreader, and Lola's daughter Pixie, who works as a reporter for the BBC; unfortunately, any more elaborate detail of the two young women's experience of diasporic living remains unforthcoming. The other two strands of Desai's novel are concerned with the memories of the Judge, Sai's grandfather, and the doomed love affair between privately educated Sai and Gyan, her lower-class tutor, desperate for social justice and mobility.

It is the very cosmopolitan ambitiousness of Desai's novel that ends up fragmenting the text and its vision, and prevents it from evolving beyond a mere re-assemblage of literary stereotypes. Despite attempts to endow the novel with semi-autobiographical authenticity (clearly Sai is designed to work as Desai's alter ego) and unfurl a colourful bouquet of mutually supportive narratives, Desai's vision remains stilted at heart and disappointingly monologic. The novel envisions a picturesque backwater invaded by the twin phenomena of globalisation and neo-nationalist agitation, yet instead of plunging the reader into this conflict-ridden scenario of a traumatically pent-up glocality and allowing it to unfold according to the inoperative rhythms of its own familial and communal dynamics, Desai moulds it didactically into a lesson on fate's alleged imbrication with history.

One cannot entirely shake off the impression that Desai takes most of her inspiration from the repertory of Anglo-Indian literature rather than real-life political commitment or locally lived cosmopolitan experience. Her representation works mainly by extraneous description rather than empathic identification, which is fiction's primary equivalent to analysis. Transported to the dilapidated imperial mansion of Cho Oyu, where Sai lives with her grandfather and his cook, discerning readers cannot help but discover that they have been to this kind of semi-derelict hill station before, and that they are also already familiar with the young lovers, the elderly sisters, the embittered patriarch, the effeminate native (Biju's father) and the couple of tragicomedic E. M. Forster-type closet homosexuals ('Father Booty' and 'Uncle Potty') who reside there. Really, Desai's only innovation, which situates her narrative securely in the twenty-first century, is her addition of the illegal migrant worker to this list of stock characters. However, throughout the narrative Biju remains as vague, bloodless and spectral as Desai's envisioning of his eventual return home at the close of the novel. He is little more than a perfunctory sketch. In vain does one wait for a more in-depth portrayal of the despair and destitution that mark Biju's diasporic experience. To compound matters, as the novel progresses, Desai's narrative succumbs without any apparent design to oddly ruptured, erratically hyphenated paragraphing. At the same time, her imagery begins to fall out of touch with any particular local specificity, blurring rather than accentuating our view of the mountainous, landbound part of India that is the novel's setting. Thus, for example, caught at a moment of pensive absent-mindedness, the Judge is described rather uncongenially as 'a creature of the Galapagos staring over the ocean' (33).

In opposition to Ghosh's subaltern blueprint of the cosmopolitan Indian writer as 'engag[ing] in a literary politics that interrupts their own global circulation and rejects an overt festishistic localism' (2004: 20), Desai proceeds, without much critical self-consciousness, to pander to a global readership's expectations of what makes a good Anglo-Indian read. *The Inheritance of Loss* paints an entirely predictable, nostalgia-ridden picture of a post-imperial idyll that finds its enormous romantic potential tragically thwarted by politics. Albeit interspersed with occasional references to the postcolonial or globalised particularities of her characters' living conditions, overall Desai's representation lacks Roy's glocalising power of the imagination, causing these references to remain isolated from her vision rather than transfused within it. Instead of political agents, her characters are subjects of fate, trapped in their allocated roles and positions. 'The laws of probability favored their slipping through life', the novel explains, 'but every now and then, somebody suffered the rotten luck of being in the exact wrong place at the exact wrong time when it all caught up – and generations' worth of trouble settled on them' (Desai 2006: 241). Far removed from Ghosh's socio-political definition of the cosmopolitan novel, Desai's vision succumbs to a sense of fateful inevitability. The novel fails to interrogate the ideological contexts that frame the conflicts it describes; nor does it bother to uncover any potential for cosmopolitan subalternity. In Desai's novel nothing ever changes – nothing *can* change. The world takes its course not as history propelled by human desire, intention and initiative, but as a massive tidal undercurrent that eludes any detailed analysis or imaginative crystallisation.

Ghosh's principal criterion for identifying a contemporary Indian novel as genuinely cosmopolitan is the invocation of 'a social imaginary where the cosmopolitical writer acts in solidarity with [. . .] "minority" communities, disenfranchised urban migrant labor, *adivasis* (tribal and indigenous peoples) and *dalits* (low-caste subjects), the rural poor, and other politically and culturally "displaced" subjects of nationalizing and globalizing "development"' (22). Certainly Desai's novel gestures in this direction. Ultimately, however, it is her project to write a best-selling novel about a handful of people in a world that could be beautiful and perfect were it not for the awkward interference of misguided politics and economic injustice. Her characters remain locked into the novel, always immediately at her authorial heel and castrated of whatever inoperative potentialities they may own. The novel is irritatingly formulaic and devoid of mobility. A poignant example in this context is Desai's portrayal of Biju's eventual return from New York and his melodramatic reunion with his father, which closes the novel: 'Sai looked out and saw two figures leaping at each other as the gate swung open.' Initially worrying only because it seems so disappointingly inconsequential in political terms, this final scene turns out to be not quite the novel's last word. Against the background of Biju's reunion with his father Desai invokes a crypto-epiphanic truth that sounds a bit like a magical afterthought: 'The five peaks of Kanchenjunga turned golden with the kind of luminous light that made you feel, if briefly, that truth was apparent. All you needed to do was reach out and pluck it' (324). As the denouement to a novel that has consistently presented its characters as deprived of agency, such an invocation of individual freedom and the whole world at your feet must appear, to put it mildly, incongruous.

The incongruity of the novel's ending highlights Desai's monologic disposition, her inability to develop a truly empathic sense of solidarity with the plight of her characters. The universalised 'you' in Desai's final vision identifies an observer unaffected by the tale of Biju and his father, reducing the latter's reunion to a fairy-tale tableau securely fixed in the background. This 'you' at once addresses and incorporates the heroine, the author and – by implication – the reader, universalising in other words Sai's own perspective as that of 'a westernized Indian brought up by English nuns, an estranged Indian living in India' (Desai 2006: 210). Desai's final vision begs not only the question which, or whose, truth precisely the author may have in mind, but also who might be suitably equipped and sufficiently at leisure to avail themselves of it. Downplaying globalisation's callousness, the novel's ending signals severe failure on the part of the author to respond adequately to Biju's humiliation and his father's dashed hopes for his son to make a better life for himself in the USA. As a result, Desai's Anglo-Indian novel seems devoid of any genuinely cosmopolitical, world-creative sensibility; instead, it appears keen in its final vision to project a facile get-up-and-go conception of Third World subjectivity that smacks precariously of current US American neo-liberalism. Possibly it could also be seen to be signalling, as Rüdiger Kunow suggests in his reading of Salman Rushdie's most recent work, that unless we proceed with great caution and always reflect on whose story we are actually in the process of recounting, our world may be at risk of becoming one in which even 'the subaltern cannot but speak American' (2006: 383).

In *The Inheritance of Loss* Biju's experiences as an illegal immigrant in New York never unfold into a story line that would allow us to acquire a sense of the specific diasporic locale in which it is set. Cursory and clichéd depiction takes the place of empathic enquiry, and ultimately what we are dealt is a plethora of truisms and platitudes. For instance, it is revealed to us that the USA is a capitalist upstairs/downstairs society, which, as political statements go, is neither news nor indeed a discovery that captures a USA-specific truth. In the same way that Desai's portrayal of Cho Oyu is strongly reminiscent of the representation of similar localities in other Anglo-Indian writing, her portrayal of contemporary New York's underbelly of economic exploitation appears informed neither by hands-on research nor by visionary inspiration; indeed, it seems predicated entirely on the notions and imageries typical of politically correct hearsay or human-interest media coverage. Ironically, aiming for a sense of global complexity, Desai cannot imagine the exact specificity of Biju's plight and, as a result, her novel falls flat in terms of cosmopolitan world-creation.

At one point Desai adopts the perspective of Biju's 'cosmopolitan' employers as they skim the international news section in the *New York Times*. The aim is presumably to capture the whole noisy clamour of postcoloniality, its unwieldy commotion of demands and accusations, and its wild, hysterical scramble for justice. In the end, however, what we are presented with by Desai is a mere listing of nationalities, the names of international corporations and governmental bodies, interspersed with muddled allegations of cause and effect – a listing, in other words, that fails spectacularly to register the horror and outrage of a single instance of actual suffering in the world:

> It was overwhelming.
>   Former slaves and natives. Eskimos and Hiroshima people, Amazonian Indians and Chiapas Indians and Chilean Indians and American Indians and Indian Indians. Australian aborigines, Guatemalans and Colombians and Brazilians and Argentineans, Nigerians, Burmese, Angolans, Peruvians, Ecuadorians, Bolivians, Afghans, Cambodians, Rwandans, Filipinos, Indonesians, Liberians, Borneoans, Papua New Guineans, South Africans, Iraqis, Iranians, Turks, Armenians, Palestinians, French Guyanese, Dutch Guyanese, Surinamese, Sierre Leonese, Malgasys, Senegalese, Maldivians, Sri Lankans, Malaysians, Kenyans, Panamanians, Mexicans, Haitians, Dominicans, Costa Ricans, Congoans, Mauritanians, Marshall Islanders, Tahitians, Gabonese, Beninese, Malians, Jamaicans, Botswanans, Burundians, Sudanese, Eritreans, Uruguyans, Nicaraguans, Ugandans, Ivory Coastians, Zambians, Guinea-Bissauans, Cameroonians, Laotians, Zaireans coming at you screaming colonialism, screaming slavery, screaming mining companies screaming banana companies oil companies screaming CIA spy among the missionaries screaming it was Kissinger who killed their father and why don't you forgive third-world debt; Lumumba, they shouted, and Allende; on the other side, Pinochet, they said, Mobutu; contaminated milk from Nestlé, they said; Agent Orange; dirty dealings by Xerox. World Bank, UN, IMF, everything run by white people. Every day in the papers another thing! (133–4)

What this section amounts to is a declaration of narrative defeat. Desai's enumeration works to harden the world from a diverse, heterogeneous hive of activity into one plaintive, turgidly homogeneous mass. The world is reduced to one huge, noisy blur of grief, impervious to all analytical or imaginative unravelling, subaltern initiative or political intervention. The implied 'you' avalanched by this global welter of postcolonial agitation is once again the heroine, the author and the reader, that is, members of a certain class, world-political positioning and influence, whose jaundiced response to this daily surge of world-wide fury Desai is able to envisage adequately enough. By contrast, whatever feebly ventriloquised fabrication of a voice Biju is equipped with in the novel succumbs to erasure, drawing attention to the glaring imbalance in Desai's representation between the privileged few, whose lives are portrayed in pithy, fleshed-out detail, and the destitute masses, whose lives scarcely substantiate even as apparitional adumbrations. Desai's novel ends up doing very little justice to local specificity; nor does it adequately picture, let alone grasp, globalised complexity. Left unglocalised, the world's potential for convivial connectivity, its potential for correlation beyond anachronistic binaries, is stifled into mere agglomeration. In effect, what Desai offers us here is a most disheartening sample of *representational* 'heapage', or literary glomicity.

Though without doubt well-intentioned, Desai's anti-globalist stance is marred by her middle-class bias and moral self-righteousness, her political naivety, as well as a most unfortunate penchant for generalisations. According to her, 'from other kitchens, [Biju] was learning what the world thought of Indians', namely that 'if they could, they would throw them out' (77). Once again, characteristic of the author's apparent disdain for detail and elaboration, what follows this allegation adds up only to a random listing of some of the nation states believed to harbour a particular dislike for Indians, including Nigeria, Madagascar, Germany and Italy but – perhaps surprisingly – not the United Kingdom. What this listing occludes is that surely there must be differences in the treatment of foreigners by countries that do have some level of anti-racialist and equal-opportunities legislation and those that do not, between democracies and dictatorships or corrupt oligarchies. In any case it would be highly unproductive to subscribe to Desai's proposition that most of the world is against Indians. Does this in any way reflect her own experience as an expatriate? The kind of welcome she received whilst being educated in Britain and the USA? Is this how one ought to interpret her winning of the Booker Prize? Loath as it clearly is to figure out subtle nuances and crucial differences, in the end the cosmopolitan vision of *The Inheritance of Loss* looks acutely under-developed. Desai cannot see the world outside the gridwork of nation-alist enclaves; her agglomerative mantra of nation states confirms the novel strictly as a *tour d'horizon* rather than a *tour du monde*. Desai thinks of her characters solely in terms of the passports they hold, and she fails to imagine any new, alternative (multitudinous, cosmopolitan, inoperative) forms of belonging. It registers with her as no contradiction that Nigerians and Malagasys feature in her listings as both riotous postcolonials and anti-Indian xenophobes. Unlike that of Roy, who zooms in on the whole world through concentration on just one of its innumerable microcosmic manifestations, Desai's vision is always already globalised and remains out of focus throughout. As a result, her novel's promise of cosmopolitan subalternity expends itself in abrupt bouts of self-righteous polemicising rather than unfolding into a sustained effort at world-creative glocalisation.

Another striking difference between Desai's and Roy's novels resides in their portrayal of the correlation between sexual love and politics, which in the former are discretely juxtaposed as separate spheres, whereas in the latter they emerge as inextricably entwined. In *The God of Small Things* the destruction of love and desire is portrayed as the 'work' of politics, its œuvre and dark apotheosis. Illicit, unruly intimacy is shown to collide with the power of the state – that is, the power of a systemically organised, ideologically fortified, communal order. As in any sacrificial ritual, the hope and the horror illuminate each other: thus, Velutha's untouchable singularity is at its most radiant at the moment of its destruction when it imprints itself traumatically on the community. By comparison, in *The Inheritance of Loss* there is no such mutual implication or sacrificial subsumption of one within the other. Sai and Gyan's love is never imbued with any particular communal significance or incorporative power; indeed, it is represented as disruptive, otherworldly and thoroughly apolitical. While her elders discuss 'terrorists, guerrillas, insurgents, rebels, agitators, instigators, and they all learn from one another, of course – the Neps have been encouraged by the Sikhs and their Khalistan, by ULFA, NEFA, PLA; Jharkland, Bodoland, Gorkhaland; Tripura, Mizoram, Maipur, Kashmir, Punjab, Assam', Sai can think only of 'how she turned to water under Gyan's hands' (128–9). When eventually their love is destroyed by circumstance, its demise appears as little more than collateral damage, devoid of any crucial expurgatory power.

Desai ruminates on 'the unfairness of things; justice [. . .] might snag the stealer of chickens, but great evasive crimes would have to be dismissed because, if identified and netted, they would bring down the entire structure of so-called civilization' (200). Roy, by contrast, demonstrates not only that crime and justice are not always so easily told apart, but also that in an increasingly globalised world it proves virtually impossible to distinguish between 'great' and 'small' crimes (see also Dallmayr 2005: 77–93). The greatest and most horrific crimes are surely those involving the individual and the humiliation, persecution and erasure or extermination of his or her singularity. The 'small' crime of killing an untouchable is at once the 'great' crime of killing the God of Small Things. The cruelty of Velutha's execution eviscerates the system of whatever ideals it may believably have owned, but that is not to say the system must collapse. Civilisation has been fed to its own operative monstrosity a thousand times before. Unlike Desai, who purports to be interested in identifying justice and guilt on a global scale,

Roy suggests that perhaps it is at home, in our immediate neighbour-hood, where the world is best observed in the process of un/working itself, full at once of hope and of potential horror.

Unlike Roy's and Desai's novels Hari Kunzru's *Transmission*, set across a vertiginous range of locations from India, California and London to the Scottish Highlands and cyberspace, is neither unfolding from nor directed towards a homecoming; rather, the narrative opens on the preparations for a departure. The novel then grows into the account of an Indian migrant worker's ill-omened effort to succeed professionally in the USA, followed by a global Wanted Man chase and, eventually, a mysterious vanishing act. In its final pages the novel somehow loses sight of Arjun Mehta, the protagonist, who becomes untraceable, quite as if he had made his escape through a thin partitioning into another world whence occasionally, during a momentary lapse of real-world concentration, he rematerialises as a fleeting world-creative promise of subaltern resistance.

The majority of locations in *Transmission* – from India's outsize urban-boom industrial estates, office complexes and chic apartment blocks to California's inner-city highways and retail parks and London's luxury penthouses and high-spec towers housing glitzy, elaborate busi-ness suites – fit perfectly Marc Augé's category of the 'non-place', the kind of purely functional, agglomerative space that is so ubiquitous in our supermodern life-world and 'which cannot be defined as relational, or historical, or concerned with identity' (1995: 77–8). As Augé explains:

> The new towns produced by technicist and voluntarist urbanization projects have often been criticized for failing to offer 'places for living', equivalent to those produced by an older, slower history: where individual itineraries can intersect and mingle, where a few words are exchanged and solitudes momentarily forgotten, on the church steps, in front of the town hall, at the café counter or in the baker's doorway: the rather lazy rhythm and talkative mood that still characterize Sunday mornings in contemporary provincial France. (66–7)

Not only inhibitive, but deeply suspicious of neighbourly sociability and in fact any kind of spontaneous inoperative encounter, our immedi-ate life-world has in certain extreme cases become so regulated, pre-scribed and self-alienated that, as Kunzru notes, 'anyone on foot in suburban California is [perceived as] one of four things: poor, foreign, mentally ill or jogging' (38). Even a place like the Scottish Highlands, renowned for its local splendour and no stranger to flaunting its com-munal history, is shown to bring about no genuine cultural exchange, but appears only as the carefully cordoned-off backdrop for the shooting of a scene in a Bollywood movie, into which its cultural identity is worked as a quaintly decorative, momentary distraction. Wherever Kunzru's novel transports us exposes the same globalised scenario governed by questions of marketability, the hustle and bustle of public relations, the cult of celebrity, and the ceaseless scramble for advertising space and other commercial ventures. Invariably, these pursuits are granted centre-stage priority over the dull quotidian struggle for human dignity, or plain and simple economic survival. *Transmission* depicts humanity on the brink of absorption into the man-made artifice of the virtual, at once abstract, make-believe, and relentless in its impact on real life. Life itself is being marginalised, as connectivity and conviviality have shifted from an actual experience of community to defining people's virtual on-screen interaction, be it mediated by mainstream cinema, computer games or the internet. Life has begun not only to mirror or imitate virtuality, but to be eclipsed and drowned out by it. In such a context globalisation comes to look like a direct corollary of 'Virtual World Syndrome' (289), within whose scope all is well as long as 'Player Mehta [is happy to] proceed' according to plan (23), that is, as long as he can be relied upon never to do anything unheard-of, let alone venture into writing his own programs or going cosmopolitan.

Transmission tells the story of two kinds of mobility, that of Arjun Mehta and that of Guy Swift who, representative of a new hot-shot breed of young British entrepreneurs, runs an international advertising and PR agency in the City. The novel complicates the categorical division of humanity – so common within globalisation studies and postcolonial theory – into the rich and privileged, on the one hand, and the utterly dispossessed, on the other. Introducing Arjun as a talented and ambitious college graduate from a solidly middle-class background, the narrative wedges open a third, in-between space rapidly colonised by a growing number of migrant professionals – Indians who are not embarked on either one of Roy's convoys, whose journey (let alone their ultimate destination) remains subject to imaginative conjecture, who are neither traditional Anglo-Indians like Sai and her grandfather, nor members of the servant classes like Gyan or Biju. Strikingly reminiscent of the anti-heroic disposition of James Kelman's Jeremiah Brown in *You Have to Be Careful in the Land of the Free*, Arjun succumbs to the allure of the American Dream and leaves home in the hope of launching himself in the USA. Once there, however, he finds himself swiftly degraded to the status of a second-class citizen or, more aptly speaking, that of a highly skilled, yet entirely disenfranchised serf.

Arjun is the victim of an exploitative recruitment agency that specialises in luring trusting young Indian professionals to the USA, where they are hired out on the cheap as disposable labour before eventually being deported home, humiliated and penniless. It is only due to his exceptional talent and resourcefulness that Arjun is able to begin forging for himself a possible way out of this vicious circle of economic commodification and systematised invisibility. Obviously he remains worlds removed from sharing 'the sublime mobility of those who travel without ever touching the ground', yet, unlike Biju in Desai's novel or Kelman's underdog Americans, he has what it takes to resist 'the other mobility, the forced motion of the shopping-cart pushers, the collectors of cardboard boxes' (47). Displaying a conspicuously American individualism, Arjun emerges as an exotic subaltern who not only acquires passable proficiency in speaking the language of his oppressors, but avails himself of the right to have his own say, however momentarily, by inserting a disruptive counter-code of his own making, shutting up everybody by stopping the system dead. Admittedly, he overshoots the mark: temporarily employed by an anti-virus software-development firm, Arjun is so keen to demonstrate his expertise that he designs and unleashes a new virus, for which he subsequently intends triumphantly to provide the cure. But the virus, manifesting as a pop-up video clip from Arjun's favourite Bollywood movie starring his idol and secret love interest, the actress Leela Zahir, develops a life of its own, and the damage it causes to the system worldwide veers catastrophically out of control:

> Experts have estimated her damage to global business at almost 50 billion US dollars, mostly in human and machine downtime, but financial calculation doesn't capture the chaos of those days. During Leila's brief period of misrule, normality was completely overturned. Lines of idle brokers chewed their nails in front of frozen screens. Network nodes winked out of existence like so many extinguished stars. For a few weeks she danced her way around the world, and disaster, like an overweight suburbanite in front of a workout video, followed every step. (4)

The carnivalesque subalternity that is Leela's unsolicited dance routine taunts the world of globalised commerce by rendering it inoperative, making her a potent in-your-face icon of cosmopolitan subalternity.

As it rampages through the strongholds of global capitalism, Arjun's super-virus spreads like a new form of advertising, not only promoting Bollywood cinema and Leela's celebrity in particular but also, more significantly, alerting the world to an increasingly arresting Third World presence that will no longer be confined to the margins. As the novel asserts, 'Leela was in the system like a quintessence, a breath' (157). In comparison to the topical relevance, vivacity and devastating impact of Arjun's virus, the PR business run by Guy Swift, formerly so brilliant at flogging intangible visions and 'convincing people to channel their emotions, relationships and sense of self through the purchase of products and services' (122), must look rather flat and uninspired, even slightly anachronistic. Guy's futurist aspirations, his love for boundless supermodern abstraction, and his knack for thriving in relationally uncharted 'non-places' (like airports) that keep his identity safely off the ground and help continually 'to ease his transition into the next world' (22), contrast markedly with Arjun's cosmopolitan rootedness in real life's immediate heres and nows. Although he would undoubtedly describe himself as a self-aware, on-the-pulse cosmopolitan, Guy's understanding of the world is in fact remarkably blinkered and old-fashioned; his busy, jet-setting, globalised lifestyle has left him unequipped with a suitable cosmopolitan vision.

As his work for PEBA (Kunzru's dystopian projection of a Pan-European Border Agency) signals, Guy cannot conceive of the world as mutually permeable or inextricably interdependent. Instead, he continues to subscribe to what is essentially a national-imperialist outlook, even if the nation-cum-empire in question is now that of a United Europe or, in Guy's formulation, 'Club Europa – the world's VIP room' (257). 'Offer[ing] the opportunity to brand the entire combined European customs and immigration regime. Logos, uniforms, the presentation of a whole continent's border police' (229), Guy's work on behalf of PEBA enables Kunzru to expose the fortress mentality of contemporary European Union politics, a politics predicated on the exclusion and even categorical abjection of components unquestionably integral to itself such as, for example, 'Third World' Albania. Europe becomes simply yet another business venture, a self-professed corporate giant oblivious to how the ranking-by-numbers of parts of the world ignores their crucial mutual embedment in one another as well as their ultimate parity as indispensable nodes – however underdeveloped or 'rogue' – in one and the same network, a network that remains dangerously vulnerable to subaltern – or 'terrorist' – contagion. Guy's politics, and that of people like him, is defined not by attempts to redesign or recast the global body politic, but by regularly fitting it out with new, glamorous attire. History is reduced to a mere flurry of swiftly manufactured and equally swiftly discarded surfaces. As long as power is ensured to look as though it has the x-factor, it is guaranteed to persist uncontested:

> The whole look and feel of immigration, customs, border police – all these things are so old-fashioned at the moment. The uniforms! My God, it's like some twentieth-century bad dream. If you could make it more – more *funky*,

instantly it would be so much better, more acceptable to modern people. All the protest they get, all the negativity, most of it is about the *feel* of these things. People don't give a shit about power, not really, not if it looks cool. (261–2)

Unchecked, Guy's attitude and outlook will 'imagineer the future' (227) into the kind of nightmare world depicted by David Mitchell in 'An Orison of Sonmi-451' in *Cloud Atlas*, a world in which other human beings are reduced to mere conveniences, perfectly instrumentalised enhancements of one's own privileged lifestyle, pliant ancillaries with no desires of their own. Notably, Guy perceives a flight attendant who is waiting on him as 'just a tool, the uniformed probe-head of the large corporate machine in which he was enmeshed' (13). This reflects of course exactly the kind of commodification and radical eclipse of his humanity that Arjun rebels against in *Transmission*.

Unlike Biju in Desai's representation, which centres on the powerless exposure of Third World economic migrants to the exploitative forces of globalisation, Arjun is portrayed as endowed with the promise of cosmopolitan agency. Yet far from putting this promise to unequivocally emancipatory use, Kunzru shrewdly manipulates it to capture the potentially tragic complicity of the victim in his own ruination. In *Transmission* the lines between European players and Third World pawns are blurred, as globalisation is revealed to be so all-encompassing because absolutely nobody on the planet is inured to the appeal of its mail-order catalogues of desire and logo-imprinted shopping bags of branded dreams. Though quite literally travelling on different planes and in opposite directions – Guy Swift playing Terris on his laptop in air-conditioned business class, while 30,000 feet below him Arjun Mehta daydreams among a throng of people on a dilapidated Third World bus – the lives of both men also run parallel to each other, if by no means perfectly in tandem. Both Arjun and Guy have their eyes fixed on the future. The ideas they have of themselves are thoroughly globalised in the sense that both of them are prepared to give in to total cultural deracination and self-estrangement from any specific locality, which is the price one allegedly pays for global mobility. In the grip of neo-liberalism's myth of unlimited self-fulfilment through economic success, neither displays any interest in ethical fair play or cosmopolitics. Kunzru's grasp of Arjun's alienation in this context is particularly striking. 'Lost in his inner retail space, he stared blankly out of the window', it reads, 'his eyes barely registering the low roofs of patch-worked thatch and blue polythene by the roadside, the ragged children, standing under the tangle of illegally strung power-lines' (11). Arjun's vision of his future is globalised, yet far from projecting the wretched passivity or hybrid self-empowerment cited in much academic theorising. Only misfortune turns him into a cosmopolitan subaltern in the end, but even then his intransigence is inadvertent rather than due to a natural or culturally determined disposition, any clear-cut political design, plan or intention. Arjun takes after the 'citizens of the postcolony' who, according to Simon Gikandi, are 'likely to seek their global identity by invoking the very logic of Enlightenment that postcolonial theory was supposed to deconstruct', and who are, 'Bhabha notwithstanding, tethered to the myth of progress' (2001: 630, 642).

Kunzru's novel mentions a random news item concerning the discovery of the bodies of two Ghanaian boys frozen to the undercarriage of a Boeing 747 at London Heathrow (127). The item is based on a real-life incident, discussed at length by Gikandi, namely the retrieval of the bodies of two Guinean teenagers from the cargo hold of a plane to Brussels in August 1998. Identifying these two boys 'as representatives of hundreds of other migrants who die every day trying to get "there" to be "like you"' (643), Gikandi demolishes the categorical idealisation of Third World migrancy in some highly theorised postcolonial discourse. As Gikandi protests, these boys 'were neither seeking cultural hybridity nor ontological difference. Their quest was for a modern life in the European sense of the word; their risky journey from Africa was an attempt to escape both poverty and alterity.' According to Gikandi, the boys' deaths must be understood as a direct result of their conviction 'that their salvation could only come from [. . .] Europe' (630–1). Similarly, in *Transmission* – even though from the start he is immeasurably better equipped for his journey than the two Guinean boys, who had neither money nor education – Arjun believes he is destined to fulfil himself in the West; in fact, nowhere else than US America (certainly not India) will do. What Arjun wants is unequivocal; he dreams of becoming a US citizen. Rather than entrusting his life to an incessant proliferation of new cultural positions, or settling in an *ou*-topian 'third space' of intercultural encounter (which might ultimately prove uninhabitable), he wants to free himself of the yoke of postcoloniality and quite simply live, and be at home, in America. Put in Gikandi's words, like the two Guinean boys' Arjun's 'identification with globality is not ethical but material; [he does] not seek to occupy the interstitial spaces between nations and cultures, but to leave what he consider[s] to be a failed polity for a successful one' (2001: 643). Accused by his Indian employer of acting unpatriotically by leaving the country and thus depriving his people of his talent and expertise, Arjun remains unmoved, musing that 'if India had wanted him for something it would probably have asked' (2004: 24).

Arjun's departure to the USA is not so very far removed from the Americanisation of a whole generation of middle-class Indians who decide to stay at home. As Vijayasree Chaganti and Kanukolanuk Ravichandra document, there are countless 'well-qualified university graduates employed in call centres [who] live to American timings, sleeping when their society is awake and staying awake when their families and the world are fast asleep' (2006: 216). Rather than becoming Americans, or 'citizens of the world' for that matter, these young Indians never exceed the status of mere 'IT coolies', which is of course a label equally applicable to Arjun. *Transmission* highlights the distinction that must be upheld between the processes of globalisation and cosmopolitanisation. Whereas the former requires individuals to give up their local affiliation and allow themselves to be absorbed into the homogeneous, economically driven chimera of one and the same globalised dream, the latter promotes world-creative self-formation predicated on the belief that one can only make a worthwhile contribution to world culture by drawing on the local specificity of one's origin. Tomlinson explains globalisation's economic determination of the world by arguing that due to the ways in which we have become used to working and living, we cannot but internalise and disseminate what he calls 'the ethos and values of corporate capitalism and consumerism', which results in the creation of 'a cultural totality – a "way of life" and a "developmental path" for developing nations to follow' (1999: 82). Tomlinson questions the inevitability of this world-communal trajectory of globalisation, its unilateralism and seemingly unstoppable unilinearity, proposing that 'movement between cultural/geographical areas always involves interpretation, translation, mutation, adaptation, and "indigenization" as the receiving culture brings its own cultural responses to bear, in dialectical fashion, upon "cultural imports"' (84). In his view, the world's infinite spectrum of local diversity is well equipped to resist being globalised into one homogeneous whole. Therefore, lest it serve as a finely tuned discourse in support of economic globalisation, cosmopolitanism must forever insist on its rootedness in the multitudinous heterogeneity of the locally specific. That even someone as irremediably globalised as Arjun harbours huge cosmopolitan potential is revealed only by accident. Notably, however, this accident discloses his Indianness unmistakably and beyond doubt, as it manifests itself for the whole world to behold in the corporeality of Leela, his one and only true love.

In terms of conceptual organisation *Transmission* falls into two sections: 'Signal' and the much shorter, coda-like 'Noise', which has only about 25 pages and concludes the novel by speculating on the future of the central characters following Arjun's mysterious disappearance on the US–Mexican border. Kunzru's design corresponds in interesting and illuminating ways with Jean-Luc Nancy's faith in the remedial power of the inoperative, not as chaos, but as a promise of unforeseeable, original world-creation opening up beyond the grasp of systemic capture. 'Signal' is defined as 'perfect information [. . .] transmitted from a sender to a receiver without loss, without the introduction of the smallest uncertainty of confusion' while, as Kunzru reminds us, 'in the real world [. . .] there is always noise' (271). Ingeniously, the novel loosens its grip on its characters and events, bringing about a deliberate dis-emplotment, which causes the narrative not so much to unravel as fruitfully to disperse. The characters are released into a radical freedom that possesses no clearly identifiable, definitive shape lest it tighten into another formative imposition. Kunzru's novel hands itself over to the inoperative productivity of Nancean interruption, after which something new is shown to emanate into the world, something that would relinquish its power should it show or declare itself too unequivocally. It is tempting to liken the ending of *Transmission* – or, rather, its gradual dispersion into an all-encompassing global 'noise' – as a narrative rendition of Roland Robertson's idea of 'deglobalisation', by which he means all 'attempts to undo the compression of the world'. Robertson reminds us 'that movements, institutions and individuals have not merely been implicated in actions that have propelled the overall globalization process but that quite frequently there has been resistance to this' as well (1992: 10). Arjun's sabotage of the system, however inadvertent or accidental it may be, sets in motion exactly such a dynamic of deglobalisation, which also radically recasts the shape and trajectory of his own life.

Both of Kunzru's central protagonists – Guy as hero and Arjun as anti-hero (or vice versa if you will) – are shown to drop out of the overarching narrative of globalisation. Guy becomes the victim of a case of mistaken identity. Confused with an illegal immigrant from Albania, he finds himself at the receiving end of PEBA's new, aggressive immigration laws and is swiftly deported, no questions asked. On his return to Britain he is a changed man. When the journalists catch up with him he is running a pottery in a ramshackle hut somewhere in rural England, probably the world's least likely convert ever to reclusive local living. Recovering from 'geopathic stress', Guy now sees the dislocated urban lifestyle he used to lead as a symptom of increasing glomicity, with large cities causing 'an immense distortion of the earth's natural energy field, a distortion which inflicts physical and psychological suffering on the people forced to live inside it' (277). Meanwhile Arjun avoids being tracked down by the authorities and their security forces through a miraculous vanishing act, the exact details of which remain undisclosed. What the novel does intimate, however, is that in his new undercover existence Arjun is joined by Leela, who has also run away, seeking refuge from her impending iconisation as Bollywood's next rising star.

Together the lovers accomplish the impossible, namely to be in the world, yet lead deglobalised lives. Their new cosmopolitan subalternity affords them a barely imaginable freedom. 'How is it possible', the novel marvels, 'in a world of electronic trails, log files, biometrics and physical traces of every kind to slip so completely away?' (291). While retaining their apparitional elusiveness and indeterminacy, Arjun and Leela also appear to encompass the whole of humanity. 'She is seen begging in the streets of Jakarta and talking on the phone in the back of New York cabs', the novel concludes, while 'he is spotted one day at an anti-globalization demo in Paris and the next coming on to the pitch in a hockey match in rural Gujarat' (297). And yet, however joyously inoperative at last, their lives are by no means exempt from being systemically put to work. Propelled by people's 'hope that the genius hacker might also be a revolutionary' (287), the truant couple are elevated to the status of grassroots celebrities. The story of their lives falls prey to organised use within a newly emergent spectrum of anti-globalisation movements, the political agendas of which prove too ideologically fraught to be identified as truly cosmopolitan in the Nancean sense of the term.

As it closes on the final vision of two renegade lovers walking carefree into a tropical sunset (most sightings of Arjun and Leela are reported from countries of the Pacific Rim), *Transmission* identifies itself as a novel that bears immense potential for postcolonial myth-making. This potential, however, is resisted by Kunzru, who indicates, on the one hand, that 'there is only one possible explanation, only one pattern that makes sense' while, on the other, he instantly disparages such absolute certainty by attributing it to the feverish imagination of 'conspiracy theorists' (297). In both Roy's and Kunzru's novels, the promise of cosmopolitan world-creation resides firmly with the lovers, the delicate smallness and desperate fragility of whose 'tomorrow' (Roy 1997: 340) stands in stark contrast to Desai's incongruously triumphant reference to a universally applicable truth at the close of *The Inheritance of Loss*. Very similar in their final vision to Mitchell's novels, both *Transmission* and *The God of Small Things* subvert the global standard of big, over-arching structures of meaning by introducing their own cosmopolitan aesthetics of the personal and 'small'. Resonating with Kunzru's conceptual distinction between 'noise' and 'signal', Roy's locally inflected language of familial turmoil creates a powerful semiotic undercurrent to the unbending absolutes of Indian tradition and state bureaucracy. Both novels are aimed not at problematising or re-envisioning nationalist and neo-imperial politics but simply at their interruption. In the novels' cosmopolitan representation, even US America seems at times about to disclose itself as a mere locality rather than a superimposed globalising structure or system of world governance. By contrast, Desai yields without reservation to US America's hegemonic self-abstraction as a set of principles and universal way of life; not once does her novel shift from its globalised perspective and achieve the kind of local insider's immersion that recommends Roy's and Kunzru's narration. As cosmopolitical worldings go, Biju's homecoming simply cannot compare to Arjun's disappearance at the end of *Transmission*, his radical dislocation, which Kunzru somehow contrives to present to us as a promise of ubiquitous glocalisation, opening up and spreading in between the increasingly piled-up surfaces of corporate glomicity.

Towards the end of 'Myth Interrupted' Nancy asserts that 'each writer, each work inaugurates a community'. Literature fulfils itself – albeit never in the sense of definitive self-completion – 'in coming to the limit, in letting the limit appear as such, in interrupting the myth' (1991: 68), and each limit is a point of renewed departure. Therefore, beyond whatever realist aspirations and political commitments it may be in pursuit of, the cosmopolitan novel *as* literature invariably opens up onto something new. From the foreseeable and expected it veers off into representational territory beyond its own comprehension. Roy's and Kunzru's narration yields to this dynamic. As a result, their novels are fruitfully incapacitated from delivering closure. Desai's novel, by contrast, follows a given blueprint; at every turn the author appears to know exactly what it is she will convey. Unequivocally Desai's end product is an Anglo-Indian novel that accommodates twenty-first-century globalisation as a theme, yet never allows it to initiate a communal unfolding against, let alone beyond, the given formula. Keen to be recognised as fitting the brand of the Anglo-Indian novel, *The Inheritance of Loss* contributes to the library of postcolonialist myth.

According to Nancy, 'the most solitary of writers writes only for the other', adding that 'anyone who writes for the same, for himself [sic!], or for the anonymity of the crowd is not a writer' (66). It seems to me that Desai is never out there on her own; she would not know how to practise the kind of narrative exposition Nancy envisages as occurring between author, character(s) and reader. Intended to appeal to a particular community of readers, her novel is written for a clearly defined market. Desai's is a postcolonial novel in which cosmopolitanism and subalternity are of necessity delegated to different, mutually exclusive spheres. To conceive of cosmopolitan subalternity, which would necessitate the inauguration of an altogether different community, never occurs to her.

Chapter 5

Suburban Worlds: Rachel Cusk and Jon McGregor

There is no imagining of the world that does not commence at home, that does not crystallise out of, and remain coloured by, at least some degree of local specificity. But what if the specificity of the place within which such an imagining of the world is grounded is peculiarly – even purposely – bland and non-descript, not so much reduced to uniformity and compliance by a process of global homogenisation as simply mirroring the agglomerative and self-compartmentalised way in which in the developed world many of us have become accustomed to living? The indifference and functional artifice of suburbia leave little room for either spontaneous or indeed operative assemblages of people into *the* people. Suburbia's pronounced lack of identity, coupled with communal anonymity and inertia, is precisely what defines its identity. Suburbanites tend to assume they have a lot in common with their neighbours, and that therefore their neighbourhood is right for them, but mostly this sense of affinity remains purely imagined, as not much social intercourse that would verify or contest the assumption ever occurs.

My final chapter is dedicated to a reading of Rachel Cusk's sixth novel, *Arlington Park* (2006), and Jon McGregor's debut, *If Nobody Speaks of Remarkable Things* (2002), both of which focus on representations of suburbia. Unequivocal in their contemporary Englishness, the novels differ markedly from McEwan's depiction of city life in *Saturday*, in which there is no mention of neighbours, while staying equally removed from the kind of village communities traditionally associated with portrayals of the English countryside. My main concern will be with the novels' representation of individuality and communal dynamics, the degree to which their narratives open up and aim at creating the world, and the particular ways in which the authors' chosen perspectives and representational techniques facilitate or impede processes of glocalisation, as well as the manifestation of other cosmopolitan habits, modes and states of communal being-in-common.

The Nancean conception of community, which throughout this study has been extended as a model for imagining a cosmopolitan world community of the future, envisages 'a bond that forms ties without attachments, or even less fusion [. . .] a bond that unbinds by binding', leading on to the question of how every one of us might or ought to make sense of 'our multiple, dispersed, mortally fragmented existences, which nonetheless only make sense by existing in common.' How might we conceive of ourselves as being simultaneously an integral part of and forever existentially removed from the totality of everybody else? As one of Nancy's most pressing questions from his preface to *The Inoperative Community* suggests, literary fiction – and the novel in particular – could play a special pioneering role not only in attempting such a daunting feat of the imagination but also in carrying it to fruition: 'How can the community without essence (the community that is neither "people" nor "nation," neither "destiny" nor "generic humanity," etc.) be presented as such?' (1991: xxxix–xl). The suburban novel appears well suited to expose and explore communal living that is at once claustrophobically close and entirely without intimacy, at the same time neighbourly and marked by mutual indifference and anonymity, both tautly uniform and randomly open to all. At first glance uninterested in world-political goings-on, Cusk's and McGregor's novels turn out to comprise detailed, concentrated rehearsals of suburban community, tracing the coincidentally convergent lives of largely unremarkable, adjacent selves.

Both *Arlington Park* and *If Nobody Speaks of Remarkable Things* immerse us in monochromatic English-suburban atmospheres, in which daily lives are for the most part being lived uneventfully. Only McGregor's title alerts us to suburbia's epiphanic potential for a discovery of the miraculous in the ordinary, a feature characteristic of much modernist writing. While Cusk introduces characters desperate to maintain a sense of individual selfhood against the common indistinctiveness they share, McGregor presents us with an intricate network of anonymous next-door strangers who dwell within closest proximity, yet never meet properly. Both Cusk's and McGregor's portrayals of community appear conspicuously Nancean in that even their neighbourhoods' occasional pulling together does not work to unify them into operative wholes; rather, they always quickly relapse into broken mosaics of irremediably atomised subjectivities, who touch and do not touch on one another, who – however closely interconnected – never form an entirety. In this respect they merit comparison with the radically deconstructive cosmopolitan communities Jessica Berman has detected in the works of several modernist writers in her study *Modernist Fiction, Cosmopolitanism, and the Politics of Community* (2001), communities that in Berman's view open up private interpersonal spaces whose peculiar sense of intimacy and estrangement lays the microcosmic foundation for new modes of global communication and belonging.

What will come under close scrutiny in this chapter is the Nancean concept of 'compearance', which describes people's coming into being in necessary relation to one another while retaining their unique separateness. According to Nancy, human living proceeds communally, yet inoperatively, which means that people's self- and world-formation as contemporaries occur in significant, even crucial, yet ultimately arbitrary and purposeless exposition to one another. As Ana Luszczynska puts it in her painstaking exegesis of Nancy's work, 'there is no common, essential, substance in which beings would partake or share and which would exist in a totality superior to them' (2005: 186). Nancean community does not designate everybody's assimilation or organised subscription to a collective entirety, but instead signifies an ordinary being-in-common, at times intensifying or shoring itself up, yet mostly manifesting as simple compearance in gentle communal oscillation.

One crucial difference between Cusk's and McGregor's representations of suburbia is that the former introduces Arlington Park as a residential enclave of fixed containment that summons its inhabitants into a mutually shared identity. The people who live there slot in on arrival, as the place quickly pervades their very sense of self. Strictly demarcated from the city to which it is affiliated, Arlington Park comprises a particular suburbia whose identity asserts itself as distinctly separate from any other's. By contrast, McGregor's section of an unnamed street assumes representational specificity without thus setting itself off or closing itself in. It resists overtly allegorical or mythical signification at the same time as it refuses to reveal any definitive shape or entitative substance. It is unlikely that the implicit communality of McGregor's suburbia would suddenly unravel and disperse beyond house numbers 11 and 27, which delimit the topographical scope of the novel; rather, one imagines it as running on in mutable variation, spreading rhizomatically in all directions. Instead of sharing the same fate or being bound by a common sense of identity, the inhabitants of McGregor's street are simply contemporaries, linked to one another as much by their strictly anonymous adjacency as by a vague, residual sense of neighbourly conviviality and solicitude. Ultimately, what holds them together is compearance rather than identity, crystallising into a more traditional semblance of community only momentarily when a near-fatal car accident disrupts the quotidian uneventfulness of life in the street.

As Berman indicates, excellent illustrative examples of Nancean compearance can be found in the modernist novel, such as Virginia Woolf's portrayal of the parallel lives of mutual strangers Septimus Smith and Clarissa Dalloway in *Mrs Dalloway*, or the central chapter in *To the Lighthouse*, in which contemporaneity takes shape as the loosely correlational coming-into-being and vanishing of atomised selves at both specifically local and broadly global levels. Similarly pronounced cases of compearance characterise the relationship of Perowne and Baxter in McEwan's *Saturday*, that of Guy Swift and Arjun Mehta in Kunzru's *Transmission*, as well as all the characters in Mitchell's *Ghostwritten* and – in a bold complication of the concept by implementing it diachronically – those in *Cloud Atlas*, too. It is important in this context to heed Nancy's explanation that 'compearance is of a more originary order than that of the bond. It does not set itself up, it does not establish itself, it does not emerge among already given subjects.' According to Nancy, compearance 'consists in the appearance of the *between* as such: you *and* I (between us) – a formula in which the *and* does not imply juxtaposition, but exposition' (1991: 29). Accordingly, compearance is never a matter of choice, the upshot of purposeful deliberation or significatory design; it is an existential link that is always already there, coeval and intimately entwined with everybody's original coming-into-being. Emerging in mutual exposition one to the other, we are invariably communally interrelated:

> Community is given to us with being and as being, well in advance of all our projects, desires, and undertakings. At bottom, it is impossible for us to lose community. A society may be as little communitarian as possible; it could not happen that in the social desert there would not be, however slight, even inaccessible, some community. We cannot not compear. (1991: 35)

Compearance, then, cannot ever be exclusively reserved for particular, outstanding individuals, as, for instance, the two protagonists in contradistinction to a novel's background cast of supernumeraries. As McGregor appears to understand, any authentic representational capture of compearance demands for everybody, all our contemporary lives, to be involved: that of 'the boy from number eighteen', 'a man with a long beard', 'the girl with the boots', 'the boy with the pierced eyebrow', and so forth. Compearance is not only radically anti-hegemonic; more crucially, it insists that no one is ever an individual, that in effect 'community cannot be conceived from the point of view of the individual, as the individual is a figure of the absolute and, therefore, utterly without relation' (Luszczynska 2005: 173).

Any novel concerned with imagining compearance must depart from the novel's traditional preoccupation with the individual. Initially *Arlington Park* appears more progressive in this respect since it is focalised through five different perspectives, rather than just one as is the case with McGregor's novel. However, the five women characters brought to life by Cusk remain tethered to the interiors of particular households that despite their obvious commonalities continue to constitute strictly compartmentalised and self-encapsulated, as well as fiercely heteronormative, realms. By contrast, McGregor's decision to focalise his narrative through one single perspective is considerably softened not only by his choice of a male-to-female cross-written view (the narrative voice is that of a young woman confronting the prospect of single motherhood), but also because the narrative voice is designed not primarily to assert itself, nor to control and manage the orchestration of the voices of others. Neither does it set out to conceal its interdependency, that is, its own implication within the network of lives it is deployed to mediate. In fact, whatever individuation is undergone by McGregor's focal character emanates from her exposition within a gradually broadening vista of suburban being-in-common, delicately sustained by a choral mix of singular and collective perspectives. Unlike *Arlington Park*, which records the difficult struggle of female selves to assert themselves against their oppressive entanglement and subsumption within suburban family life, *If Nobody Speaks of Remarkable Things* embeds the self's genesis and ascent to communal intelligibility in processes of cross-written compearance, demonstrating how selves must always materialise out of each other's mutual adumbration.

Nancean thinking entails that novels concerned with the creation of community, let alone global world-creation, are well advised to dispose of the genre's fixation on the individual. According to Nancy, 'the individual is merely the residue of the experience of the dissolution of community. By its nature – as its name indicates, it is the atom, the indivisible – the individual reveals that it is the abstract result of a decomposition' (1991: 3). Rather than representing community's most elementary and original building block the individual induces an infestation at the heart of communal life, causing the latter to lose coherence, crumble and disintegrate. The novel's focus on the individual proves counterproductive to whatever envisioning of community it may be seeking to accomplish at the same time. This is due to the individual's monolithic immobility, its non-negotiable, rigidly autonomous self-enclosure. A radical reconceptualisation of subjectivity is required because, so Nancy insists, 'one cannot make a world with simple atoms'. To facilitate community the self needs to be more generously defined, more malleable and accommodating, as an entity that is pure energy, a particle that is essentially also a measure of radiation, a definite location that nimbus-like always reaches beyond itself, establishing the self first and foremost as a relation instead of a fixity. As Nancy explains, 'there has to be a *clinamen*. There has to be an inclination or an inclining from one toward the other, of one by the other, or from one to the other. Community is at least the *clinamen* of the "individual".' Much of *The Inoperative Community* must be seen as Nancy's endeavour to envisage precisely 'this declination or decline of the individual within community [. . .] outside itself, over that edge that opens up its being-in-common' (1991: 3–4). Importantly, Nancy's investigation is not aimed at the discovery of a 'different' or 'new' kind of self, a self that would make a splendid alternative to the individual; rather, 'according to Nancy, the individual being, [traditionally] conceived, not only reflects an impoverished perspective but is ultimately a logical impossibility' (Luszczynska 2005: 169). Individuality – of which individual*ism* is the globalised inscription – perpetrates a distortion of the human; it is an ideological chimera incapacitating community and crippling the self.

Nancy conceives of the self as a singularity that can only exist in plurality, thus revealing the link between the self and community as intrinsic and coeval instead of contingent. As an immediate corollary, being human – and indeed humanity *per se* – becomes an ethical impulse. In Nancy's view, 'singularity is the passion of being'. Human existence is inseparable from communal responsibility as society is synonymous with 'com-passion', unfolding a blueprint for cosmopolitan living that melds the experiential and the ethical into one:

> The singular being [. . .] is in the passion – the passivity, the suffering, and the excess – of sharing its singularity. The presence of the other does not constitute a boundary that would limit the unleashing of 'my' passions: on the contrary, only exposition to the other unleashes my passions. Whereas the individual can know another individual, juxtaposed to him both as identical to him and as a thing [. . .] the singular being does not know, but rather experiences his *like (son semblable)*. (Nancy 1991: 32–3)

The difference between Cusk's and McGregor's representations of community, then, is rooted in their divergent renditions of subjectivity. Cusk's novel is informed – and, as we shall see, petrified in ethical terms – by the myth of the individual and her unique separateness from her partners and peers, which creates the illusion that the self is able to withdraw and step back into the community at her own free will. By contrast, McGregor's singular beings compear in mutual inextricability as both neighbours and strangers until, in the end, their diversity as variations on the same likeness of contemporary humanity is shown to culminate in a momentary conflagration of communal compassion. McGregor's suburbanites inhabit a world that *is* the *clinamen* of their conviviality, a world that is their experiential-ethical opening up *as* community. Steeped in each other's lives, they are worlds removed from Cusk's hardcore individuals portrayed as solitary islands of thought, feeling and self-reflection, who fastidiously brush themselves down after each agoraphobic venture into the community.

Like Nancean philosophy, McGregor's literary representation asserts that 'humans are fundamentally social in a much more vital and radical sense than is generally thought' (Luszczynska 2005: 192). *If Nobody Speaks of Remarkable Things* will not tolerate individual self-seclusion; in McGregor's rendition of community everybody's every move, feeling and thought are forever accentuated, reflected, contrasted, paralleled or otherwise cast into relief by everybody else's. In McGregor's vision communal relatedness precedes whatever bonds we are socialised into or choose to form consciously. By contrast, oblivious to the foundational axiomatic of compearance, *Arlington Park* fragments in an atrophy of communal compassion as Cusk uses the individual as an implement with which to vivisect community, spawning exultant egotism and abject loneliness in equal measure. Ultimately what we see in Cusk's and McGregor's divergent representations is the distinction Luszczynska makes in her astute unravelling of Nancean compearance between juxtaposition and exposition. 'What occurs in the "between" and the "and" in which compearance is, is not a side-by-sideness of you and I (a juxtaposition) but rather an exposition', she explains. 'In juxtaposition we are almost forced to see the lack of connection indicated, whereas exposition specifically gives the sense of an opening to an outside, thus implying a kind of connection' (2005: 193). Juxtaposition is of course the prevalent (anti-)communal mode of globalisation, propelled by rampant neo-liberal individualism and resulting in worldwide glomicity, whereas exposition vigorously promotes cosmopolitan world-creation. A comparison of Cusk's and McGregor's representations of suburbia highlights in miniature how the insurmountable differences between globalisation and Nancean mondialisation are mainly due to the world's ongoing and indeed increasing faith in the individual. Individualism inscribes an acute misapprehension of the human, positing the individual's precedence over what Fred Dallmayr has called humanity's 'originary sociality' (1997: 181). In effect, it threatens to pull the whole world out of joint.

Rachel Cusk is a neo-modernist writer whose work has been likened, both stylistically and thematically, to that of Virginia Woolf and other modernists. Cusk's novels are engaged in a painstaking, often unrelenting exploration of the contemporary female psyche. They comprise tales of social ineptitude and compulsive-obsessive self-absorption, ill-advised adventure, emotional misapprehension and thwarted expectation. They are also expert at unpeeling the trauma of loneliness, experienced at its starkest amidst one's friends, in the embrace of one's lover, and in the family home. Like *Mrs Dalloway* and also McEwan's *Saturday*, *Arlington Park* follows a day-in-the-life structure geared towards the hosting of a party, in this case the dinner party at the Lanhams' attended by five virtually indistinguishable suburban couples, to some of whose everyday lives we are introduced in the preceding sections of the novel. The novel's effort at building up a sense of community is tense and contrived. The unremarkably fraught marriages of Juliet and Benedict Randall, Christine and Joe Lanham, Maisie and Dom Carrington, and so forth, are presented by Cusk as variations on a ubiquitous theme, showing individuals married against rather than to each other, resulting in couples worlds removed from the cosy, intimately knotted *égoïsme à deux* of McEwan's protagonists.

Whatever fractious and volatile togetherness Cusk's couples share goes under in the vorticious agitation of the individual mind, and especially the female mind, depicted by Cusk as a kind of time-bomb at the centre of an uncharted minefield that is the family. Rather than finding shelter in love, her women must brace themselves against being stripped to the bone by marital duty and maternal affection:

> It was a dangerous place to live in, a family: it was as tumultuous as the open sea beneath a treacherous sky, the shifting allegiances, the flurries of cruelty and virtue, the great battering waves of mood and mortality, the endless alternation of storm and calm. A downpour would come or a reprieving ray of light, and in the end you didn't know what the difference was, what it all meant, what it added up to, when set against the necessity for just surviving and getting through. (Cusk 2006: 186–7)

Cusk's women find themselves exposed not in the Nancean sense within an integrative, if inoperative being-in-common, but in the sense of an elemental, life-threatening exposure. Ostensibly society's bedrock, the family is experienced not as a nurturant communal matrix, but as a poisonous tangle of snares.

Cusk paints a bleak, defeatist picture of contemporary post-feminist womanhood, suggesting that throughout the twentieth century right into our immediate present the pressure on intelligent, well-educated, middle-class women to get married, have children, and self-sacrificially surrender the prospect of a fulfilling career has continued to take its toll. Within well-heeled suburban enclaves like Arlington Park an anachronistic separation of the sexes continues to prevail, casting man in the role of breadwinner and woman in the role of home-maker. Cusk's representation starkly confirms Roger Silverstone's assessment that 'women and men experience suburbia in typically and conventionally, powerfully and divisively distinctive ways' (1997: 5). In Cusk's contemporary suburbia we find the sexes locked in a primordial battle that, both systemically and biologically, women are doomed to lose. To compound matters, post-feminist woman's sense of entrapment is exacerbated by her atomisation as an individual, her loneliness and isolation resulting in a solipsistic worldview and quasi-autistic inability to relate. Long gone are the days when women could be relied upon to be more emotionally attuned, resourceful and 'naturally' adept at establishing and maintaining relationships. Indicatively, Juliet's memory of her first encounter with her husband is that 'she saw him as a prize, her first, in the strange new field of endeavour known as human relationships' (36). In Arlington Park women get together for coffee after dropping off their kids to school, but no sense of communal solidarity develops; no sharing occurs that could pierce the individuality of their encapsulated selves. Even more pronounced is the rift between men and women, their insurmountable, categorical enmity. Not only is Juliet led to conclude that 'all men are murderers [. . .] All of them. They murder women' (18), but she is also guilty of perpetuating this excruciating heteronormativity that works to carve the body of humanity into male and female. Juliet lovingly and sympathetically identifies with her daughter while confessing to a keen, cold-hearted desire to control and discipline her son: 'Oh, how differently she felt when it came to Barnaby! How punitively she yearned to have him in uniform, to have him straitjacketed!' (29). Quite unsurprisingly, then, under such circumstances marriage fails to assume shape as an emotional bond or partnership, but invariably lapses into a mere 'state of hyphenation' (123). Symptomatically Juliet's first thought on waking up in the marital bed in the morning is that 'she and Benedict were not joined but separate' (8).

Cusk's women are victims of exactly the cultural malaise described by Zygmunt Bauman in *Liquid Love* in terms of contemporary humanity's increasing inability to relate, form enduring bonds and create communities, an inability he regards as a direct corollary of 'our world of rampant "individualization"'. Pertinently Bauman dedicates his study to:

Men and women, our contemporaries, despairing at being abandoned to their own wits and feeling easily disposable, yearning for the security of togetherness and for a helping hand to count on in a moment of trouble, and so desperate to 'relate'; yet wary of the state of 'being related' and particularly of being related 'for good', not to mention forever – since they fear that such a state may bring burdens and cause strains they neither feel able nor are willing to bear, and so may severely limit the freedom they need – yes, your guess is right – to relate . . . (2003: viii)

Not only does Juliet's 'inner conviction [. . .] that she was exceptional' (23) make her loath to relate intimately to anyone lest irretrievably she give away something essential of herself, but more significantly it also obscures to her the axiomatic fact of her compearance. It is her faith in her inalienable individuality that tragically signposts her descent into loneliness and self-hyperbole, the like of which we find expressed in her peer Amanda's neurotic need 'to have subjugated the rooms of her house, to have mastered the weekly disciplines of shopping and cooking, to have penetrated her husband, her children, her possessions with such sanitary force that their very natures seemed to recur, like laundry, in a transfigurative cycle of cleanliness' (56–7). Rather than embarking on the world as self-formative community, the kind of individualism that enthrals Cusk's characters grasps the world as an inimical object and territory to be claimed, domesticated and recast after one's own image. This of course is also how, on a much larger scale, globalisation takes its course. Signally, the estrangement and remoteness that are felt within marriage and the family are presented by Cusk as indicative of a deeper alienation and much more profound, global lack of 'fellow feeling':

> It was like when Juliet sometimes stood in front of the television with the remote control [. . .] and a fragment of news would come on the screen. She would see a war or an earthquake, the faces of people in pain or people holding guns, see regions of dust and mountains far away. She would see it, a few instants of turmoil on the other side of the world, and then she would switch over. (25)

Not only is suburbia a safely quarantined world of imperturbable routine where nothing ever really happens, but similar to an impenetrable homeostatic time-capsule its daily existence remains impervious to world events to which it is connected digitally yet without much compassion.

Suburbia shares its relationally challenged crowdedness and forbidding anonymity with Augé's non-places (such as airports, shopping malls and refugee camps). Lives are contained and processed rather than lived fulfillingly. Rather than directly by the people who live there, suburban identity is first and foremost determined functionally or, more precisely, infrastructurally. Yet unlike Augé's non-places suburbia is not 'a world thus surrendered [. . .] to the fleeting, the temporary and ephemeral' (Augé 1995: 78). Its propensity for spawning loneliness and a lack of communal belonging is not generated by too much flux and impermanence but on the contrary because suburban identity possesses very little mutability. Every suburban encounter, be it within or outside the family, serves primarily to affirm and consolidate rather than challenge and develop identity. In other words, encounters occurring within suburbia can no longer truly count as events, a fact that has massive repercussions for suburbia's sense of community. According to B. C. Hutchens, 'community is not merely a collection of selves, but the occurrence of singular events that relate individual selves' (2005: 116). As Hutchens proceeds to explain, 'a community is not an entity that consists of isolated atomic individuals into which other individuals might be introduced. It is neither a pre-existing substantial entity ("our town") nor an entity that gains a substantial identity through mimetic reflection and playing back' (158). Any superimposed model for group- or self-identification that lays greater emphasis on the imagined than on the immediately experiential must stifle whatever community is always already in circulation. Like our increasingly globalised planet, suburbia is at risk of surrendering its world-creative potential to a prefabricated, purely functional system of universal consent and manageability, sacrificing the specificity of local or indigenous community to an imported, individualist uniformity of the masses.

As if to put Arlington Park's communal resourcefulness to the test, about halfway through the novel Cusk shifts her focus momentarily from the interior of individual households to a genuinely communal space, the local commons, which indeed turns out to display a fair amount of mobility. Yet what we come to witness in the park is mainly the mechanised, self-absorbed mobility of joggers, casually scattering whatever natural clusters of conversation are forming among the other visitors of the park – mainly mothers and their children, and the elderly. The overall impression is that leisurely social intercourse is being invaded and elbowed out of the way by spurts of rushed recreational exercise reeling itself off in hectic, asocial circles:

> More people were coming: people in tracksuits and white shoes, running side by side. Two lean, grey-bearded men ran past dressed in black. A girl in a tight vest and headphones ran past. A man in shorts bounded by on long, fantastically muscled legs. A fat lady pattered along behind, her delicate feet barely leaving the ground. A woman with hair cut in steely-grey waves marched in step with her husband: they flung out their elbows, conversing in indignant tones. A young woman on rollerblades propelled a pram along the path and the couple moved aside, still conversing.
> On the grass the man struggled valiantly with his kite. A tall, drooping girl with a melancholic face loped past him, gasping. The man in shorts

came round again and the old man on the bench looked at his watch. (142)

As Christine's ruminations on the personal assets and achievements of her dinner guests in the final chapter of the novel reveal, this self-serving, aimless mobility of the joggers in the park actually makes quite a suitable image for the busy, yet largely ineffectual, disconnected everyday lives led by all the middle-class residents of Arlington Park. Albeit brimming with effort, promise and general well-intentionedness, nobody's life possesses much clout or world-creative impact. Everybody is willing to do their best, but in the end all their vision and motivation amount to is making their own lives a little less insufferable and more 'interesting':

> You worked with what you had and tried to improve it. Look at Dave and Maggie, look at Juliet: look at Maisie if you wanted, trying to make a new life for herself, giving them her own individual perspective on things. Look at Juliet, bringing her skills and qualifications to the table. Look at Maggie, just being generally inspiring, keeping herself together and inspiring them all. They all had a contribution to make, didn't they? They all did their bit, did their best to make life interesting. (235)

What markedly fails to grab the attention of the people of Arlington Park is the world at large, which in their miniature England is offered accommodation only reluctantly. Foreignness is policed by a petty, anachronistic xenophobia all the more depressing for its tedium and predictability. Christine's late father is best remembered for his stale joke that 'the only good Indian was a prawn biryani' (202) while her husband Joe, drunk and bored with making polite after-dinner conversation, listlessly suggests to his peers that 'the English race [. . .] is dying out' (217). A little later in the evening he produces an eighteenth-century colonial toy that re-enacts the scene of a decapitation, consisting of 'a pair of painted figurines beside a painted palm tree [. . .] a man in military uniform with an intricately carved moustache, holding a sword in his clasped hands. The other was a dark-skinned man in a loincloth, kneeling with his head bent forwards over a carved tree stump and his wrists delicately bound behind his back' (228). Yet the evident glee Joe takes in showing the other men how ingeniously this device works comes across as merely silly and mortifying rather than seriously offensive. Showing perhaps that indeed there persists a tenuous post-imperial sense of Englishness that unites the nation across class boundaries, Joe's cringe-worthy performance is mirrored by the brash ignorance of Katie, the Carringtons' working-class teenage baby-sitter, who enthuses about the sunny beaches of Spain, but expresses disdain for the food, which she 'can't stomach', and the people, whom she finds 'chippy'. In Katie's view, the Caribbean might make a more suitable holiday destination if only it were not for 'the natives. You know, the people who live there', whom her boyfriend cannot help but find somehow, inexplicably, objectionable: 'He just thinks he wouldn't like them' (197).

Broader environmental and humanitarian concerns are dealt with in a similarly opinionated and defeatist mode, testifying to an endemic of gross global estrangement and cosmopolitical fatigue among the suburbanites, for whom – just like the Perownes in *Saturday*, in fact – nothing that goes on in the world is ever more than the stuff of moderately heated conversation. As Christine puts it, 'it can get really heavy on a coffee morning, you don't believe me but it can' (70). Yet no calamity is ever pitiful enough, no political failure sufficiently outrageous, and no global threat alarming enough to jolt the suburbanites out of their lethargy. Rather than familiarising us more intimately with the world and introducing it to us as our home, science, the media and the new communication technologies have rendered the planet a foreign and remote, quasi-televisual reality, with us merely watching it, mesmerised yet largely incredulous. Symptomatically, during an altercation with her husband, Maisie notes distractedly that 'the top of Kilimanjaro's melted', but on reading 'that the mountain-top hadn't been visible for eleven thousand years' she dismisses the whole story as that kind of monstrously ungraspable fact 'that discredited even the most heartfelt demonstration of concern for the situation' (181). It is almost as if the people of Arlington Park did not quite live in this world, but in some secluded, securely safeguarded, parallel variant of it.

But 'what about the two million people who die each year from malnutrition?' (66). Confronted with this and similar questions, Christine finds it hard to feel genuinely affected and respond with a clear sense of ethical responsibility. Instead, individualism rears its head, the panic of missing out on self-fulfilment, which is after all every individual's principal duty: 'I get so worked up about asylum seekers and earthquake victims and abducted children and the bloody starving millions that I forget to enjoy myself. That's the tragedy here. I mean, what a waste! What a waste of a good life, not to enjoy it' (108). But can fun at all be had in a world as increasingly crowded as ours, riven by economic injustice and torn by many millions' daily struggle for bare life? Introducing a sharply glocalised perspective Cusk poignantly disrupts Christine's illusion of the world's neat compartmentalisation into various, mutually discrete locales. As the novel shows, dire living conditions elsewhere in the world protrude ever more irrepressibly into our own. Thus, idly pontificating in a shopping-mall restaurant about 'how we can't complain really' (106), Christine finds herself closely surrounded by people who can, 'dark-skinned men and women [who] slowly trawled the tables with their big plastic sacks, sweeping rubbish into them' (108), guest-working migrants on the minimum wage (should they be so lucky) whose lives have been seriously upset by the global chaos and destitution that Christine finds so discomfiting in theory.

Only Solly, another one of Cusk's female characters, engages with foreigners on a somewhat more intimate, personal level. Solly rents out a room in her family home to lodgers from various parts of the world: Taiwan, Japan, Italy. Perplexingly though, this closer contact does not lead Solly to a discovery of their common humanity; rather, faced with her lodgers' exotic difference she experiences a curious kind of regression, a descent into some unnameable, primeval amorphousness equivalent to a complete loss of civilisation, as if even in the twenty-first century the intercultural encounter must negotiate an abyss, a potential heart of darkness booming with its own unintelligibility. Thus, sparing not a single thought for the girl's own sense of alienation, which must be acute, Solly finds her Japanese lodger's rudimentary English so disconcerting that she feels:

> at the very limit of her own civilised self, vacillating there as though on the perimeter of a vast darkness. Now that she could no longer communicate, she became aware of how much of her lay shrouded in this inarticulate darkness. Yet she could not navigate it either. It was like a big black prairie she saw from her lit porch. She became a kind of animal, pantomiming enquiries and requests, acting out her own consciousness with bodily heaves and grimaces. (118)

Solly's hysterical overreaction to what is after all only a language barrier seems closely related to her peer Amanda's near-pathological solipsism. The latter is rendered by Cusk in equally hyperbolic images, satirically likening the suburbanite's estrangement from her community to being a tourist watching wildlife on safari: 'Like a settler in a new, uncharted country, Amanda was aware [. . .] of the deep habits of herds migrating and convening across the reaches of Arlington Park [. . .] She was aware of them passing and feeding and gathering in groups to graze or rest, but try as she might, she could not bridge their distance from her' (56). It is in depictions such as these that Arlington Park betrays the colonial heritage of its Englishness, and that the individual's imperviousness to marital, familial and communal intimacy broadens into an analogy of the entire nation's apparent ineptitude at embracing and effectively facilitating cosmopolitan glocalisation.

The latest arrivals in Arlington Park, Maisie and Dom Carrington, are said to have fled the city because they could no longer bear 'living

with two children in the churn of London, the great rotating machine
[. . .] always living their lives neck-deep in people and cars and chaos,
in the thick vortex of multitudinous screaming wants' (192). Yet suburbia affords them no wondrous communal relief from the relentless
glomicity of the contemporary; it only negligibly adjusts the angle of
their disenchantment. No matter whether it is the metropolis or suburbia, the world at large or one's immediate neighbourhood, in order to
rediscover any more genuinely world-creative view of the human that
would resist the production of the uniform mass as well as the loner,
our perception of and experience as individual men and women is
required to change fundamentally. Following Nancy, we are called
upon to let go of individualism and instead recognise and embrace our
singularity. As Dallmayr explains, 'whereas individuation proceeds by
detaching closed-off entities from a formless ground [. . .] singular
beings do not emerge against the background of a prior chaos, or
against the foil of an original unity, or else against a process of "becoming" and wilful construction. Rather', he continues, 'singular beings
always emerge together from the beginning; their finitude "co-appears
or compears [. . .]" in a shared world' (1997: 181). In *Arlington Park*
there is only one brief moment towards the very end of the novel when
we catch a glimpse of Cusk's couples as precisely such a communal
clustering of singularities. Ironically, however, the formation of this
suburban community coincides with its swift dispersion. As Christine
waves goodbye to her dinner guests, the latter 'moved in a body, out
into the street, into the night. And then she saw them scatter and break
apart, calling, going this way and that, like an armful of birds released
into the sky' (239).

McGregor's debut novel *If Nobody Speaks of Remarkable Things*
resembles in its entirety the kind of spontaneously uncoordinated, inoperative and swiftly re-disintegrative moment of assemblage with which
Arlington Park concludes. The people who live in McGregor's street are
at once neighbours and strangers who know, but do not really know,
each other. Their lives congregate only for an instant as they all come
to witness a near-fatal car accident happening right on their doorsteps,
rendering 'the whole street frozen in a tableau of gaping mouths' (2002:
9) until 'the knot of people in the street loosened [again], turned aside'
(11). Importantly, this communal moment does not evaporate into thin
air. Instead of being consigned to oblivion, the event inscribes itself on
the minds of all who were there, relating McGregor's central character
everlastingly to this neighbourhood of people, no matter if she can
remember everybody's name or, on moving out of the street, is likely

ever to see them again. It would therefore be very wrong to mistake this community simply for a crowd of onlookers, whose fixation on the spectacle in front of them desensitises them to each other's humanity.

Certainly it is worth noting that the moment does allow experience to translate immediately into ethically informed, neighbourly action, as 'the boy from number eighteen [is seen] moving through the locked moment like a blessing' (9), rushing to catch the little boy as he is flung through the air by the impact of the collision. Meanwhile, the man with the scarred hands, an asylum seeker who once failed to save his wife from a burning house, proceeds to knock on the door of the boy's parents to alert them to what has happened. Unlike Cusk's portrayal of suburban life, which shows the individual at the same time locked into and combatively pitted against the community, McGregor's representation identifies individual self-crystallisation and communal self-immersion not as mutually opposed but as *compearently* entwined and interdependent. In terms of both individual and communal existence, which invariably must coincide, McGregor's world constitutes itself from 'small moments captured and enlarged by the context' (8). This is reflected by the narrative itself, whose structuring principles and appearance on the printed page are designed to assert that every moment, every observation, every movement, every aspect deserves its own indentation, and that the novel as a whole is an amalgamation of segments, distinct in tone, tense and perspective whilst augmenting the same deep-structural matrix of communal connectivity and correlation.

Switching between a range of past and present time levels, McGregor's novel pursues no trajectory and remains firmly embedded within the present. Even the central character's pregnancy does not develop into a project that could rock the resolute contemporaneity of the novel. Except for the most quotidian comings and goings life is largely uneventful, to the extent at times of seeming homeostatic. It is devoid of emplotment as whatever does happen is not preceded by 'a buildup, a feeling in the air, a premonition or a warning or a clue' (10). In spite of this, the novel never sprawls into incoherence or irrelevance. Like Cusk, in terms of style and thematic concerns McGregor is probably most aptly described as a neo-modernist writer interested in exploring the workings of the individual mind and adapting his narration accordingly. The individual's sense of time is shown to be at once intricately entwined with and unstoppably unravelling from the time of the world at large. For the most part, in *If Nobody Speaks of Remarkable Things* the lived present is recounted in the past tense, burdened by the memory of the day of the accident, which is recounted in the present tense, thus not so much divorcing tense from time, and language from its grammatically accurate representation of the world, as probing and re-charting their world-creative co-alignment. Careful not to lumber his novel with too much design, McGregor none the less summons it to an effort at modernist meaning-making. Propelled by a compelling desire for epiphany, the novel never ceases to doubt 'if there was something I missed because I wasn't paying attention' (10), something wondrous and revelatory that might arise at any moment from the sobriety of everyday suburban routine. As the man with the scarred hands insists, 'if nobody speaks of remarkable things, how can they be called remarkable?' (239). This is the key to McGregor's motivation for writing the novel in the first place: to make us pay closest attention to what determines our individual and communal lives, yet for most of the time passes wholly unnoticed.

McGregor's novel makes a perfect case study in Nancean compearance, demonstrating how the life of the individual is not simply communally determined, but essentially generated by as well as generative of community as mutual exposition and being-in-common, which is tautly relational even at its most anonymous and seemingly detached. The narrative is not so much focused on, as focalised through, the life of a young woman who has just found out she is pregnant after a brief holiday affair. She is 'the girl with the short blonde hair and the small square glasses' (189), at least that is what she looked like in her student days, the vivid recollection of which (and especially the day of the accident) takes up a lot of her time. 'I don't understand why it seems so fresh in my mind, even now, three years later and a few hundred miles away', she muses, 'I think about it, and I can't even remember people's names' (11). Only in McGregor's second novel, *So Many Ways to Begin* (2006), is this woman given a name and identified clearly as Kate Carter, daughter of Eleanor and David Carter, who are allowed a shadowy appearance in the earlier novel when Kate explains that 'my mother is Scottish, my dad is not [. . .] My grandmother's funeral was the only time I've ever been to Scotland' (165), and it is during this visit to Scotland that she falls pregnant. This kind of interpermeation of consecutive novels in terms of characters, thematic concerns and even structural peculiarities, which is equally typical of David Mitchell's work, must be regarded as typical of narratives of compearance. Such narratives will not tolerate any of their cast paling into the background as purely vehicular supernumeraries; rather, these works insist that all lives are not only mirrored but crucially informed by each other. It is suggested that the circumstances of Kate's pregnancy in *If Nobody Speaks of Remarkable Things* and her father's search for his long-lost birth mother in the second novel can really only hope to begin making sense together. Resonating with the Nancean proposition of community as productively inoperative, novels of compearance take the view that life is invariably 'more complicated' than neat emplotment allows for:

> Lives were changed and moved by much smaller cues, chance meetings, overheard conversations, the trips and stumbles which constantly alter and readjust the course of things, history made by a million fractional moments too numerous to calibrate or observe or record. (McGregor 2006: 129)

Even the minutest coincidental events are likely to unfold into gravely consequential intersections of necessity, resulting in the formation of couples, groups and communities – however casual, perfunctory and momentary – that determine the history of the world as one vast, never-ending moment of compearance.

Kate has moved from a provincial university town (possibly Nottingham) to the metropolis (quite probably London), and her sense of atomised individuation is acute, which perhaps explains her preoccupation with the past when she was effortlessly immersed in a thriving network of student life. Deprived of the easy sociability she experienced then, she tries to remember 'what it was like to be near so many people who knew me' (23) and does her best to stay in touch with old friends. Yet despite the fact that 'we're not that far apart, maybe half an hour on the tube', no actual meetings take place, only occasional telephone calls: 'Once a month, maybe less, one of us will call the other and we'll say oh hi it's been ages we should try and meet up, and a plan will be made, and cancelled, or not quite made at all' (21). These telephone calls are so steeped in nostalgia they hardly touch on the present ('We talked about other people, saying do you remember when, and how funny was, and I wonder what happened to' [23]), highlighting the irremediable scattering into work and adulthood suffered by the former circle of friends: 'All the emails I get these days start with sorry but I've been so busy, and I don't understand how we can be so busy and then have nothing to say to each other' (26). It seems that Kate's life is not at all so very far removed from that of Cusk's desperate middle-class housewives; in fact, once her baby is born, single motherhood must inevitably render her suburban entrapment even more pronounced than theirs. Significantly, however, in McGregor's representation it does not appear to be adult life as such that is the problem; rather, it is the ways in which, as a society, we have become accustomed to living our grown-up lives in isolation, as singletons or frozen into coupledom and families, seeking self-fulfilment in work, inhabiting parts of town that suit and reflect our identities, leading perfectly manageable, orderly, worked-out lives.

This rigidification of our everyday existence disagrees fundamentally with the notion of life as contingent, essentially unworkable and in flux, as embraced intuitively – if somewhat naively, considering modern life's innumerable interpellative pressures – by 'the girl with the glitter around her eyes' who is going out with 'the white-shirted boy':

> The music goes doowah doowah I love you so, and she thinks about the two of them. They haven't spoken about it, they haven't said what will we do when we leave here, do you want to come with me, let's work something out, and she knows that this means they will quickly and easily drift apart, into other people's lives, into other people's arms in rooms like this. She is surprised that this doesn't make her feel sad. (31)

Sadness and frustration set in when life comes to a halt, when the last amorous embrace or self-fulfilling moment in work cease as a matter of course to lead to another, when life coagulates into the worked-out existential standstill that characterises places such as Arlington Park, patterned by relentless regularity and routine that ultimately only pure chance or sudden accidental trauma can unwork.

As McGregor intimates, all life – however spontaneous, seemingly unprecedented and ecstatic – is subject to processes of rigidification. The flux of the contemporary must inevitably stiffen into historical tableau. For example, aided by an old photograph of 'Simon and Rob and Jamie dancing naked down the street in the first pale hours of that summer, celebrating the election', Kate is able to remember vividly the Labour Party's landslide victory in May 1997, but she also recalls 'coming back from the garage at midnight [. . .] and seeing my friends' faces lit up by the shrine of the television [. . .] Already looking like ghosts' (40). Importantly, McGregor's reference to Tony Blair's euphoric rise to power, combined with the detail that the immediate present of the narrative is a Sunday – the last day of summer of the same year, which sees Kate and her newly graduated friends pack up their belongings and get ready to leave their university town for the last time – suggests that the implied time of the novel is 31 August 1997, that is, the day Princess Diana died in a car accident in Paris. If so, then the accident that happens in McGregor's street later that day, gathering the neighbourhood into one community of witnesses, is deliberately crafted after that most memorable of personal tragedies in recent history. Unprecedentedly Princess Diana's death (re-)united in grief and sympathy not only the British nation, jaded and divided after eighteen years of Conservative rule, but large parts of the global population as well. Very similar to Cusk's representation of suburbia, then, even though it presents itself as incapable of imagining even one suburban street in its entirety, McGregor's novel emerges not only as an account of the nation but of global humanity as a whole. Ordinary routines are disrupted and socially divisive barriers lifted as we behold a community constituting itself purely out of compassion, spectacularly overcoming the neo-liberalist dictum that 'there is no such thing as society. There are individual men and women, and there are families', imposed upon the nation in 1987 by the then prime minister Margaret Thatcher, and interpreted by David Harvey as an 'ideological assault' intended to dissolve 'all forms of social solidarity [. . .] in favour of individualism, private property, personal responsibility, and family values' (2005: 23). As history has demonstrated and McGregor's narrative reaffirms, '[community's] relational character is predicated on the very rupture or ecstatic transgression of compactness' (Dallmayr 1997: 179). Put differently, ultimately only trauma, extreme euphoria and widespread popular agitation are likely to possess the inoperative might required to undo the managerial work of habit and political ideology, and thus remobilise the world-creative potentialities of community.

One day, on an outing with her new friend Michael, who never quite becomes her boyfriend, Kate discovers an art installation, whose representational scope evidently encompasses the whole of humanity, consisting of 'thousands and thousands of six-inch red clay figures, as roughly made as playschool plasticine men, a pair of finger-sized sockets for eyes, heads tilted up from formless bodies' (231). The artwork shows humanity as a vast mass of singular entities, at once fully assimilated into their mutual being-in-common and existentially splintered and forlorn in each and every one's own individuality, thus creating a breath-taking spectacle of humanity's infinite multiplicity of the same. 'Each one almost identical', Kate notes, 'each one unique.' The installation in question is inspired by Antony Gormley's *Field* (1991), a version of which ('Field for the British Isles', comprising 35,000 handmade terracotta figures) won the Turner Prize in 1994, while an even larger reconfiguration ('Asian Field', comprising a staggering 180,000 figures) featured at the Sydney Biennale in 2007. Gormley's vision encapsulates a sense of the world that – like her author, as well as Mitchell in *Ghostwritten* and *Cloud Atlas* – Kate finds herself at a loss adequately to put into words: 'I wanted to count them, give them all names, make up stories for each of them, but it seemed impossible to even begin' (231). The novel can only hope to grasp humanity through focalised exemplification, by attempting, as McGregor does, to capture the trauma of coping with the loss of just one life out of so very many.

Later that day – keen to halt the world, if only for the briefest of moments – the man with the scarred hands wills all humanity to cry out

in unanimous grief for the severely injured little boy who lies unconscious in the street after the accident. Remarkably, the boy is all of a
sudden no longer an unnamed fiction but an astoundingly real, singular
person: Shahid Mohammed Nawaz. The man envisages what would:

> happen if the whole street called his name, joining with the mother's small
> voice, the whole street lifting the words and the words spreading through
> this city, taking flight like a flock of birds at dusk, clouding the sky, the voices
> all-present, across fields and forests and oceans, sent out, transmitted, broad-
> cast, on BBC and CNN, satellite and terrestrial and international optic fibres,
> on billboards and buses and videoscreens, on flyers and posters and news-
> journals and magazines, the information, the name, pouring down from the
> sky like electronic rain, out from this one street and sucked down into the
> lightning-rod antennas that bristle from mansions and shantyhouses across
> all our misconnected world, a chorus of name-saying, a brief redemptive
> span of attention. (272)

What turns this compassionate gesture into such a powerful cosmopolitical appeal is the fact that in this English suburban street it is initiated
by a Muslim refugee from some war-torn, possibly Eastern European
country. Albeit drawing on Islamic wording to alert the world to the
suffering of the injured British-Asian child, McGregor leaves no doubt
about the fundamental secularity of the man's plea for a moment of
unreserved global compassion. 'He has no faith', the novel explains,
'but the words keep coming, he thinks oh inshaallah let the whole
world hear, let the whole world listen for a moment, his name is Shahid,
Shahid Mohammed Nawaz and he is dying' (272). The contrast
between Shahid's accident and Princess Diana's – which of course
attracted exactly the kind of global attention envisaged by the man,
notably entirely without prompting – is clearly fully intentional. As
Kate remembers, 'there was nothing about [Shahid's accident] on the
news [. . .] I knew there wouldn't be but it didn't seem right' (24).
McGregor's message here is unequivocal: because it must inevitably rip
a hole in the densely woven fabric of the world, seriously disrupting its
communal network of interdependent exposition and compearance,
each and every violent death – no matter whose, without exception –
ought to be experienced as a shocking outrage.

But in the end Shahid does not die. Instead, echoing the mysterious
life–death compearance that links neurasthenic party hostess Clarissa
Dalloway to shell-shocked suicide Septimus Smith in Woolf's *Mrs
Dalloway*, the young man who runs out into the street to catch Shahid
does, suddenly struck down by a congenital heart condition triggered
by the physical exertion of his effort to save the boy. As the novel puts
it, 'there is an interruption in the way of things, a pause, something
faint like the quivering flutter of a moth's rain-sodden wings, something

unexpected. Something remarkable.' At the very moment the young man dies, Shahid – still in the ambulance on his way to the hospital and expected by everyone not to make it – 'breathes suddenly and violently through his nose' (273). It appears to be no mere coincidence either that just before he dies, the young man knocks to the floor a small clay figure strikingly similar to the ones used by Gormley in his art, which so impressed Kate. *If Nobody Speaks of Remarkable Things* is a novel keen to establish links and patterns among its cast of characters that identify the latter as a community and help illuminate the human condition as transfused by existential compearance and being-in-common. Some of these links and patterns pass unnoticed due to their unremarkability, but others are more conspicuous, dramatically honed, and obtrusive. Apart from Shahid's accident, which momentarily ties all the characters into one, McGregor's work displays some other deliberate patterning reminiscent of Mitchell's unnerving invocation of the cross-generational recurrence of a comet-shaped birthmark in *Cloud Atlas*. In McGregor's representation, however, this kind of patterning tends to retain its purely coincidental appearance while forfeiting none of its significatory poignancy. This is certainly the case with the novel's introduction of three pairs of twins, establishing a connection between Shahid and his unharmed brother, the twin babies Kate is found to be expecting towards the end of the novel, and her new friend Michael, who turns out to be the twin brother of the young man who died in Shahid's stead, and who is revealed also to have had a major crush on Kate when both of them lived in the street as students.

McGregor's second novel *So Many Ways to Begin* is informed by the same fateful contingency, following Kate's father as he uses the name given on his birth certificate to trace his Irish birth mother. His search eventually leads him to an elderly woman who, like his mother, worked as a teenage servant girl in post-war London and on finding herself pregnant by her employer had no choice but to abandon her newborn child. The woman David finds is indeed called Mary Friel, but she turns out not to be his mother: 'What you should understand, she said very quietly [. . .] is that most girls would have given false names to the nurses' (2006: 359). The irony is that the chosen false name is so common in Ireland that it connects two complete strangers, whose lives not only intimately mirror but virtually coincide with each other, many decades later uniting a mother and a son who are not related despite sharing the same story. To compound even further the extraordinary interwovenness of McGregor's two in actual fact very different novels, the prologue of *So Many Ways to Begin* depicts poor Irish country-folk in the post-war years flocking to the annual hiring fair in the nearest big town to find seasonal work in England. What is truly remarkable here is the way in which this opening vision of the novel reads like an almost perfect narrative mobilisation of Gormley's *Field*.

As Cusk's and McGregor's suburban worlds illustrate, the cosmopolitan dynamics of Nancean community are at work even where one might perhaps least expect to find them. The two portrayals of contemporary suburbia at once celebrate and problematise people's daily struggle for world-creative neighbourliness. Refining modernist modes of representation Cusk achieves a satirical exposure of middle-class England's relational self-impairment, its obsessive fixation on the individual and world-oblivious aversion to glocalisation. Meanwhile, McGregor adapts the traditional novel to enable it better to capture everyday individual and communal existence in the twenty-first century, and he does so by self-consciously pioneering a new mode of focalised representation. According to Berman, 'communities come into being to a large extent in the kinds of stories of connection we have been told or are able to tell about ourselves' (2001: 3), and this is as true about the literature of the early twentieth century with which Berman concerns herself as it is with regard to the contemporary English novel.

Arlington Park and *If Nobody Speaks of Remarkable Things* are first and foremost precisely such 'stories of connection', which, in response to the ways in which we live now, not only disclose what hampers and obstructs community but also hint at possible cosmopolitan escape routes out of contemporary society's predicament of individualist, localist and nationalist self-identification. It is here that the two novels – seemingly so focused on the ordinary, private and suburban – reveal their larger political potential. A cosmopolitan world politics loath to impose any one grand scheme of emancipation or universal salvation upon the world in its totality must learn to listen in on humanity's actual heartbeat, the everyday trials of both private self-authentication and local conviviality that play themselves out at community's most fundamental, grassroots levels. It is in this respect, then, that contemporary literature, and more specifically the novel, might come to serve as a profoundly inspirational resource, and our political culture might indeed benefit greatly from opening up 'to the varieties of "being-in-common" that are often relegated [. . .] to the kinds of voices, such as those often present within fictional narratives, that seem to speak outside of politics in general' (Berman 2001: 15).

The residents of Arlington Park live in a neatly boxed-in enclave, haunted by the spectre of bourgeois discontent and a little paranoid about being not so much under surveillance as under constant examination. They do not appreciate the contingency of nature and other extraneous uncontrollabilities as these must inevitably exacerbate their already-severe performance anxiety. For example, heavy rain in the night makes them 'feel somehow observed, as if a dark audience had assembled outside and were looking in through the windows, clapping their hands' (Cusk 2006: 5). The impression one gets from the opening of Cusk's novel is that this is a perfectly self-contained world living after a well-rehearsed script which, as the curtain is momentarily lifted, we are invited to visit and view. To facilitate our inspection, its world has been conveniently carved up into a concatenation of discrete acts, each reserved for the treatment of a particular individual case. By contrast, exposed rather than sheltered and only sketchily contoured rather than strictly demarcated, daily life in McGregor's street is always already steeped in the noise of the world at large. It forms part of the metropolitan organism of the city rather than existing separately in the form of an excrescent suburban offshoot. Its inhabitants' lives chime in with the general urban cacophony, which is also a morning song:

> The rippled roll of shutters pulled down on late-night cafes, a crackled voice crying street names for taxis, a loud scream that lingers and cracks into laughter, a bang that might just be an old car backfiring, a call box calling out for an answer, a treeful of birds tricked into morning, a whistle and a shout and a broken glass, a blare of soft music and a blam of hard beats, a barking and yelling and singing and crying and it all swells up all the rumbles and crashes and bangings and slams, all the noise and the rush and the non-stop wonder of the song of the city you can hear if you listen the song. (McGregor 2002: 3)

Whereas Cusk's novel must be read as a shrewd satire on contemporary middle-class life, intent on exposing the current state of affairs, McGregor's seems more proactively Nancean in its representation of suburban community. As Berman reminds us, 'Nancy positions community within a realm of play that not only supplants the categories of self and other, but never resolves into an entity that has an identity or performs tasks' (2001: 14). McGregor's characters never find themselves corralled, let alone consciously organised, into the fixity of a neighbourhood whose identity precedes the people who live there, assimilating each and every one of them on arrival. Random, disorderly and inoperative, McGregor's street never pulls purposely or contiguously into one; its sense of community remains spontaneous, improvised and contingent.

McGregor enacts in his narrative precisely 'the politics of connection' that Berman detects in the modernist novel. Like Woolf, he appears to conceive of 'subjectivity as coming into being always in fluctuating relation to a small group of affiliated yet singular others'. In the same vein, he conceives of communal affiliation as oppositional to 'both atomistic individualism *and* to conventional modes of construing community in which the group exists as a "monolithic, consistent, whole"' (Berman 2001: 121–2). Against this background McGregor's representation must at first seem diametrically opposed to Cusk's. However, rather than reinforcing the suburban ideal of well-managed perfection, *Arlington Park* demolishes it to disclose a human mosaic self-consciously broken into painfully individuated selves. According to Nancy, a community of individuals is a contradiction in terms that cannot exist; neither can communities modelled conceptually after the individual, such as the nation, because instead of promoting diversity they enforce subjection to their myths of homogeneity and self-containment. As with their modernist precursors, one would err greatly to regard Cusk's and McGregor's suburban novels as apolitical exercises in purely aesthetic or quaintly localist navel-gazing. Their rejection of uniformity and communal consensus is fiercely political, and so is their repudiation of dissent and ostracism as a stepping or falling out of community. Community can only thrive if it learns to embrace misunderstanding, confusion, nervous agitation, strife and alienation as wholeheartedly as it is keen to embrace unanimity, exaltation, mutual solicitude and compassion. Indeed, it is their understanding of community 'as situated within a political world predicated on the need for constant translation between and among individual speakers and [. . .] on the impossibility not only of consensus but also of discursive harmony' (Berman 2001: 24) that identifies *Arlington Park* and *If Nobody Speaks of Remarkable Things* as world-creative novels promoting a refreshing cosmopolitan realism. Defying notions of globalisation as the end of history, humanity is portrayed as unlikely ever to speak the same language or master the art of perfect communication. As Berman puts it, there will always be 'fragmentation even within affiliation'. What one ought therefore perhaps most hopefully to expect from the cosmopolitan novel is 'an unworking that interrupts the false myth of group communion or a rewriting that articulates the call to community and its limits' (123).

Throughout my investigation I have argued that the cosmopolitan novel is world-creative, and that its narrative forms and representational techniques must be taken seriously beyond their playful experimentalism as crucially and constructively informative of its vision of the world. In other words, the novel's cosmopolitanism resides as much in its form and generic disposition as in its content. As Berman most helpfully asserts, 'without claiming that we can derive a specific political doctrine from a certain textual mode, we can nonetheless recognize the possibilities it makes available and the social assumptions that, in concert with other thematic and discursive elements, a particular text enables' (21). Yet with regard to enabling Nancean community, there is a problem here because, according to Nancy, community cannot be promoted or created; it is not something we can strive towards or seek to establish. Rather, as Luszczynska explains, it is 'a constitutive aspect of being':

> We can neither enact it nor, properly speaking, even grasp it. It is with us before everything, having an absolute priority and immediacy and, therefore, could not be something that an empirical context could make more or less visible or more or less abundant. (2005: 194–5)

Community can only be uncovered, revealed, highlighted and accentuated, and this is what in my view the cosmopolitan novel sets out to achieve: to identify and expose what in our world, as it currently unfolds, eclipses and obstructs community, and beyond that to imagine and create contexts 'that would allow community, in the Nancean sense, to flourish' (Luszczynska 2005: 196). Significantly, according to Luszczynska, the most fruitful contexts in this respect 'might be those which have been least affected by a pervasive, overwhelming, and guiding notion of the individual' (197).

To achieve global community, then, humankind is required not so much to change as to recognise and accept itself for what it always already is: finite (that is, mortal and resolutely of this world), singular-plural (that is, compearing in relational being-in-common rather than crystallising as individuals separate from community) and inoperative (that is, productively unmanageable, complex and diverse, and without fixed or identifiable *telos*). Naturally, by embarking on such a quest for a discovery of who we always already are, 'we invariably run the risk of [. . .] making community into a work or project, or attempting to operate the inoperable' (Luszczynska 2005: 204). The cosmopolitan novel might be able to evade this risk. As realist fiction it appeals to our conscience as much as our imagination, yet its chief aim is not to persuade or to mobilise the reader. Rather, its aim is to make us see by involving us in an experience – always focalised and yet never entirely by proxy – of the world as it is.

Coda: The Cosmopolitan Imagination

'To globalize or not – that is no longer the question' (Krishnaswamy and Hawley 2008: 15). Rather, we must ask how globalisation, whose processes involve and impact on all of us, can be turned to our advantage so that it comes to benefit humankind in its entirety. As suggested in this study, the first step might well be to imagine ourselves as belonging to something far less securely defined and neatly limitable than the nation, that is, to conceive of ourselves first and foremost as members of humanity in all its vulnerable, precariously exposed planetarity. This is where the role of literature, and the novel in particular, comes to the fore, breaking up the old identitarian myths of self-containment in order to make us take another look at ourselves and acknowledge our actual position within the world, which is simultaneously aspirational and free, finite and framed.

Put differently, globalisation reopens the question of community, how we connect one to the other, starting with the most intimate levels of everyday existence (our lives as family members, lovers and friends) via our communal neighbourhoods right up to the abstract heights of the nation and the globe as a whole. What do we expect or hope to contribute to world society, always making the most of our immediate boundedness in the local? Let us remember in this context that 'the question of the concrete character of the impending world society or global family of peoples' (Dallmayr 1997: 176) must remain seriously fraught due to its inbuilt utopian fallacy. Experience warns us to steer clear of any seemingly workable global management plans – such as Communism, neo-liberalism or religious fundamentalism – because these are prone to totalisation, either disenfranchising and subsuming the individual or recklessly fetishising the self at the expense of society. Influenced by Nancean philosophy, Fred Dallmayr reminds us of 'the need for a differential strategy beyond global synthesis and its denial: that is, for a kind of double move or double gesture proceeding cautiously in the interstices of affirmation and negation' (1997: 189). What must taint the implementation of any exclusive design of globalised living is its inevitable lack of realism and acute disregard for humanity's multitudinousness, that is, in other words, its inability to embrace imperfection, which is probably humanity's most inalienable trait. Therefore, as Jessica Berman understands, in order to build a viable, cosmopolitan future for the world as a whole, we must learn 'to imagine a political realm where incomplete communication or disagreement over shared values is the norm, and where translation is always fraught with difficulty' (2001: 201–2).

The greatest cosmopolitical challenge is to inspire a global politics that circumvents the pitfalls of both totalisation and atomisation by radically recasting the relationship between self and other in terms of what – with recourse to Nancean thought – Christopher Watkin describes as 'the irreducible primordiality of being-with'. As Watkin proceeds to explain, the self's fundamental condition is that 'I am not *in* relation; I *am* singular plural relation.' What this means is that the relational dynamic informing any kind of society, as in fact that of humanity in its entirety, is not so much grounded in or determined by 'a shared value or essence, or even a reciprocal pact to "look out for each other" [as] simply this: that its participants have nothing in common; they *are* in-common' (Watkin 2007: 61). Accordingly, communal responsibility, sharing and compassion are not second nature to us; they *are* our nature. We may not be family exactly, but we are always society. No matter if we attempt to ignore, ostracise, deport or even exterminate our *semblables*, the injury we inflict, as well as the ensuing trauma, will invariably be our own. This is what makes it imperative that we repair our warped post-Enlightenment conception of subjectivity and alterity, which lurks at the root of so much contemporary world-political conflict.

Cosmopolitanism encourages us quite literally to dis-close ourselves and to abstain for good from globalisation's agglomerative practices of segregation, partitioning and self-enclosure. What is needed to accomplish this feat is first and foremost an act of the imagination, informed by an understanding of how literature, critical theory and politics might coalitionally come to (re-)create the world. Inspired by Nancy, Watkin analyses the ongoing eruption of allegedly irresolvable conflict in the world as follows:

> The recurring tragedies of Bosnia, Kosovo, Congo, East Timor, Chechnya, Pakistan, Afghanistan, Ireland and Corsica [. . .] show that we have been unable to dismantle or discourage recourse to [. . .] an essentializing 'we' that functions with the self-identity of an 'I'. The fire of conflict is stoked by the

inability to disengage from the dichotomy of self-identity and absolute alterity, and the flames are further fanned by an intimately related but opposite
global process whereby infinite generality dissolves all definite coexistence.
These equal and opposite problems – the infinite generality of globalization
and the bellicose intensity of fundamentalist essentiality – are mutually compounding, with the latter feeding off the former, and they derive from a
primary 'we' resolving on the one hand to an undifferentiated 'one' and on
the other hand to the essential dichotomy of same and other. (Watkin 2007:
52)

With the way things currently are, people continue to crave a national
identity, whose absolute distinctiveness they perceive as threatened by
erasure or absorption into other identities. Against such a background
it seems vain to argue, like Jeremy Waldron, that 'one culture does not
need to be clearly and importantly *different* from another [. . .] in order
to be the culture that it is', asserting that 'a culture just is what it is, and
its practices and rituals are constitutive of it in virtue of their place in a
shared way of life, not in virtue of their perceived peculiarity' (2000:
233). National identity is still commonly perceived as an essential component of the self, deprived of which one is left to feel shamefully
denuded or mortally humiliated. As long as national identity continues
to be articulated in such absolutist and exclusivist terms, always defined
in contradistinction to somebody else's from which it is believed to
differ non-negotiably in essence rather than in kind, it effectively
presents itself as an imagined inalienability sustained most effectively
by alienating the other.

The best global community one might be able to hope for under
these circumstances would be based on multicultural juxtaposition.
Transnational exposition, in terms of a cosmopolitan opening up and
mingling with the other, must inevitably conjure the spectre of an
impending extinction of national identity in the form of cultural attenu-
ation, contamination or assimilation. As long as identity is imagined as
something we own, and therefore something that can be taken away
from us by others, we remain worlds removed from 'the coexistence of
singular pluralities [. . .] equidistant from juxtaposition and integration'
(Watkin 2007: 60) identified by Nancy as the actual, originary condition of human life on earth. Cosmopolitanism, then, continues to be
obstructed by the daily vying for self-assertion of a margin of peripher-
ons, organised in ever more cellular configurations, battling against one
overbearing hegemon, whose actual vertebrate tangibility decreases in
direct proportion to the pervasive ubiquity of its power. From a cosmopolitan perspective the real challenge of any viable future world politics
is to abolish for good this imperialist dynamic of psycho-geographical
self-determination and instead begin to think of ourselves beyond

territory, conquest and resistance as a Nancean community of world citizens, that is, 'to think "we" otherwise than in terms of the mutually compounding dyad of globalization and fundamentalism' (Watkin 2007: 52–3).

It is the role of art and literature to provide the cosmopolitan imagination needed to facilitate this fundamental shift in the way in which we conceive of ourselves in relation to one another. Exploring 'glimpses of cosmopolitanism in the hospitality of art' Nikos Papastergiadis touches on this complex issue in his enquiry of what precisely it might be 'that art does that is so exquisite in its execution of the political that differentiates it from politics'. Papastergiadis asserts that 'artists do not deliver documents which reveal the condition of cosmopolitanism, but rather that they take an active role in the mediation of its emergence', and mediation in this context he understands as 'the process of working out the next step for living together in times when the perplexity of difference is almost overwhelming' (2007: 149–50). The novel has always been a superb instrument for capturing the spirit of the age, as well as anticipating the imminent future, without resorting to facile projection or crass proselytising. As my reading of a handful of contemporary British novels has shown, the cosmopolitan novel continues in this tradition, thus fulfilling the genre's promise as literature's 'first truly planetary form', endlessly flexible, resourceful, and entirely deserving of Franco Moretti's emblematic description of it as 'a phoenix always ready to take flight in a new direction, and to find the right language for the next generation of readers' (2006: 9).

Still it is crucial to stay alert to what may be standing in the way of the contemporary novel in its effort to fulfil its communal and civilisational function. Most conspicuously, there is the increasingly common categorical dismissal of serious literature as arcane, elitist and out of touch, which has become almost standard among cultural theorists, media studies experts and even literary critics, who tend to view newer, more popular media, such as music, television, cinema and the internet, as somehow more interesting and reliable in their representation of the contemporary human condition. Little thought is given in this context to popular culture's much greater susceptibility to manipulative indoctrination and its proclivity for distorting rather than illuminating reality. This is particularly worrying with respect to popular culture's wholesale surrender to neo-liberalist thought, undoubtedly today's world's most hegemonic discourse, which – as David Harvey demonstrates – 'has become incorporated into the common-sense way many of us interpret, live in, and understand the world'. In fact, the academic turn to the new media at the expense of more traditional modes and

means of representation might well be part of neo-liberalisation's 'creative destruction [. . .] not only of prior institutional frameworks and
powers [. . .] but also social relations [. . .] ways of life and thought [. . .]
attachments to the land and habits of the heart' (2005: 3). Critics ought
to be aware that whatever they deem relevant, authentic and hence
worthy of scholarly attention, as well as their preferred methodology,
constitutes in itself an indicator of ideological indoctrination and
control. Instead of embracing as democratically progressive and even
emancipatory the decline of an 'elitist' reading culture, I wonder if such
a point-blank dismissal of solitary world-creation in favour of more
gregarious and often tediously formulaic 'reality' genres ought not to
elicit our gravest concern. Might it not be possible that eye-opening
innovation is still mainly initiated by the singular, privately secluded
mind rather than conglomerates of hot-desking studios sponsored by
the state and/or corporatist power?

The novel, even though still mostly single-authored, has not been
able to escape consumer-led mass production, and in this respect the
British publishing conventions no longer greatly differ from the global
– that is, US American – standard. As James English and John Frow
discover:

> The 'blockbuster' paradigm that first emerged in American-based publishing
> houses during the 1970s, and the corresponding emphasis both on short-
> term profits and on a thoroughly rationalized business plan even for what
> we think of as high-cultural production, are seen as propelling a global shift
> in literary life toward the kind of polarized, winner-take-all economy that
> characterizes American society in general. (2006: 42)

What strikes me as worrying in this context is that, rather than brows-
ing more eclectically and compiling their own lists informed by their
own expert criteria, many literary scholars seem now very happy to
allow their reading and research choices exclusively to be determined
not only by a popular canon that is always already pre-selected by pub-
lishers, but also by titles that are hyped in the media, awarded prizes
decided on largely by lay or celebrity juries, or recommended to the
TV-watching public by the likes of Richard & Judy and Oprah Winfrey.
The texts and authors that find their way into university curricula, that
are critiqued and widely written about, are now often identical with
those that feature on chat shows and televised book quizzes. The names
of Zadie Smith, Monica Ali and Lloyd Jones are virtually everywhere;
'their literary peers, meanwhile, however indistinguishable or even
superior in terms of perceived artistic merit, struggle ever harder simply
to get their works into print' (English and Frow 2006: 42). This trend
seems exacerbated by a ceaseless popular craving for the next new

thing, causing the market to be inundated by an ever-growing number of debut novels by Creative Writing graduates commissioned by literary agents whilst still in the process of being written. These novels often demonstrate great craftsmanship with regard to character and plot development, yet their trained rendition tends to lack in imaginative scope and inquisitive rigour. They make acceptably middle-brow, yet otherwise undemanding and entirely forgettable airport reads that help people while the time away. In my view, they are best described as novels of no consequence, devoid of truth, beauty and community, though never shy of using an aspirational title, such as Smith's much-lauded *On Beauty* (2005) (see also Thomas 2006).

Cosmopolitan fiction meets the challenge of imagining pan-global community – for example, by transporting the English novel, as David Mitchell does on a regular basis, beyond the usual post-imperial frontiers into the non-English-speaking world. The cosmopolitan novel also helps expose a growing anglophone parochialism that in virtually all walks of life contrives to hide its shortcomings by feverishly limelighting its cultural hegemony. The common assumption is that anything of global interest or import is available in English, or about to be translated. The actual impoverishment and cultural narrow-mindedness of contemporary British society are shockingly brought to light by the results of a recent sociological study, which might just as well have been conducted in Rachel Cusk's Arlington Park. In fact, the study relies on research into the glocalising role of mediascapes conducted among largely middle-class communities in Greater Manchester. Examining their respondents' habits of cultural consumption by asking questions about people's English and non-English referents in the visual arts, music, cinema and television, Mike Savage and his team discovered that:

> Fully 70% of all cultural references are to English sources. Of the remainder, the vast majority, 75%, are to references from the United States [. . .] a mere 7.5% of references are to cultural products which come from outside England or the USA. Of this very small number, about half (3% of the total) are to European sources, and another half (3%) to Australian or Canadian ones. Only 1% of references are to other parts of the world, including all of Asia, Latin America, and Africa. (2005: 173)

These figures refute the initial impression of Britain as one of the most cosmopolitan places on earth. The nation's cultural worldliness turns out to be an illusion, kept alive by the chauvinism of some of its most prominent artists, academics and cultural critics. Thus Krishan Kumar, a British-Asian sociologist and currently professor at the University of Virginia, insists that 'English society is now more "multicultural" than ever it was before', adding that 'even if it is largely due to American influence, the fact that English has become so widely spoken on the Continent certainly should be an aid to English integration in Europe' (2003: 17). Seemingly unconcerned about Britain's increasing Americanisation, Kumar considers it the most natural thing in the world that English (or does he in actual fact mean 'British'?) Europeanness should be safeguarded by other peoples' bilingualism. Does Kumar not realise that there is much about Europe that remains unexpressed in English, and surely also that integration is a matter of reciprocity and ought not to rely entirely unilaterally on the hospitality of others? Due to Britain's increasing monocultural parochialism, exacerbated by Americanisation, what Gianni Vattimo refers to as 'the European spirit' – that is, 'a different view of existence, a different notion of what constitutes a "good life," a different existential plan' (2005: 31; 33) – is quite likely to elude the British. This does not bode at all well for Britain's world-creative capabilities, the country's cosmopolitan outlook and general transcultural responsiveness to the spirit of the world as whole.

None the less, as the present study has demonstrated, it is possible to detect a world-creative consciousness beginning to stir within the imaginative realm of the contemporary British novel. Inexpert and improvised at best, the cosmopolitan novel shows itself willing to open up to globality, submit to it, and thus possibly assist in shaping future globalisation from within. Its ethos is to home in on the daily life of all of us as the world's one chief purpose and intention, to imagine humanity in global coexistence as determined by, yet not wholly incarcerated in, ideological frames, and to conceive of real cosmopolitics as a communal tackling of global threats beyond the requirement for perfect, enduring unanimity. I agree with Dominic Head that 'the cosmopolitan identity often emerges as our single main resource of hope in combating the worst effects of globalization', and certainly also that, as he suggests, 'the novel is sometimes deemed to be a useful instrument in that endeavour' (2008: 96). Like him, I regard the literary as 'an alternative imaginative space, with a social function' (9). Unlike him, however, I have much greater faith in the cosmopolitan imagination. This study is my defence of the novel's power not only to react to the world, but to recast it.

Bibliography

Acheson, James and Sarah C. E. Ross (eds). *The Contemporary British Novel*. Edinburgh: Edinburgh University Press, 2005.

Al-Azm, Sadik J. '*The Satanic Verses* Post Festum: The Global, the Local, the Literary.' *Comparative Studies of South Asia, Africa and the Middle East* 20:1–2 (2000), pp. 44–76.

Aldama, Frederick. 'Postcolonial Imaginings: A Conversation with Hari Kunzru.' *Interdisciplinary Literary Studies: A Journal of Criticism and Theory* 8:1 (2006), pp. 110–17.

Anderson, Benedict. *The Spectre of Comparisons: Nationalism, Southeast Asia, and the World*. London: Verso, 1998.

Anderson, Benedict. *Imagined Communities: Reflections on the Origin and Spread of Nationalism*. Revised edition. London: Verso, 2006 [1983].

Anderson, Perry. 'European Hypocrisies.' *London Review of Books* 29:18 (20 September 2007), pp. 13–21.

Appadurai, Arjun. *Modernity at Large: Cultural Dimensions of Globalization*. Minneapolis and London: University of Minnesota Press, 1996.

Appadurai, Arjun (ed.). *Globalization*. Durham, NC: Duke University Press, 2001.

Appadurai, Arjun. *Fear of Small Numbers: An Essay on the Geography of Anger*. Durham, NC: Duke University Press, 2006.

Appiah, Kwame Anthony. 'Cosmopolitan Patriots.' In Cheah and Robbins (1998), pp. 91–114.

Appiah, Kwame Anthony. *Cosmopolitanism: Ethics in a World of Strangers*. London: Allen Lane, 2006.

Armstrong, Nancy. *How Novels Think: The Limits of Individualism from 1719–1900*. New York: Columbia University Press, 2005.

Augé, Marc. *Non-Places: Introduction to an Anthropology of Supermodernity*. Tr. J. Howe. London: Verso, 1995 [1992].

Barratt, Robert. 'Marabar: The Caves of Deconstruction.' *Journal of Narrative Technique* 23:2 (1993), pp. 127–35.

Bauman, Zygmunt. *Globalization: The Human Consequences*. Cambridge: Polity, 1998.

Bauman, Zygmunt. *Community: Seeking Safety in an Insecure World*. Cambridge: Polity, 2001.

Bauman, Zygmunt. *Liquid Love: On the Frailty of Human Bonds*. Cambridge: Polity, 2003.

Beck, Ulrich. 'The Cosmopolitan Manifesto.' *New Statesman* 20 (1998), pp. 38–50.

Beck, Ulrich. 'The Cosmopolitan Perspective: Sociology in the Second Age of Modernity.' In Vertovec and Cohen (2002), pp. 61–85.

Beck, Ulrich. *The Cosmopolitan Vision.* Tr. C. Cronin. Cambridge: Polity, 2006 [2004].

Beck, Ulrich and Edgar Grande. *Cosmopolitan Europe.* Tr. C. Cronin. Cambridge: Polity, 2007 [2004].

Beck, Ulrich and Natan Sznaider. 'Unpacking Cosmopolitanism for the Social Sciences: A Research Agenda.' *British Journal of Sociology* 57:1 (2006), pp. 1–23.

Bentley, Nick (ed.). *British Fiction of the 1990s.* London: Routledge, 2005.

Berman, Jessica. *Modernist Fiction, Cosmopolitanism, and the Politics of Community.* Cambridge: Cambridge University Press, 2001.

Bhabha, Homi K. (ed.). *Nation and Narration.* London: Routledge, 1990.

Bhabha, Homi K. 'Unpacking My Library . . . Again.' In Chambers and Curti (1996), pp. 199–211.

Bindé, Jérôme. 'Toward an Ethics of the Future.' In Appadurai (2001), pp. 90–113.

Binnie, Jon, Julian Holloway, Steve Millington and Craig Young (eds). *Cosmopolitan Urbanism.* London: Routledge, 2006.

Breckenridge, Carol A., Sheldon Pollock, Homi K. Bhabha and Dipesh Chakrabarty (eds). *Cosmopolitanism.* Durham, NC: Duke University Press, 2002.

Brennan, Timothy. 'The National Longing for Form.' In Bhabha (1990), pp. 44–70.

Brennan, Timothy. *At Home in the World: Cosmopolitanism Now.* Cambridge, MA, and London: Harvard University Press, 1997.

Brennan, Timothy. 'Cosmo-Theory.' *South Atlantic Quarterly* 100:3 (2001), pp. 659–91.

Butler, Tim. 'Living in the Bubble: Gentrification and Its "Others" in North London.' *Urban Studies* 40:12 (2003), pp. 2469–86.

Calhoun, Craig. 'The Class Consciousness of Frequent Travellers: Toward a Critique of Actually Existing Cosmopolitanism.' In Vertovec and Cohen (2002), pp. 86–109.

Carpenter, Rebecca. '"We're Not a Friggin' Girl Band": September 11, Masculinity, and the British–American Relationship in David Hare's *Stuff Happens* and Ian McEwan's *Saturday.*' In Keniston and Quinn (2008), pp. 143–60.

Chaganti, Vijayasree and Kanukolanuk Ravichandra. 'Macaulay to Microsoft: Globalization and the Indian Academy.' In Joseph and Wilson 2006, pp. 209–23.

Chambers, Iain and Lidia Curti (eds). *The Post-Colonial Question: Common Skies, Divided Horizons.* London: Routledge, 1996.

Cheah, Pheng and Bruce Robbins (eds). *Cosmopolitics: Thinking and Feeling beyond the Nation.* Minneapolis: University of Minnesota Press, 1998.

Chomsky, Noam. *Hegemony or Survival? America's Quest for Global Dominance.* London: Penguin, 2003.

Connell, Liam. 'Global Narratives: Globalisation and Literary Studies.' *Critical Survey* 16:2 (2004), pp. 78–95.

Connell, Liam. 'Business as Usual: The Image of the Corporation in the Cultures of Globalisation.' In Smith (2006), pp. 161–80.

Connell, Liam. 'Post-colonialism and Globalization: The Literal and Figurative Economies of Difference.' In Dayal and Murphy (2007), pp. 190–208.

Connor, Steven. *The English Novel in History, 1950–1995*. London: Routledge, 1996.

Craig, Cairns. 'Resisting Arrest: James Kelman.' In Wallace and Stevenson (1993), pp. 99–114.

Crystal, David. *English as a Global Language*. Second edition. Cambridge: Cambridge University Press, 2003 [1997].

Culler, Jonathan. 'Anderson and the Novel.' In Culler and Cheah (2003), pp. 29–52.

Culler, Jonathan and Pheng Cheah (eds). *Grounds of Comparison: Around the Work of Benedict Anderson*. New York: Routledge, 2003.

Cusk, Rachel. *Arlington Park*. London: Faber, 2006.

Dallmayr, Fred. 'An "Inoperative" Global Community? Reflections on Nancy.' In Sheppard et al. (1997), pp. 174–96.

Dallmayr, Fred. *Small Wonder: Global Power and Its Discontents*. Lanham, MD: Rowman & Littlefield, 2005.

Damrosch, David. *What Is World Literature?* Princeton: Princeton University Press, 2003.

Dasgupta, Samir and Ray Kiely (eds). *Globalization and After*. New Delhi: Sage, 2006.

Davies, Rhiannon. 'Enduring McEwan.' In Lea and Schoene 2003, pp. 105–23.

Dayal, Samir and Margueritte Murphy (eds). *Global Babel: Questions of Discourse and Communication in a Time of Globalization*. Newcastle: Cambridge Scholars, 2007.

Delrez, Marc. 'Escape into Innocence: Ian McEwan and the Nightmare of History.' *Ariel* 26:2 (1995), pp. 7–23.

Denzin, Norman K. and Yvonna S. Lincoln (eds). *9/11 in American Culture*. Walnut Creek: Altamira, 2003.

Desai, Kiran. *The Inheritance of Loss*. London: Penguin, 2006.

Dumbrell, John. *A Special Relationship: Anglo-American Relations from the Cold War to Iraq*. Second edition. Basingstoke: Palgrave, 2006 [2000].

Eagleton, Terry. *The Illusions of Postmodernism*. Oxford: Blackwell, 1996.

Easthope, Anthony. *Englishness and National Culture*. London: Routledge, 1999.

Eco, Umberto. 'An Uncertain Europe between Rebirth and Decline.' In Levy et al. 2005, pp. 14–20.

English, James F. (ed.). *A Concise Companion to Contemporary British Fiction*. Oxford: Blackwell, 2006.

English, James F. and John Frow. 'Literary Authorship and Celebrity Culture.' In English (2006), pp. 39–57.

Featherstone, Mike, Scott Lash and Roland Robertson (eds). *Global Modernities*. London: Sage, 1995.

Ferguson, Frances. 'The Way We Love Now: Ian McEwan's *Saturday* and Personal Affection in the Information Age.' *Representations* 100 (2007), pp. 42–52.

Ferguson, Marjorie. 'The Mythology about Globalization.' *European Journal of Communication* 7:1 (1992), pp. 69–93.

Fine, Robert. 'Taking the "ism" out of Cosmopolitanism: An Essay in Reconstruction.' *European Journal of Social Theory* 6:4 (2003), pp. 451–70.

Fine, Robert. *Cosmopolitanism*. London: Routledge, 2007

Fine, Robert and Vivienne Boon. 'Introduction: Cosmopolitanism: Between Past and Future.' *European Journal of Social Theory* 10:1 (2007), pp. 5–16.

Finney, Brian. *English Fiction since 1984: Narrating a Nation*. New York: Palgrave, 2006.

Forster, E. M. *A Passage to India*. Penguin: Harmondsworth, 1985 [1924].

Friedman, Thomas. *The World Is Flat: The Globalized World in the Twenty-first Century*. London: Penguin, 2005.

Gane, Gillian. 'Migrancy, the Cosmopolitan Intellectual, and the Global City in *The Satanic Verses*.' *Modern Fiction Studies* 48:1 (2002), pp. 18–49.

García-Moreno, Laura and Peter C. Pfeiffer (eds). *Text and Nation: Cross-Disciplinary Essays on Cultural and National Identities*. Columbia: Camden House, 1996.

Garton Ash, Timothy and Ralf Dahrendorf. 'The Renewal of Europe: Response to Habermas.' In Levy et al. 2005, pp. 141–5.

Gauthier, Tim S. *Narrative Desire and Historical Reparations: A. S. Byatt, Ian McEwan, Salman Rushdie*. New York: Routledge, 2006.

Ghosh, Bishnupriya. *When Borne Across: Literary Cosmopolitics in the Contemporary Indian Novel*. New Brunswick: Rutgers University Press, 2004.

Gikandi, Simon. 'Globalization and the Claims of Postcoloniality.' *South Atlantic Quarterly* 100:3 (2001), pp. 627–58.

Gilroy, Paul. *After Empire: Melancholia or Convivial Culture?* London and New York: Routledge, 2004.

Glomb, Stefan and Stefan Horlacher (eds). *Beyond Extremes: Repräsentation und Reflexion von Modernisierungsprozessen im zeitgenössischen britischen Roman*. Tübingen: Narr, 2004.

Griffiths, Philip. '"On the Fringe of Becoming": David Mitchell's *Ghostwritten*.' In Glomb and Horlacher (2004), pp. 79–99.

Gunesch, Konrad. *Multilingualism and Cosmopolitanism: Meanings, Relationships, Tendencies*. Saarbrücken: VDM Verlag, 2008.

Habermas, Jürgen. *The Divided West*. Tr. C. Cronin. Cambridge: Polity, 2006 [2004].

Habermas, Jürgen and Jacques Derrida. 'February 15, or What Binds Europeans Together: Plea for a Common Foreign Policy, Beginning in Core Europe.' In Levy et al. 2005, pp. 3–13.

Hadley, Elaine. 'On a Darkling Plain: Victorian Liberalism and the Fantasy of Agency.' *Victorian Studies* 48:1 (2005), pp. 92–102.

Hagemann, Susanne. 'Postcolonial Translation Studies and James Kelman's *Translated Accounts*.' *Scottish Studies Review* 6:1 (2005), pp. 74–83.

Hall, Stuart. 'Political Belonging in a World of Multiple Identities.' In Vertovec and Cohen (2002), pp. 25–31.

Halliday, Fred. *The World at 2000*. Basingstoke: Palgrave, 2001.

Hannerz, Ulf. 'Cosmopolitans and Locals in World Culture.' *Theory, Culture & Society* 7 (1990), pp. 237–51.

Hardt, Michael and Antonio Negri. *Empire*. Cambridge, MA, and London: Harvard University Press, 2000.

Harvey, David. *A Brief History of Neoliberalism*. Oxford: Oxford University Press, 2005.

Haylett, Chris. 'Working-class Subjects in the Cosmopolitan City.' In Binnie et al. (2006), pp. 187–203

Head, Dominic. The *Cambridge Introduction to Modern British Fiction, 1950–2000*. Cambridge: Cambridge University Press, 2002.

Head, Dominic. *Ian McEwan*. Manchester: Manchester University Press, 2007.

Head, Dominic. *The State of the Novel: Britain and Beyond*. Chichester: Wiley-Blackwell, 2008.

Held, David. 'Culture and Political Community: National, Global, and Cosmopolitan.' In Vertovec and Cohen (2002), pp. 48–58.

Hopkins, Terence K. and Immanuel Wallerstein (coordinators). *The Age of Transition: Trajectory of the World-System, 1945–2025*. London: Zed Books, 1996.

Huggan, Graham. *The Postcolonial Exotic: Marketing the Margins*. London: Routledge, 2001.

Hutchens, B. C. *Jean-Luc Nancy and the Future of Philosophy*. Chesham: Acumen, 2005.

Hutcheon, Linda. *The Poetics of Postmodernism: History, Theory, Fiction*. New York: Routledge, 1988.

Iñárritu, Alejandro González (dir.). *Babel*. Paramount Pictures, 2006.

Jackson, Ellen-Raïssa and Willy Maley. 'Committing to Kelman: The Art of Integrity and the Politics of Dissent.' *Edinburgh Review* 108 (2001), pp. 22–7.

James, Ian. *The Fragmentary Demand: An Introduction to the Philosophy of Jean-Luc Nancy*. Stanford: Stanford University Press, 2006.

Jay, Paul. 'Beyond Discipline? Globalization and the Future of English.' *PMLA* 116:1 (2001), pp. 32–47.

Jenkins, Jennifer. *English as a Lingua Franca: Attitude and Identity*. Oxford: Oxford University Press, 2007.

Jones, Joseph. *Terranglia: The Case of English as World-literature*. New York: Twayne, 1965.

Joseph, Clara and Janet Wilson (eds). *Global Fissures – Postcolonial Fusions*. Amsterdam: Rodopi, 2006.

Kagan, Robert. *Of Paradise and Power: America and Europe in the New World Order*. New York: Knopf, 2003.

Kalb, Don. 'Localizing Flows: Power, Paths, Institutions, and Networks.' In Kalb et al. (2000), pp. 1–29.

Kalb, Don and Marco van der Land. 'Beyond the Mosaic: Questioning Cultural Identity in a Globalizing Age.' In Kalb et al. (2000), pp. 273–80.

Kalb, Don, Marco van der Land, Richard Staring, Bart van Steenbergen and Nico Wilterdink (eds). *The Ends of Globalization: Bringing Society Back In*. Lanham, MD: Rowman & Littlefield, 2000.

Kalliney, Peter. 'Globalization, Postcoloniality, and the Problem of Literary

Studies in *The Satanic Verses.*' *Modern Fiction Studies* 48:1 (2002), pp. 50–82.

Kant, Immanuel. *Perpetual Peace, and Other Essays on Politics, History, and Morals.* Tr. T. Humphrey. Indianapolis: Hackett, 1983 [1795].

Kelly, Aaron. 'James Kelman and the Deterritorialisation of Power.' In Schoene 2007, pp. 175–83.

Kelman, James. *A Disaffection.* London: Vintage, 1999 [1989].

Kelman, James. *Translated Accounts.* London: Secker and Warburg, 2001.

Kelman, James. *You Have to Be Careful in the Land of the Free.* London: Penguin, 2005 [2004].

Keniston, Ann and Jeanne F. Quinn (eds). *Literature after 9/11.* New York: Routledge, 2008.

Kiely, Ray. *Empire in the Age of Globalisation: US Hegemony and Neoliberal Disorder.* London: Pluto, 2005.

King, Bruce. *The Internationalization of English Literature.* Oxford: Oxford University Press, 2004.

Kneale, Matthew. *Small Crimes in an Age of Abundance.* London: Picador, 2005.

Kövesi, Simon. *James Kelman.* Manchester: Manchester University Press, 2007.

Krishnaswamy, Revathi and John C. Hawley (eds). *The Postcolonial and the Global.* Minneapolis: University of Minnesota Press, 2008.

Kristeva, Julia. 'Women's Time.' In Moi (1986), pp. 187–213.

Kumar, Krishan. 'Britain, England and Europe: Cultures in Contraflow.' *European Journal of Social Theory* 6:1 (2003), pp. 5–23.

Kumar, Krishan. 'The Question of European Identity: Europe in the American Mirror.' *European Journal of Social Theory* 11:1 (2008), pp. 87–105.

Kunow, Rüdiger. 'Architect of the Cosmopolitan Dream: Salman Rushdie.' *American Studies* 51:3 (2006), pp. 369–85.

Kunzru, Hari. *Transmission.* London: Penguin, 2004.

Lea, Daniel and Berthold Schoene (eds). *Posting the Male: Masculinities in Post-war and Contemporary British Literature.* Amsterdam: Rodopi, 2003.

Lehner, Stefanie. 'Subaltern Scotland: Devolution and Postcoloniality.' In Schoene 2007, pp. 292–300.

Levy, Daniel and Natan Sznaider. 'Memories of Europe: Cosmopolitanism and Its Others.' In Rumford (2007), pp. 158–77.

Levy, Daniel, Max Pensky and John Torpey (eds). *Old Europe, New Europe, Core Europe: Transatlantic Relations after the Iraq War.* London: Verso, 2005.

Luszczynska, Ana. 'The Opposite of the Concentration Camp: Nancy's Vision of Community.' *Centennial Review* 5:3 (2005), pp. 167–205.

McCallum, Pamela and Wendy Faith (eds). *Linked Histories: Postcolonial Studies in a Globalized World.* Calgary: University of Calgary Press, 2005.

McClure, John A. *Partial Faiths: Postsecular Fiction in the Age of Pynchon and Morrison.* Athens: University of Georgia Press, 2007.

Macdonald, Graeme. 'A Scottish Subject? Kelman's Determination.' *Etudes Ecossaises* 8 (2002), pp. 89–111.

McEwan, Ian. *Black Dogs.* London: Picador, 1992.

McEwan, Ian. *Saturday.* London: Vintage, 2005.

McGregor, Jon. *If Nobody Speaks of Remarkable Things*. London: Bloomsbury, 2002.

McGregor, Jon. *So Many Ways to Begin*. London: Bloomsbury, 2006.

Malcolm, David. *Understanding McEwan*. Columbia: University of South Carolina Press, 2002.

Melas, Natalie. *All the Difference in the World: Postcoloniality and the Ends of Comparison*. Stanford: Stanford University Press, 2004.

Mignolo, Walter. 'The Many Faces of Cosmo-polis: Border Thinking and Critical Cosmopolitanism.' In Breckenridge et al. 2002, pp. 157–87.

Milne, Drew. 'Broken English: James Kelman's *Translated Accounts*.' *Edinburgh Review* 108 (2001), pp. 106–15.

Mitchell, David. *Ghostwritten: A Novel in Nine Parts*. London: Sceptre, 1999.

Mitchell, David. *number9dream*. London: Sceptre, 2001.

Mitchell, David. *Cloud Atlas*. London: Sceptre, 2004.

Mitchell, David. *Black Swan Green*. London: Sceptre, 2006.

Moi, Toril (ed.). *The Kristeva Reader*. Oxford: Blackwell, 1986.

Moretti, Franco. *Atlas of the European Novel, 1800–1900*. London: Verso, 1998.

Moretti, Franco (ed.). *The Novel*. 2 volumes. Princeton: Princeton University Press, 2006.

Morrison, Jago. 'Narration and Unease in Ian McEwan's Later Fiction.' *Critique* 42:3 (2001), pp. 253–68.

Morrison, Jago. *Contemporary Fiction*. London and New York: Routledge, 2003.

Moses, Michael Valdez. *The Novel and the Globalization of Culture*. New York: Oxford University Press, 1995.

Mouffe, Chantal. 'Cosmopolitan Democracy or Multipolar World Order?' *Soundings* 28 (2004), pp. 62–74.

Mullaney, Julie. *Arundhati Roy's The God of Small Things: A Reader's Guide*. New York: Continuum, 2005.

Munck, Ronaldo. *Globalization and Contestation: The New Great Counter-Movement*. Abingdon: Routledge, 2007.

Nancy, Jean-Luc. *The Inoperative Community*. Tr. P. Connor, L. Garbus, M. Holland and S. Sawhney. Minneapolis: University of Minnesota Press, 1991 [1986].

Nancy, Jean-Luc. *Being Singular Plural*. Tr. R. D. Richardson and A. E. O'Byrne. Stanford: Stanford University Press, 2000 [1996].

Nancy, Jean-Luc. *The Creation of the World or Globalization*. Tr. F. Raffoul and D. Pettigrew. New York: SUNY Press, 2007 [2002].

Nava, Mica. *Visceral Cosmopolitanism: Gender, Culture and the Normalisation of Difference*. Oxford: Berg, 2007.

Nederveen Pieterse, Jan. *Globalization and Culture: Global Mélange*. Lanham: Rowan and Littlefield, 2004.

Nicoll, Laurence. 'Facticity, or Something Like That: The Novels of James Kelman.' In Acheson and Ross 2005, pp. 59–69.

O'Brien, Susie and Imre Szeman. 'Introduction: The Globalization of Fiction/ the Fiction of Globalization.' *South Atlantic Quarterly* 100:3 (2001), pp. 603–26.

Papastergiadis, Nikos. 'Glimpses of Cosmopolitanism in the Hospitality of Art.' *European Journal of Social Theory* 10 (2007), pp. 139–52.

Parrinder, Patrick. *Nation and Novel: The English Novel from Its Origins to the Present Day.* Oxford: Oxford University Press, 2006.

Pitchford, Nicola. 'How Late It Was for England: James Kelman's Scottish Booker Prize.' *Contemporary Literature* 41:4 (2000), pp. 693–725.

Pollock, Sheldon. 'Cosmopolitan and Vernacular in History.' In Breckenridge et al. (2002), pp. 15–53.

Preuss, Ulrich. 'The Iraq War: Critical Reflections from "Old Europe".' In Levy et al. 2005, pp. 167–85.

Pynchon, Thomas. *The Crying of Lot 49.* London: Picador, 1979 [1965].

Ray, Amit. '"Indianness" and Contemporary Cosmopolitan Fictions: Of Bookers and "Spice" and Everything Nice.' In Shands (2008), pp. 127–34.

Ray, Larry. *Globalization and Everyday Life.* London: Routledge, 2007.

Rée, Jonathan. 'Cosmopolitanism and the Experience of Nationality.' In Cheah and Robbins (1998), pp. 77–90.

Robertson, James. *Joseph Knight.* London: Fourth Estate, 2003.

Robertson, Roland. *Globalization: Social Theory and Global Culture.* London: Sage, 1992.

Robertson, Roland. 'Glocalization: Time-Space and Homogeneity-Heterogeneity.' In Featherstone et al. (1995), pp. 25–44.

Rofe, Matthew. '"I Want to Be Global": Theorising the Gentrifying Class as an Emergent Elite Global Community.' *Urban Studies* 40:12 (2003), pp. 2511–26.

Rothenberg, David and Wandee J. Pryor (eds). *Writing the World: On Globalization.* Cambridge, MA: MIT, 2005.

Roy, Arundhati. *The God of Small Things.* London: Flamingo, 1997.

Roy, Arundhati. *The Cost of Living.* London: Flamingo, 1999.

Roy, Arundhati. *Power Politics.* Cambridge, MA: South End Press, 2001.

Rumford, Chris (ed.). *Cosmopolitanism in Europe.* Liverpool: Liverpool University Press, 2007.

Rushdie, Salman. *Midnight's Children.* London: Cape, 1981.

Rushdie, Salman. *The Satanic Verses.* Dover, DE: Consortium, 1992 [1988].

Ryan, Kiernan. *Ian McEwan.* Plymouth: Northcote House, 1994.

Sankaran, Chitra. 'Ethics, Aesthetics and the Globalized Other in Arundhati Roy's *The God of Small Things.*' In Joseph and Wilson (2006), pp. 103–19.

Saussy, Haun (ed.). *Comparative Literature in an Age of Globalization: The 2004 American Comparative Literature Association Report on the State of the Discipline.* Baltimore: Johns Hopkins University Press, 2006.

Savage, Mike, Gaynor Bagnall and Brian Longhurst (eds). *Globalisation and Belonging.* London: Sage, 2005.

Scheffler, Samuel. 'Conceptions of Cosmopolitanism.' *Utilitas* 11:3 (1999), pp. 255–76.

Schoene, Berthold (ed.). *The Edinburgh Companion to Contemporary Scottish Literature.* Edinburgh: Edinburgh University Press, 2007.

Schoene, Berthold. 'Cosmopolitan Scots.' *Scottish Studies Review* 9: 2 (2008), pp. 71–92.

Shands, Kerstin (ed.). *Neither East Nor West: Postcolonial Essays on Literature, Culture and Religion.* Huddinge: Södertörns Högskola, 2008.

Sheppard, Darren, Simon Sparks and Colin Thomas (eds). *On Jean-Luc Nancy: The Sense of Philosophy.* London: Routledge, 1997.

Silverstone, Roger (ed.). *Visions of Suburbia.* London: Routledge, 1997.

Smith, Stan (ed.). *Globalisation and Its Discontents.* Cambridge: Brewer, 2006.

Smith, Zadie. *On Beauty.* London: Hamish Hamilton, 2005.

Spinks, Lee. 'In Juxtaposition to Which: Narrative, System and Subjectivity in the Fiction of James Kelman.' *Edinburgh Review* 108 (2001), pp. 85–105.

Szerszynski, Bronislaw and John Urry. 'Cultures of Cosmopolitanism.' *Sociological Review* 50:4 (2002), pp. 461–81.

Szerszynski, Bronislaw and John Urry. 'Visuality, Mobility and the Cosmopolitan: Inhabiting the World from Afar.' *British Journal of Sociology* 57:1 (2006), pp. 113–31.

Tew, Philip. *The Contemporary British Novel.* Second edition. London: Continuum, 2007 [2004].

Tew, Philip and Rod Mengham (eds). *British Fiction Today.* London: Continuum, 2006.

Thomas, Susie. 'Zadie Smith's False Teeth: The Marketing of Multiculturalism.' *Literary London: Interdisciplinary Studies in the Representation of London* 4:1 (2006), www.literarylondon.org/london-journal/march2006/thomas. html.

Tickell, Alex. '*The God of Small Things*: Arundhati Roy's Postcolonial Cosmopolitanism.' *Journal of Commonwealth Literature* 38:1 (2003), pp. 73–89.

Tomlinson, John. *Globalization and Culture.* Cambridge: Polity, 1999.

Toremans, Tom. 'An Interview with Alasdair Gray and James Kelman.' *Contemporary Literature* 44: 4 (2003), pp. 564–86.

Trumpener, Katie. 'World Music, World Literature: A Geopolitical View.' In Saussy (2006), pp. 185–202.

Vattimo, Gianni. 'The European Union Faces the Major Points of Its Development.' In Levy et al. 2005, pp. 28–33.

Vertovec, Steven and Robin Cohen (eds). *Conceiving Cosmopolitanism: Theory, Context, and Practice.* Oxford: Oxford University Press, 2002.

Waldron, Jeremy. 'What Is Cosmopolitan?' *Journal of Political Philosophy* 8:2 (2000), pp. 227–43.

Walkowitz, Rebecca L. *Cosmopolitan Style: Modernism beyond the Nation.* New York: Columbia University Press, 2006.

Wallace, Elizabeth K. 'Postcolonial Melancholia in Ian McEwan's *Saturday*.' *Studies in the Novel* 39:4 (2007), pp. 465–80.

Wallace, Gavin and Randall Stevenson (eds). *The Scottish Novel since the Seventies: New Visions, Old Dreams.* Edinburgh: Edinburgh University Press, 1993.

Wallerstein, Immanuel. *Geopolitics and Geoculture: Essays on the Changing World- System.* Cambridge: Cambridge University Press, 1991.

Wallerstein, Immanuel. 'The Global Possibilities, 1990–2025.' In Hopkins and Wallerstein (1996), pp. 226–43.

Waters, Malcolm. *Globalization.* Second edition. London: Routledge, 2001 [1995].

Watkin, Christopher. 'A Different Alterity: Jean-Luc Nancy's "Singular Plural".' *Paragraph* 30:2 (2007), pp. 50–64.

Wells, Lynn. 'The Ethical Otherworld: Ian McEwan's Fiction.' In Tew and Mengham (2006), pp. 117–27.

Welsh, Irvine. *Trainspotting*. London: Minerva, 1994 [1993].

Werbner, Pnina. 'Global Pathways: Working-Class Cosmopolitans and the Creation of Transnational Ethnic Worlds.' *Social Anthropology* 7:1 (1999), pp. 17–35.

Will, George. 'The End of Our Holiday from History.' *Jewish World Review* (12 September 2001), www.jewishworldreview.com/cols/will091201.asp.

Xie, Shaobo. 'Is the World Decentred? A Postcolonial Perspective on Globalization.' In Joseph and Wilson 2006, pp. 53–75.

Young, Iris Marion. 'De-centering the Project of Global Democracy.' In Levy et al. 2005, pp. 153–9.

Ziarek, Krzysztof. 'Is All Technological? Global Power and Aesthetic Forces.' *New Centennial Review* 2:3 (2002), pp. 139–68.

Index